What Must Be
FORGOTTEN

Judaic Traditions in Literature, Music, and Art
Ken Frieden and Harold Bloom, *Series Editors*

Chaim, Ethel, and Chaya Segal *(on the right),* with workers and goat, Ra'anana, Palestine; photograph by Zev Segal, author's collection.

WHAT MUST BE
FORGOTTEN

THE SURVIVAL OF YIDDISH
IN ZIONIST PALESTINE

Yael Chaver

Syracuse University Press

Copyright © 2004 by Syracuse University Press
Syracuse, New York 13244–5160

All Rights Reserved

First Edition 2004

04 05 06 07 08 09   6 5 4 3 2 1

Published with the assistance of a grant from the Littauer Foundation.

The paper used in this publication meets the minimum requirements
of American National Standard for Information Sciences—
Permanence of Paper for Printed Library Materials,
ANSI Z39.48–1984.∞™

Library of Congress Cataloging-in-Publication Data
Chaver, Yael.
  What must be forgotten : the survival of Yiddish in Zionist Palestine /
Yael Chaver.— 1st ed.
    p. cm. — (Judaic traditions in literature, music, and art)
  Includes bibliographical references.
  ISBN 0-8156-3050-6 (cloth [hardcover] : alk. paper)
  1. Broches, S. (Samuel), b. 1886—Criticism and interpretation. 2.
Rives, A., 1900–1963—Criticism and interpretation. 3. Poòtash,
Riòkudah, 1906–1965—Criticism and interpretation. 4. Hebrew
language—Political aspects—Palestine. 5. Zionism. I. Title. II. Series.
  PJ5129.B74Z63 2004
  839'.10995694—dc22

                                            2004013670

Manufactured in the United States of America

I dedicate this effort to three figures of blessed memory.

The first is Zev Segal (1903–69), my Jerusalem-born father. His passion and intellect—his particular combination of interest in all the varied strands of Jewish culture and experience and steadfast commitment to the Zionism that was a guiding principle of his life—form an unvoiced background and commentary to my own life and work.

The second is my uncle Elazar Goelman (1913–99), who began an uncompleted study of Yiddish in Israel after a distinguished career in Jewish education in the United States and gladly shared with me his immense knowledge and great love for *yiddishkeyt* in lively and enthusiastic dialogue.

The third is my mother, Chaya Goelman Segal (1910–2004), whose love, warmth, and wisdom are constantly present and continue to provide rich sustenance. It is her voice, with its Bialystok Yiddish accent, more familiar to me than my own, that I hear when I read Yiddish, true *mame-loshn.*

Yael Chaver was raised and educated in Israel and in the United States; received her academic degrees from the Hebrew University, Jerusalem, and the University of California, Berkeley; and has taught, written, and translated in Hebrew, English, and Yiddish. She currently teaches Yiddish at the University of California, Berkeley, and is working on a new book.

Contents

Illustrations

Acknowledgments

This project owes its existence to the many who have encouraged, challenged, and accompanied it over its long course of development. I have had the pleasure to work with peerless academic mentors and companions at the University of California, Berkeley. Chana Kronfeld's incomparably detailed professional engagement and extraordinary personal support have been crucial to the project from its inception. I have benefited greatly from Robert Alter's wide-ranging research, refined insights, and nuanced critical readings. Naomi Seidman's consistently fresh viewpoint has enhanced my understanding of cultural processes and literary texts. Karl Britto provided an invaluable broad perspective on the topic. I am indebted to Aviva Fuchs for graciously permitting me to use the poetry and photograph of her mother, Rikuda Potash; to Michael Ardon of the Hebrew University, Jerusalem, for sharing memories of his father, Mordecai Ardon, and for permitting me to include copies of two of his father's works; and to Bezalel Narkiss of the Hebrew University, Jerusalem, for reminiscences of his aunt, Rikuda Potash. Avraham Novershtern of the Hebrew University, Jerusalem, contributed generous, meticulous, and unfailing support. My thanks to Daniel Boyarin of the University of California, Berkeley, for revitalizing my interest in Yiddish; David Stronach, Ann Kilmer, Bluma Goldstein, and Ariel Bloch, all of the University of California at Berkeley, and Michael Gluzman of Tel-Aviv University for ongoing dialogues; Vera Solomon of the Hebrew University, Jerusalem, Itzik Gottesman of the *Forward* and Zippora and David Talshir of Ben-Gurion University for useful information and productive suggestions; Shalom Luria of Haifa University for details of the Palestinian and Israeli Yiddish scene.

Thanks to David Shneer, Matthew Hoffman, Sheila Jelen, and Todd Hasak-Lowy, who commented on early drafts of the project. I also owe special thanks to Chana Bloch, who introduced me to Rikuda Potash's work and helped refine my translations of Potash's poetry, and to Hadass Bar-Yosef for her impressions of Rikuda Potash. I am grateful to Eli Katz and Chava Turniansky for assisting with the fine points of Yiddish translation; to David Shneer, Victoria Motchalova, Stefania Rubinsky, and Ilan Roth for facilitating translations from Russian and Polish; and to Achi Ben-Shalom for providing information about popular songs of the Yishuv. Eliyah Arnon, Clint Reed, Inbar Zamir, Paul Hamburg, Dan Eisenstein, and Rami Geller were invaluable technical supporters. Special thanks go to my daughter, Tamar Baskind, for her invaluable help with indexing. My thanks to staff members of the editorial and production departments at Syracuse University press for their attention to detail while enabling the overall result. The dissertation that forms the basis of this book was completed with the aid of a University of California Chancellor's Dissertation-Year Fellowship and a doctoral grant from the Memorial Foundation for Jewish Culture, both in 1999–2000. The book took final shape with the aid of a Fellowship Grant from the Memorial Foundation for Jewish Culture in 2001–2002.

My family and friends have been the other pole of support for this project. First and foremost, I thank my spouse and partner, Aaron Chaver, for the unwavering love, challenge, and support that have been the foundations of our long joint adventure. Our children—Alon, Yair, and Tamar—have followed my work with enthusiasm and encouragement; and our granddaughters, Abigail, Rahel, Shira, and Rivca—as well as their classmates—decorated innumerable sheets of discarded drafts with their artwork, creating yet another layer of this cultural palimpsest. My dear friends in Israel and the United States, some going back forty years, have steadfastedly shared in my excitement for the project. Thus, in many ways, this has truly been an adventure enabled by my different communities, to all of which I owe more than I can express.

Introduction

This study considers the unfolding of a prolonged formative moment in the development of Israeli culture, a moment that was the focus of profound personal and communal ambivalence: the key process of fulfilling the Zionist imperative to relinquish Yiddish, the mother tongue of the Ashkenazi majority, in favor of Hebrew, the ancient language that Zionism valorized exclusively. Eastern European Jewish culture, with Yiddish as its major language, was the originary location of the Zionists who immigrated to Palestine in the early decades of the twentieth century and created the Yishuv. These immigrants aimed to divest themselves of all the attributes of their former homes in order to be reconstituted as a new nation in the ancient homeland. Perhaps most crucial for the topic of this study, they were enjoined to abandon their Yiddish language in favor of Hebrew, the sacred language that was being revived for everyday use. Yiddish was derisively labeled as "jargon," identified with the diasporic culture, and stigmatized by Zionism as negative and therefore irrelevant.[1] Mainstream histories have in fact taught generations of Israelis and non-Israelis that the pioneers instantaneously and totally repudiated their mother tongue. The dominant Israeli national narrative construes this total reconfiguration of the individual and the collective as a complete success: according to this view, the Zionist

---

1. Linguists, historians, and cultural thinkers have extensively discussed the complex relationship between Hebrew and Yiddish. Thus, for a first modern comprehensive overview of the development of Yiddish, see M. Weinreich 1980; the historical development of Yiddish literature is surveyed in Shmeruk 1978; Harshav (1990, 1993a) presents cultural and linguistic analyses of Yiddish; for a detailed analysis of modern Yiddish literary prose, see Miron 1996; the evolution of modern literary Hebrew is delineated in Alter 1988. Seidman (1997) examines the complicated and changing gender relations between the two languages; chapter 4 in her book is particularly relevant to my topic.

pioneers forsook all aspects of their former lives and were indeed "reborn." [2]

However, a closer examination of this rebirth narrative in the light of Israeli neoformalist "polysystem theory," developed by Itamar Even-Zohar in a series of studies, reveals assumptions that beg to be challenged. Even-Zohar defines *polysystem* as a dynamic, "heterogeneous, open structure . . . a multiple system, a system of various systems which intersect with each other and partly overlap, using concurrently different options, yet functioning as one structured whole, whose members are interdependent . . . a dynamic system" (1990c, 11). According to this view, the nascent Hebrew culture of Palestine was a "polysystem-in-the-making" (Even-Zohar 1981, 174), with cultural opposition between the "Old Jew" and the "New Hebrew" a constitutive imperative (172). Hebrew had historically been an integral component of multilingual Jewish culture, functioning as a more prestigious language than Yiddish or the other Jewish vernaculars such as Judeo-Spanish (known to its speakers as Ladino or Spanyolit) or Judeo-Arabic, to name the best-known ones. In a curious inversion, the "old" Hebrew language now became the basis for the "new" culture; Hebrew emblematized the antithesis to the diasporic polysystem and culture that were to be jettisoned. Once Zionism contrasted New Hebrew with Old Jew, the components of the opposition were in place.

But what actually happened to Yiddish, to its culture, and to the native speakers who were commanded to abandon it? European Jews had spoken Yiddish for more than one thousand years; in 1918, the literature written in it was described as having served as a "territory" for a people that had no physical homeland (Bal-Makhshoves 1994, 75). The term *Yiddishland,* often used for this particular Jewish home, was taken beyond the realm of literature by the major Yiddishist figure Chaim Zhitlovsky in 1937: "A spiritual-national home . . . 'Yiddish-land' we call it today—whose atmosphere consists of the fresh air of our folk language and where with every breath and every word one helps maintain the national existence of our people" (1953, 403).[3] In Palestine, however, Jews whose "homeland" had been the text (Steiner 1985, 22) were creating a physical home identified with a language

---

2. See, among others, B. Eli'av 1979, Erez 1964, Ettinger 1969, Karmi 1997, Talmi and Talmi 1981.

3. All translations from Yiddish and Hebrew are my own, unless otherwise noted. Translations of biblical texts are from *The New Oxford Annotated Bible* (1977).

that was only one part of the millennium-old culture. Zionism caused the European "Yiddishland" culture to undergo a singular upheaval. In one revolutionary stroke, that culture was both dispossessed and refigured in a double-valenced location: the linguistic "home" of Hebrew and the physical homeland of the Land of Israel. Yet Yiddish did not vanish overnight. Discussing the emergence of a native Hebrew culture in Palestine, Even-Zohar notes the lingering of "a remarkable mass of 'old culture' " (1981, 175); such persistence can be explained only by the continued presence of both consumers and suppliers. The overwhelming majority of Yishuv members, in its early decades, were native Yiddish speakers. They continued to use the language because Hebrew was unable to function as a complete polysystem. The former "complete" polysystem of Jewish culture with its multiplicity of languages (including Yiddish) was now deficient with Hebrew alone; it lacked the means to perform the colloquial functions that Yiddish formerly fulfilled (Even-Zohar 1990a, 125). Benjamin Harshav adds the critical social and psychological dimension to this somewhat mechanistic analysis when he describes the difficulty of "changing the individual's base language [Yiddish] to a language [Hebrew] that is not yet the base language of any society" (1993a, 138). Those people whose mother tongue was Yiddish naturally tended to continue using it, with its long colloquial history and its well-established literary tradition.

Given the ambivalence that accompanied the obligation to abandon Yiddish in favor of Hebrew, the development of a Yiddish literature in the Zionist Yishuv is therefore hardly surprising. Equally unsurprising is the fact that Israeli literary historiographers, intent on establishing the exclusivity of a Hebrew culture, have ignored the existence of this literature. Yet, as I show, Yiddish literature flourished in the Yishuv beginning with the work of Zalmen Brokhes during the period of the Second Aliyah between 1904 and 1913. In some respects, the Yiddish literature of the Yishuv was a branch of its European counterpart. Many European Yiddish writers of the 1920s and 1930s were affiliated with general European modernist trends and combined avant-garde features with the expressive advantage that Yiddish enjoyed over Hebrew at this time.

A few words on the relevant qualities of the two languages are in order. Max Weinreich defines Yiddish as a "fusion language," in which components from four unrelated linguistic groups (Hebrew as well as Latin-derived Romance, Germanic, and Slavic languages) combine and "fuse" in various aspects of vocabulary and grammar, giving rise to a new linguistic structure

(1980, 29–30). However, the term is not quite accurate because the resonances of the different language components remain explicit and audible to varying degrees, conferring fluidity of expression and flexibility of range and register. Harshav notes that it is typical of Yiddish conversation "to borrow expressions from beyond the language border and to shift for a while from Yiddish proper to pieces of discourse in other languages and back" (1990, 28). Yiddish style incorporated the particular structure of each language, "stressing the counterpoints rather than the linguistic melting pot"; the different components could be set off against each other. This was not only possible, but necessary: David Roskies notes that the effectiveness of the Yiddish style at its peak (the work of Sholem Aleichem at the turn of the twentieth century) "depended entirely for its success upon a milieu sensitive to nuances in Yiddish, Hebrew, Ukrainian, Polish, Russian, German, and English" (1985, 163), all languages that functioned within the Jewish polysystem. In his 1878 Yiddish *Masoes Binyomin ha-Shelishi* (Travels of Benjamin the Third), for example, S. Y. Abramovitch (1835–1917, considered the "father" of modern Yiddish literature) was able to delineate complex relations between Jews and non-Jews by inserting partially or wholly untranslated dialogues between members of the two communities in a Slavic language to which his readers would be attuned (1947, 79).[4] Thus, representing the language of the "other" is a natural feature of Yiddish literature. In Yiddish, Harshav remarks, "you speak several languages in one sentence" (1993b, 25).

The language components of Yiddish could be manipulated for various purposes. Because the Hebraic component is ubiquitous in all Yiddish dialects, and because it is the most freighted by association with the domain of the sacred, it was the most susceptible to ideological attacks in an age of secularization. Perhaps the most striking illustration is the Soviet Yiddishists' elimination of the Hebrew spelling of Hebraic root words in Yiddish in the 1920s in an attempt to erase its religious and nationalist cultural valence. Deprived of their original orthography, the Hebrew words in Soviet Yiddish

4. See Miron 1996 for an illuminating account and analysis of Abramovitch and his work. Symptomatic of the linguistic ambivalence of European Jewish culture at this time is the fact that Abramovitch himself (often conflated with his better-known literary persona Mendele Mokher-Sforim [Mendele the Bookseller]) began his literary career in Hebrew in 1862 and continued to write in both Hebrew and Yiddish. He published a Hebrew version of *The Travels of Benjamin the Third* in 1896.

texts appear distorted and may have unintentionally become more notice-able instead of the reverse. In a different society, the introspectivist poets of the In Zikh group in the United States (1919) stressed the use of the "spoken language" (Harshav 1990, 83) and presented Hebrew words according to phonetics rather than in their Hebrew spelling in an attempt to secularize the traditionally sacred language.[5] In early-twentieth-century Europe, in con-trast, Jewish non-Zionist expressionists writing in Yiddish assigned particu-lar poetic value to Hebrew. The Yiddish literary critic Maks Erik defined Hebrew words as " 'sinewy,' heavy, weighty" (1922, 17) and therefore desir-able. Some Yiddish expressionist poets used Hebrew innovatively. Perets Markish, in "Oyf Markn un Yaridn" (At markets and fairs)—part of his 1921 *poema Di Kupe* (The pile), which memorializes the Horodishtsh pogrom on the day after Yom Kippur 1920—recontextualizes the Hebrew word *ne'ila* (in Yiddish pronunciation, *nile,*) to great effect. *Ne'ila* (literally, "locking up") is the name of the last part of the Yom Kippur service, when the gates of heaven draw shut and sentences of life and death can no longer be reversed. *"S'iz nile-tsayt"* (it's locking-up time), Markish says, defamiliar-izing the freighted Hebrew term—which in Yiddish discourse refers exclu-sively to the end of the period of divine grace on Yom Kippur—by relocating it in the marketplace (1921, 14). Reconfiguring the holiest moment in the Jewish year shocks the reader into a new perception. As Even-Zohar puts it, the "naturalness, immediacy and prolific variants" of Yiddish were of signif-icant importance (1990b, 156). Yiddish could incorporate Hebrew overtly, but the reverse—though implicitly practiced, as we shall see—was not acceptable.

The situation of Hebrew was essentially different. In the early twentieth century, the capacities of modern Hebrew literature were circumscribed by a literary norm resulting from its relatively short tradition.[6] The normative He-

5. The In Zikh poets desacralized Christian terms as well and made them part of "spoken" language; Yankev Glatshteyn, for example, drew the title of his 1929 volume *Kredos* from Catholic ritual, instead of using the Hebrew liturgical expression *ani ma'amin* (I believe), of which the Latin *credo* is a translation and which is normally used in Yiddish.

6. The first Hebrew novel, Abraham Mapu's *Ahavat-tziyon* (Love of Zion) appeared in 1853. Although Robert Alter notes that Hebrew "was never a dead language" (1988, 18), the works produced in it before the mid-nineteenth century belonged mostly to genres that did not require a vernacular: legalistic, exegetical, and philosophical genres. The highly stylized rich He-brew poetry written in Spain and Italy during the tenth to fourteenth centuries did not require a vernacular either (Pagis 1991).

brew prose style of the late nineteenth century (the *nusach*), created before a
Hebrew vernacular existed, was developed in Europe (virtually single-
handedly by S. Y. Abramovitch; many European Jewish writers were profi-
cient in both languages) as a flexible synthesis of historically diverse elements
of Hebrew style and was revolutionary for its time. It drew chiefly on rabbinic
sources, with biblical and other layers of the language such as liturgy and medieval exegesis, to form a medium for vernacular expression. The *nusach,*
which became the "authoritative model of good literary Hebrew," had a
wider register than did its predecessor, the stilted neobiblical Haskalah (Enlightenment) Hebrew of the early nineteenth century, which incorporated
melitsah, "a lifeless pastiche" of biblical phrases (Alter 1988, 45, 24).[7] Yet for
all its initial innovativeness, the *nusach* quickly became an inflexible norm. As
early as 1918, the critic and writer Shlomo Tzemach argued that the *nusach*
had become an obstacle to personal expression: "Today the style dominates
creative work, suffocating and burdening it through its very domination"
(1968, 57). Writers at the turn of the century, perhaps most notably Yosef
Chaim Brenner (1881–1921) and Uri Nissan Gnessin (1879–1913), upset the
formal balance of the *nusach* in their attempt to express modernist concerns
such as aesthetic integrity and representation of individual consciousness.
However, they were the exception rather than the rule and were often considered uncouth (Brenner) or unnecessarily aestheticizing (Gnessin). Accord-
ingly, their canonical status remained problematic for decades.

The normativity of the *nusach* was well suited to the standards of Yishuv
society, which was essentially becoming shaped by a socialist Zionist ideology that emphasized the collective. Gershon Shaked (1988) argues that the
uniformity of the ideological society existed to a great extent in the literature
as well, in both style and thematics. Brenner's seminal essay of 1911, "ha-
Zhaner ha-Eretz-yisre'eli ve-Avizraihu" (The Palestinian genre and its features), is perhaps the first detailed attempt to deal with the shortcomings of
contemporaneous Hebrew Palestinian literature, arguing, in effect, that no
such genre was possible. Among his major concerns in the essay was genre
writers' emerging idealization of the harsh daily realities with which the
Yishuv struggled, one result of which was a lack of authentic insight into the
individual's sensibility—the *"hemyat ha-nefesh"* (murmurings of the soul)

7. Chaim Rabin makes the fine point that Haskalah Hebrew prose incorporates the high
biblical registers of poetry, prophecy, wisdom, laws, and narrative but does not re-create actual
biblical usage (1985, 19).

(1985, 574). Following Brenner's terminology, Shaked draws an important distinction between genre and antigenre literature of the early Yishuv, although he correctly notes that there was "no absolute line dividing the genrists from the anti-genrists" (2000, 66, 80). Shaked terms as *genre* the romanticizing writing locally perceived as positive and describes the creators of genre literature in the 1920s and 1930s as naïve writers who "shaped reality according to their vision" (1983, 35). He posits that the antigenre writers challenged the mainstream's view of the Zionist experience—a view that continued to dominate Hebrew fiction until at least the 1950s (67). Amos Oz speaks of the "ecstatic" (genrist) view versus the "sober" (antigenrist) view of Israel in local fiction following 1948 (1993, 15). Nilli Sadan-Loebenstein presents her notion of what Brenner might have construed as antigenre: fiction that is self-exposing and that breaks stereotypes, whose content indicates a very unheroic reality, pessimistic and depressing in character (1991, 26).

One of the most prominent genre writers was Moshe Smilansky, who in his early romantic fiction idealized the settlers and their achievements in opposition to the Arabs, who were depicted, on the whole, as the enemy.[8] Meir Vilkansky was another writer who, in Shaked's view, ignored the objective conditions and instead created a dreamland, turning history into myth (2000, 65–67). Brenner's own clear-eyed and critical writing may be classified as antigenre, as was the work of others, most notably Shmuel Yosef Agnon (who was a singular figure and is addressed separately later). One important antigenre literary figure of the Second Aliyah was Aharon Re'uveni (1886–1971), who began in Palestine as a Yiddish writer and journalist and eventually switched to Hebrew; his major Hebrew trilogy *Ad Yerushalayim* (Unto Jerusalem) originally appeared as three separate novels in the 1920s. A highly critical and individualistic participant in the Zionist project, Re'uveni depicts the problematics of life in Jerusalem during the First World War; his characters, struggling with ideology, include non-Zionist members of the Old Yishuv.[9] Several antigenre writers of the 1920s and 1930s, such as Dov

8. That the lines between genre and antigenre were fluid is demonstrated, for example, by Smilansky's eventual change of tone in relation to the local Arabs. As Yaffa Berlowitz points out, Smilansky's later stories (1921–34) criticize the tendency among the Jewish settlers to isolate themselves totally from their Arab neighbors and call for a dialogue between the communities (1996, 159–66).

9. Re'uveni's linguistic "wanderings" may serve to indicate the cultural and linguistic fluidity that characterized European Jewish writers at the turn of the century. Re'uveni, born in Poltava, Ukraine, began writing in Russian and shifted to Yiddish during a stay in the United

Kimchi and Nathan Bistritsky, strove toward a more individual voice within this seemingly uniform society and tried to express some of the paradoxes and problematics of the Zionist project. Thus, Palestinian Hebrew literature was, in effect, less univocal than it seemed on the surface.

Yet its means of expression were hampered. In the absence of an accepted local literary vernacular, Palestinian Hebrew literature—which construed itself as an expression of the collective experience—characteristically employed the *nusach* to represent all registers of speech and inner sensibility, regardless of their connection with the style's source culture. As late as 1937, the European Jewish *nusach* served to reproduce the speech of a non-European, Yemenite Jew in the Yishuv (Chanani 1937). Even more incongruously, the rabbinic-dominant idiom of the *nusach* was used to represent the speech of non-Jews, such as an Arab fisherman (Shmeterling 1935). In his introduction to Nilli Sadan-Loebenstein's study on Yishuv prose of the 1920s, Avidov Lipsker notes that Hebrew prose language at the time, aware of its stylistic constraints, was deeply engaged in a struggle to shape and enrich itself (1991, 12). Shaked discerns attempts to shift from *nusach* to a new style but notes that these attempts fell short of success: "Hebrew fiction still suffered from the appearance of having been translated, as if the written language were only a representation of some other, oral language" (2000, 103–4).

Creating a literary representation of daily discourse was a difficult undertaking. Because Hebraist ideology negated the use of other languages in Jewish discourse, non-Hebrew phrases had to be identified clearly as foreign. Brenner, for example, fragmented the stilted conversational style of the *nusach* even further by interpolating other languages; he often represented a European language such as English, German, and Russian in its original orthography or set it off in quotation marks, intensifying the choppy, disjointed effect of his dialogues (1978, 1541–47) and blatantly disregarding the edict to preserve the "purity" of Hebrew. In 1926, Nathan Bistritsky used the *nusach* to convey the modernist anguish of a kibbutz member undergoing an ideological crisis of faith (1978, 157–68). Seeking stylistic solu-

---

States (1904–1905). After immigrating to Palestine (1910), he began publishing in *ha-Achdut*; his articles were translated from Yiddish by Brenner and others. Only in 1918 did he start writing in Hebrew, while continuing to write in Yiddish (Pilowsky 1991, esp. 8–11; Sadan-Loebenstein 1994). He apparently continued to write in Yiddish at least as late as 1923 (Pilowsky 1986, 257, 339–40n. 14).

tions to their poetic dilemmas, both these writers resorted, among other means, to ellipses and dashes in order to represent the untidy, halting processes of thought articulation within the normative style; these liberally scattered punctuation marks effectively disconnect the spoken phrases.[10] In actual fact, Israeli Hebrew eventually became a "fusion language" as well, enabling the incorporation of components from other languages (Harshav 1993a, 167–72). This is hardly surprising because Hebrew, as a language in constant written use, was always absorbing linguistic and cultural influences. Even-Zohar astutely points out that elements from Yiddish, such as intonation, that were not readily recognizable as Yiddish—and thus did not conflict with Zionist ideology—were admitted into modern Hebrew (1990a, 126). Oz Almog, in a path-breaking study of native Israeli culture, explains the inclusion of many Yiddish words in Hebrew slang of the 1940s and 1950s as owing to "the repugnance for Yiddish, which symbolized Diaspora culture, [and] made Yiddish words into inside jokes" (2000, 201). Yet Yosef Guri notes that about one-fifth of the one thousand idioms in spoken Hebrew are calques from Yiddish (1997, preface, n.p.). I do not deal here with the complexity of the Yishuv's changing attitudes toward Yiddish following the destruction of Europe's Jewish community in the Second World War. However, it is significant that David Grossman's major novel *Ayen Erekh Ahavah* (see under Love [1986]), for example, which addresses the Holocaust and its ramifications in Israeli society, contains a massive Yiddish subtext.

Yiddish literature, in contrast, was not bound by such stylistic or historical constraints; its tradition included epics, romances, novelettes, Hasidic legend, and hagiography.[11] The variegation that was a central feature of Yiddish proved to be an asset that facilitated the representation of social and ideological difference; Even-Zohar states that Yiddish was at the time "far superior to Hebrew from the point of view of its possibilities" (1990b, 157). The established and decisive vernacular tradition of the literature and many Yiddish writers' organic links with European modernisms enabled Yiddish

10. Distortion of syntax was one of the techniques used by precursors of Hebrew modernist prose such as M. Y. Berdichevsky in the late 1890s and by modernist writers such as David Fogel in the 1930s (Alter 1988).

11. Studies of older Yiddish literature are numerous. Among the most illuminating is Shmeruk 1978; see also Miron 1996 for an account of S. Y. Abramovitch's Yiddish literary antecedents.

writers in the Yishuv to admit and express the heterogeneity and problematics of local society and culture. Yiddish literature could reproduce the natural flow of the multifaceted language that most pioneers spoke. Moreover, because Yiddish did not bear the same ideological significance as Hebrew, its literature could be less orthodox in thematics as well. Differences could be voiced through the introduction of Yiddish idioms, dialects, and registers, as well as by the practice, conventional for Yiddish, of representing other languages in Yiddish orthography. The Zionist Yiddish writers of Palestine combined the full range of the Yiddish vernacular with inserts from other languages—a situation that was perfectly natural to their linguistic medium—and thus created an unforced, richly patterned polyphony that reflected the heterogeneity of the early Yishuv. As Harshav notes, "most creative work is done at an intersection of several cultural strains" (1994, 84). It was at precisely such an intersection that the Yiddish writers of the Yishuv were located, enabling their multifaceted work.

The personal experience of many native Israelis born before statehood echoed the conflict concerning language use. Yiddish was spoken in many homes, usually by the parents, and thus took on a positive aura of intimacy. Its identification with "the old," which Zionism negated, was problematic. The ambivalence created by this position, though suppressed, continued to reverberate and affect the nascent Hebrew culture. The vehemence with which Yiddish was ostracized in the Yishuv seems to indicate the extent of the internal struggle, a situation whose implications and ramifications have still not been fully acknowledged or examined. The persistent presence of the old language was buttressed by the fact that it was the first language of the majority.[12] The ambivalent position of *mame-loshn,* the mother tongue, both beloved and rejected, may be said to have haunted the prestatehood culture of Israel despite this culture's conscious allegiance to Hebrew and the eventual predominance of that language. Mainstream Israeli historians usually gloss over the ensuing psychological hardships, viewing them as a necessary hurdle on the way to attaining personal and collective goals. Yet careful readings of contemporaneous reports, discussions, and personal accounts in Hebrew and of later documents and memoirs indicate the extent of the problematics involved in the process of cultural rehoming. Cultural shift occurs at

---

12. Paradoxically, Yiddish speakers and their descendants are still perceived as dominating Israeli culture, although they became a numerical minority in the State of Israel after the massive influx of Jews from Arabic-speaking countries in the 1950s.

the crucial intersection of ideology and personal practice. A process of cultural archaeology such as I undertake here can provide insight into the founding process of a dynamic, living culture.

This study, then, lies in the indeterminate ground between historical and literary study. I illuminate the interplay of these two fields by alternating the focus between them because, as the cultural process unfolds, literature and history necessarily inform each other. The first and third chapters are historical in nature. Chapter 1 examines the unique role of language in the Zionist narrative in light of theories of nationalism and the construction of a national high culture. A series of close readings probes Hebrew Zionist documents of the twentieth century's second decade, uncovering and explicating the ideological subtexts of polemical essays written by people who were extremely conscious of the valence of language. These readings tease out some of the dilemmas inherent in the Zionist language imperative, such as the way in which the choice of Hebrew or Yiddish took on the additional implications of class difference carried over from European Jewish socialist attitudes (which considered Hebrew speakers elitist and Yiddish speakers populist). Chapter 3 charts the course of the conflict through the 1920s and 1930s, decades that were crucial to the formation of Yishuv culture. I analyze two paradigmatic clashes over the language issue in 1927, incidents that sparked an intense public debate verging on physical violence. Close readings of the reactions by leading Hebrew literary figures of the Yishuv juxtapose their explicit positions with unacknowledged practices and biases.

The continued de facto bilingualism of the Yishuv community provided the basis for the development of a local Yiddish literary culture. Chapters 2, 4, and 5 focus on this locally produced literature. The choice of writers examined reflects some of the different generational, ideological, and poetic features of the literature, with special emphasis on determining the poetic significance of the particular expressive capacities of Yiddish polyglotism. Chapter 2 presents short stories by Zalmen Brokhes, the Second Aliyah author who may be considered the first protomodernist Yiddish writer in Palestine. Brokhes, whose early work is largely non-Zionist, delineates a vision of Palestine that is more inclusive than the one depicted in contemporaneous idealizing Zionist presentations of the pioneering settlers and their surrounding culture: Muslims, Christians, and Jewish residents. Chapter 4 analyzes fiction by the Zionist and socialist Avrom Rivess as a manifestation of modernist writing serving local concerns. The Palestinian work of Rivess, an expressionist Yiddish writer, reconciles his ideology with his language. Using the receptivity of Yiddish to other languages, he was able to limn the cultural and ideological diversity of the Yishuv by giving voice to marginal figures within the community as well as to outsiders such as Arabs and non-Jews. Finally, in chapter 5, I examine the distinctive nativizing poetry of Rikuda Potash, who continued to write until 1965. Potash points the way toward a possible alternative Israeli culture that can reconcile the ideological opposites reified in the language choice. She combines a modernist sensibility with ancient European and Near Eastern traditions, refracting this poetic and thematic blend through the prism of Yiddish, the paradigmatic diasporic language, to create a distinctive new amalgam.

My attempt to recover the Yiddish culture of the Yishuv has teased out unexpected riches. The literature was popular and widely distributed: twenty-six Yiddish literary magazines were produced in Palestine between 1928 and 1946. Fiction, poetry, essays, and reviews by local Yiddish writers fill hundreds of pages. The perspectives and insights that emerge from these magazines provide an invaluable counterversion to the view presented by contemporaneous mainstream Hebrew literature. Discussing Kafka, the quintessential modern outsider, Gilles Deleuze and Felix Guattari remark that a writer who is "in the margins or completely outside his or her fragile community [is allowed] the possibility to express another possible community and to forge the means for another consciousness and another sensibility" (1993, 154). Although Deleuze and Guattari refer to minor literature written in the major language, Chana Kronfeld has shown that minor literature can in fact be written in a minor language (1996, 1–17). It is precisely this unacknowledged possibility that my study presents.

What Must Be
FORGOTTEN

CHAPTER ONE

Nationalism, Zionism, and the Formation of a National Narrative

Both the impulse which led to the creation of modern spoken Hebrew,
and the circumstances which led to its successful establishment, are too
unusual to set a general example.

— E. J. Hobsbawm, *Nations and Nationalism since 1780*

Hebrew in the Zionist Imaginary

Modern theories of nationalism recognize that the origins and course of Zionism, the national movement of the Jewish people, are unusual if not unique among late-nineteenth-century national movements. Major thinkers have expressed their awareness of this singularity in terms that imply varying degrees of mystification. Ernest Gellner considers the State of Israel, the outcome of Zionism, "the most famous and dramatic case of a successful diaspora nationalism," noting that "the human transformation involved in the Jewish case went counter to the global trend" (1983, 106–7). Gellner's choice of words such as *dramatic* and *transformation* to characterize the developments that culminated in the founding of Israel intimates the scholarly consensus, which notes the peculiarity of the phenomenon without elaborating on what makes it so. Benedict Anderson expresses his perplexity concerning Zionism in more striking language: "The significance of the emergence of Zionism and the birth of Israel is that the former marks the reimagining of an ancient religious community as a nation, down there among the other nations—while the latter charts an alchemic change from wandering devotee to local patriot" (1991, 149n. 16)

Although it is curious that this enigmatic passage does not address—or

1

even acknowledge—the causal connection between the two elements, Zionism and the State of Israel, it does indicate the general puzzlement at the manifestation of Jewish nationalism. When Anderson characterizes the effect of Zionism as alchemic, he seems at a loss to categorize the movement or the processes that led to its success: *alchemic* signifies an inexplicable, mysterious process of transmutation. According to this scenario, the Jews, recognized for centuries as a deterritorialized religious community, were somehow transformed into a national community anchored in a physical territory. Anderson does not analyze the way in which the Jews were "reimagined." Remarkably, though he is so keenly aware of the crucial significance of language in the development of national consciousness, he somehow misses its pivotal role in Zionism. Unique among national movements, Zionism might be said to have been conceived in language.

The lack of attention by such a seminal thinker to the key position of language in Zionism underscores an essential way in which "the Jewish case" calls into question some of the major assumptions of Western theories of nationalism. Thus, for example, the role of territory—a requirement that was a key component of national movements in the nineteenth century—was problematic in Jewish nationalism, where, in a sense, language replaced territory as the focus of national awakening. Nineteenth-century nationalist thought almost exclusively addressed the situation of nations that, though living in their homelands, were denied political independence. In fact, a foundational assumption of nationhood was the sustained physical location of the nation in its homeland—a specific geographical area—during a longer or shorter period of occupation by other powers, an occupation that had led to the marginalization of the previously dominant nation in its homeland.

The Jews, however, had overwhelmingly not remained in their ancestral homeland of Palestine during centuries of occupation (although a Jewish community, usually small, did exist there almost continuously, fed by constant immigration since the final loss of Jewish autonomy in 70 C.E.).[1] Since antiquity, they had been dispersed throughout the world, living in communi-

---

1. Detailed documentation of this minority Jewish community has been done, mostly by Israeli scholars interested in establishing its presence. See, for example, relevant articles and chapters in Avi-Yonah 1980, Cohen 1981, Kedar 1988, and Ya'akobi and Tsafrir 1988. Gellner's argument that "[n]early two thousand years of history had left no Jewish territorial base whatever, least of all in the land of Israel" (1983, 107) is based on his concept of a dominant population as a crucial base for nationhood.

ties sometimes totally isolated from each other. Thus, a "real" territorial base, which would satisfy conventional criteria, was not available to supply a basis for nationhood. Jewish nationhood obviously rested on a different foundation—that of a shared culture in which history, religion, and, in particular, language and its textual heritage were intertwined to occupy a central position. The territory, refigured as "Zion,"[2] became a powerful nation-forming locus of prayer and dream in the people's imaginary.

That culture as collective memory can provide a theoretical basis for this type of nationhood is clear from Ernest Renan's seminal definition in his Sorbonne lecture of 1882: "A nation is a soul, a spiritual principle. Two things, which in truth are but one, constitute this soul or spiritual principle. One lies in the past, one in the present. One is the possession in common of a rich legacy of memories; the other is present-day consent, the desire to live together" (Renan 1990, 19). Interestingly, Renan's flexibility of thought and ability to view the intangible as legitimate seem more modernist than the ideas of contemporary theorists, who still often apply the criterion of territoriality, thereby rejecting Renan's position. Gellner, for example, seems unhappy with culture as a criterion and qualifies it as inadequate for the understanding of nationalism (1983, 7). He explicitly challenges Renan in a chapter whose title—"What Is a Nation?"—is taken from Renan's essay. He concedes that "when general social conditions make for standardized, homogeneous, centrally sustained high cultures, pervading entire populations and not just elite minorities, a situation arises in which well-defined educationally sanctioned and unified cultures constitute very nearly the only kind of unit with which men willingly and often ardently identify. The cultures now seem to be the natural repositories of political legitimacy" (55). Gellner seems to be applying Benedict Anderson's concept of print capitalism, according to which "print-as-commodity" is "the key to the generation of wholly new ideas of simultaneity" (Anderson 1991, 37). Yet for Jews, whose ritual literature was mostly in the Jewish lingua franca of Hebrew, print capitalism was hardly a prerequisite or a necessary condition of nationalism. Most Jewish men were at least minimally literate in Hebrew, and all of them used the language in daily religious practice; European Jewish women and uneducated men read religious literature in Yiddish, written in Hebrew characters. Language and textual culture had been an integral part of quotidian

---

2. This biblical synonym for Jerusalem became expanded metonymically to designate the entire land. It was appropriated by the Jewish national movement and provided its name.

life for centuries, and the advent of widely circulated printed products hardly signaled a cultural revolution.

Gellner, in line with his essentializing tendencies, attempts to construct a typology of nationalisms. According to this typology, the territorial aspect is still the main criterion for nationhood even for minorities that lack territory ("diaspora nationalisms"): "For a dispersed urban population, the major problem is, of course, the acquisition of the required territorial base" (1983, 106). As I noted earlier, Gellner makes no attempt to address the "typological" anomalies of Zionism and Israel beyond the fact that they exist. He cites the State of Israel almost as a curiosity, without offering any explanation, quoting briefly from Hugh Trevor-Roper: " '[Zionism is] the last, least typical of European nationalisms' " (106–7).

What, then, makes Zionism and its end product, Israel, so atypical? Gellner ascribes the rise of Jewish nationalism mostly to persecutions of the Jews: "[T]his extraordinary transformation was achieved, no doubt thanks in large part to the incentive provided by the persecutions, first in eastern Europe and then throughout Europe during the period of the Holocaust" (1983, 107). Although he leaves open the issue of the other factors that led to the transformation of the Jews, admitting to the decisive function of a common culture in the formation of Zionism would seem to contradict his assumptions about the centrality of territory in national consciousness.

It is nevertheless true that a key unifying element in this culture was the traditional link with the ancestral homeland, expressed through language, which was an integral part of Jewish spiritual practice over the centuries. Exile from the homeland strengthened the sense of community and enabled the imagining of the nation, in Anderson's terminology. In the culture of exile, Eretz-Israel[3] became the site of national longing. The link with the long-lost homeland was expressed in countless prayers and ritual practices of Judaism. This bond was the basis for the foundational assumption of mainstream political Zionism: a national revival, complete with economic, political, and cultural autonomy, could take place only in Eretz-Israel.

Organized political Zionism was preceded by Chibat-Tziyon, the European proto-Zionist movement of the early 1880s that developed in the wake of pogroms in Russia. The very name of this movement, which means "Love of Zion," expressed its adherence to the traditional Jewish connection with

---

3. "Eretz-Israel"—the Land of Israel—is the traditional Hebrew name (adopted by Zionists) for the area that became known in late antiquity as Palestine.

Palestine. Impelled by a perceived need to address the problematics of Jewish life in the Diaspora, members of Chibat-Tziyon immigrated to Palestine in an attempt to lay the groundwork for an economically independent Jewish community there. By the end of the nineteenth century, these pioneers of the First Aliyah[4] (1882–1903) had established more than twenty-five Jewish agricultural settlements in Palestine. The political World Zionist Organization was founded in 1897, with the Land of Israel as the focus of its aspirations and efforts.[5]

It is important, however, to note that Zionists were a minority among European Jews; other solutions to "the Jewish problem" (all linked with language) had been suggested earlier within the community, and they continued to be proposed in the early years of the twentieth century. The Haskalah Jewish Enlightenment movement (roughly 1780–1880) had promoted "European culture, secular values, and aesthetic forms of behavior and writing" (Harshav 1993a, 59), with the aim of achieving political and cultural equality for the Jews within the states in which they lived, aspiring to an assimilation that would include language. One heir to Haskalah was Yiddishism, which evolved in the first decade of the century as a counterforce to Zionism in a continuation of efforts to attain civic equality in Europe. Yiddishists envisioned the survival of eastern European Jews as a distinct community enjoying emancipation as a national group, with Yiddish as their national language (Goldsmith 1976, 107–8). At the 1908 First Yiddish Language Conference in Czernowitz, after heated debates between Zionists and Yiddishists, Yiddish was in fact proclaimed as a national language of the Jewish people.[6]

---

4. The Hebrew term for immigration to Palestine signifies a move to a higher plane of existence, as it were, with the move to the Holy Land. Zionism appropriated the term to mean waves of immigration motivated by Zionist ideology. Individual immigrants were and are still termed *olim* (ascenders). The different backgrounds and ideological trends of each *aliyah,* as well as the reaction to each group of newcomers, were crucial for the formation of Zionist culture in Palestine.

5. In 1903, the movement's leader, Theodor Herzl, made a short-lived attempt to shift the practical emphasis of Zionism from Palestine to East Africa (the "Uganda Plan"), almost causing the dissolution of the organization. This alternative plan, suggested by the British, to establish a Jewish national home in Africa was diametrically opposed to the traditional link with Eretz-Israel and was rejected by the Sixth Zionist Congress (Shimoni 1995, 98–99).

6. It is not clear whether this ambiguous proclamation was addressed to Jews or non-Jews or both. There is scant information about the reaction to the Czernowitz conference in the ruling circles of the Hapsburg Empire. However, an effort in 1910 to include Yiddish as one of the

Another movement, the socialist Jewish Bund of Russia and Poland (founded in 1897), at first limited its Jewish program to the struggle for equal civil and political rights in those states, viewing Zionism as a reactionary, utopian, and petit-bourgeois phenomenon that would harm the Jewish masses (Goldsmith 1976, 80–85). The Bund allied itself with Yiddishism when it defined Yiddish as *the* Jewish national language and entered into an extreme confrontation with Zionism. Within Zionism, a territorial faction that considered other physical locations for Jewish settlement eventually seceded from the World Zionist Organization and formed the Jewish Territorialist Organization. An alternative form of Zionism was the nonpolitical "cultural Zionism" propounded by the influential Jewish writer Asher Ginzberg (better known by his pen-name Achad ha-Am, One of the People), who believed in 1901 that the establishment of a spiritual (rather than political) national center in Palestine would provide "a 'safe refuge' for our nation's *spirit*" (1921, 129, emphasis in the original) and would serve as a safeguard against assimilation.[7] Yet it was political Zionism that eventually succeeded in realizing its goal in the traditional Land of Israel.[8]

Zionism, with its roots in the deterritorialized diasporic "location" of Jewish culture, aspired to reterritorialize the Jewish nation at the expense of the same diasporic culture. The movement focused on a yearning to return to the homeland, negating diasporic life in its goal of creating a new culture. The tension inherent in a movement that strives to overthrow its own base—by disowning its immediate past and present for the sake of the future—reverberated significantly in the formative stages of the Yishuv. Far from being resolved by the gradual realization of the Zionist dream, this tension continued to lie at the core of the Yishuv throughout its formative stages and exists perhaps even in the Israel of today.

The opposition between the old values of the deterritorialized culture and the envisioned values of a reterritorialized nation was cardinal. Benjamin Harshav, expanding on what he terms "the force of negation" (1993a, 17–23), notes that the "Jewish revolution" at the turn of the twentieth century consisted in a negation of the three deictics "here, now, I." The impera-

official languages of the Austro-Hungarian Empire was unsuccessful. For a detailed survey of Yiddishism and of the First Yiddish Language Conference, see Goldsmith 1976.

7. For a discussion of Achad ha-Am as well as of the territorialist orientation within Zionism, see S. Almog 1987, 129–41, 238–304.

8. See, for example, Shimoni 1995 for a detailed history of Zionism and its various facets.

tives, therefore, were: "not here"—that is, out of the shtetl to the city or to another country altogether; "not like now"—that is, a struggle for political and personal change; and "not me"—that is, a need to refashion one's own personality (which, as we shall see, often led to a mobilization of the individual subject to the needs of the collective). It was part of the Zionist credo that a refiguring of the self would lead to a refiguring of the nation. Zionism integrated these three imperatives in its vision of a new Jewish character and culture that would be forged in the ancestral homeland. The revolutionary makeover was embodied in Hebrew—the ancient, sacred language common to all Jews and a fundamental component of their culture, which the founders of Zionism sought to adopt for everyday use. Although Renan did not consider language an indisputable criterion of nationhood, other European theorists clearly regard it as an integral component, perhaps the most crucial one, of national culture—though not, as noted, in the case of the Jewish nation. Anderson refers to the late-eighteenth-century romantic European conception of "nation-ness as linked with private-property language" that begins with Johann Herder (1991, 67–68). Classic Zionist ideology designated Hebrew as the "private-property" language of the Jewish people, and its use became a signifier of nationhood.

The revival of Hebrew had begun earlier, during the Haskalah. Its writers began creating secular literature in biblical Hebrew, the traditional Jewish language of "high culture." Hebrew, as Robert Alter notes, "had always been the most valued language of Jewish culture . . . and had long been the medium of refined literary exercises and epistolary art" (1988, 13). Its cultural prestige was unique. As the language of a tradition of Jewish learning that had been identified with men over the centuries, it was also a marker of masculinity.

Yiddish, in contrast, the vernacular of most eastern and some central European Jews, was the language of quotidian discourse and as such was considered a signifier of "low culture." Although both men and women used it in daily life, texts and religious books for girls and women were written in Yiddish (as Harshav notes, however, they were "also read and enjoyed by men albeit as a peripheral or secular genre" [1990, 23n. 4]). The perception of Yiddish as a marker of femininity was to figure significantly in the Hebrew-Yiddish conflict.[9] At the outset, Haskalah ideological writers used both Yiddish and Hebrew, each for a different purpose: they used Yiddish as an

9. Shmuel Niger's 1913 essay "Di Yidishe Literatur un di Lezerin" (Yiddish literature and the female reader [1985]) is a ground-breaking attempt to delineate the gender implications of

initial vehicle for disseminating Haskalah ideas and construed the new secular Hebrew (as distinct from the traditional language of ritual) as a familiar yet higher-ranking language of transition between "low" Yiddish culture and the eventual adoption of European cultures. With the extinction of the Haskalah dream of assimilation following the Russian pogroms of the early 1880s, there seemed to be no further purpose for the secular use of Hebrew.

For most Jewish ideologists, the Hebrew-Yiddish opposition was emblematic of modernization. Mainstream Zionism, however, gave *Hebrew* a new valence beyond the name of a language. Zionists considered the full-scale revival of the ancient language for everyday use both a prerequisite for and a sign of the projected national renewal. *Hebrew* came into use both as an adjective and a proper noun, to describe the future Jewish society and the individual of the Yishuv. In 1905, the ardent young Zionist Vladimir Jabotinsky painted (in Russian) a vivid portrait of the future Palestinian "Hebrew" that, as Amnon Rubinstein points out, was derived from a conscious juxtaposition with the prevalent image of the Diaspora Jew:

> Our starting point is to take the typical Zhid [Jew] of today and to imagine his diametrical opposite . . . because the Zhid is ugly, sickly. . . . [W]e shall endow the ideal image of the Hebrew with masculine beauty. . . . The Zhid is trodden upon and easily frightened, and the other one ought to be proud and independent. The Zhid is despised by all, and the other one ought to charm all. The Zhid is accustomed to surrender, and therefore the other one ought to learn how to command. The Zhid prefers to conceal his identity from strangers, and the other one ought to march forth with courage and dignity, look the world straight in the eye and flaunt his banner: "I am a Hebrew!" (Jabotinsky 1958, 99)

This passage encapsulates contemporary Zionists' attitude toward diasporic culture as concentrated in the anti-Semitic persona of the "Zhid." Jabotinsky did not invent this pejorative term for Jews—it was commonly used in Slavic countries—but his (or his translator's) use of it is a stunning example of an internalization of anti-Semitic stereotypes that fueled the Zionists' own sense of themselves as revolutionaries.[10] As Naomi Seidman notes,

---

Yiddish. For a finely nuanced analysis of the role of gender in the Yiddish-Hebrew opposition, see Seidman 1997.

10. For a detailed examination of the psychosexual implications of this internalization, see Boyarin 1997.

"the disempowered diaspora existence . . . was often consciously or unconsciously perceived as having emasculated or feminized the Jewish collective" (1997, 110). The choice of *Hebrew* to designate far more than the language at this early stage of Zionism is telling; expressing the Zionist ideal, the word identifies a reinvented public and private persona. The Zhid is ugly, sickly, cowardly, despised, and submissive, whereas the ideal Hebrew will be beautiful, healthy, proud, commanding, and self-assertive. But let us note Jabotinsky's use of a subjunctive conditional mode rather than a straightforward future tense in this description. The wishful *tzarikh lihiyot* (ought to be) instead of the confident *yihiyeh* (will be) seems to subvert the certainty of conviction that he expressed so forcefully in other writings. The overtone of doubt foreshadows the inherent tension and ambivalence that complicated the individual's decision to abandon native cultural values and reinvent the national subject.

Yid, the English version of the slur, evokes Yiddish, the name of the language identified with the Diaspora and its values. The standing of Yiddish as a language was further weakened by quasi-scientific opinion; the mother tongue of most Zionist immigrants to Palestine was termed *jargon*.[11] Paradoxically, the term—derogatory to this day—was internalized by the Jews whose culture it disparaged and was widely used in Jewish letters as early as the Haskalah;[12] Haskalah ideologues viewed Yiddish as an unavoidable tool toward Enlightenment, to be discarded as soon as Jews were able to use other languages. In the nineteenth century, the term *jargon* lost much of its negative valence for European Jews and was in widespread use by Jews and non-Jews alike as the name of the language. It was only in 1903 that *zhargon* was replaced by *Yiddish* in the masthead of the popular European Yiddish

---

11. Of course, Zionism and the Yishuv included Jews who did not speak Yiddish, a fact that mainstream histories largely gloss over. Alcalay (1993) makes a seminal effort to balance the mainstream emphasis on the role of European Jews in the Yishuv and to place this role in a larger context. Interestingly, as seen in later chapters, it was Yiddish writers in Zionist Palestine who were not only keenly aware of the cultural and emotional situation of the Zionist non-European minority, but gave it unique expression.

12. An authoritative 1960 definition of *jargon* runs, in part, *"(a)* a language, speech or dialect that is barbarous or outlandish; *(b)* a hybrid speech or dialect arising from a mixture of languages . . . or one artificially made up. Specifically: Yiddish" *(Webster's)*. By 1987, the reference to Yiddish had been dropped, but *Webster's* definition retains the elements of incomprehensibility and nonnormativity : *"(a)* confused unintelligible language; *(b)* a strange, outlandish, or barbarous language or dialect."

newspaper *Der Fraynd*. Viewed in this light, Yiddish seemed to bear out nineteenth-century racist European notions that people speaking a hybrid language were somehow inferior and incapable of clear, intelligible, and sophisticated thought. Thus, according to Zionism, the language had to be discarded if the people were to improve and reinvent themselves.

The choice of Hebrew as the national language was a corollary of Zionism's selective relationship with the nation's history. At the 1901 conference of Russian Zionists in Minsk, Achad ha-Am (Asher Ginzberg) stated: "A nation has no national language except that which was its own when it stood on the threshold of its history, before its national self-consciousness was fully developed" (1921, 126). Achad ha-Am here echoed prevalent nationalist terminology, with its roots in romanticism. An intimate kinship with the classical past is central for a nation whose culture idealizes antiquity. For the Jewish nation, "the threshold of its history" was the pre-exilic period, antedating diasporic existence. In Jewish collective memory, the biblical period—emblematized by Hebrew, the language of the Bible—came to be viewed as a time of purity in heart and purpose (discounting the Bible's own diatribes against the people's disobedience of divine law).[13] Anderson places this particular bond within the context of nineteenth-century nationalism: "Nations to which they [nation-states] gave political expression always loom out of an immemorial past" (1991, 11). Elaborating on the Zionist construction of a collective identity, Yael Zerubavel comments: "The selective reconstruction of Antiquity was part of the historical mission of reviving the ancient national roots and spirit. Antiquity became both a source of legitimation and an object of admiration" (1995, 25).[14]

Interestingly, a similar analysis was made in the Yishuv as early as 1914, with a highly negative conclusion. A major thinker of the Po'alei Zion (Workers of Zion) Labor Party, Alexander Chashin, spoke of Yishuv educators as "teaching our youth to hate the Diaspora and with it—its language.

---

13. The Bible itself contains examples of such tendentious construals of the past as a time of absolute righteousness. Taking the nation to task for sins in his own time, Jeremiah evokes an idealized earlier era in a famous evaluation of the post-Exodus wanderings in the desert: "Thus saith the Lord, I remember the devotion of your youth, your love as a bride, how you followed me in the wilderness, in a land not sown" (Jer. 2:2). Applying the common biblical metaphor of Israel as a wife, Jeremiah is disregarding here the Bible's numerous mentions of Israel's transgressions precisely during that period.

14. See Yael Zerubavel for a cogent analysis of the selective memory involved in what she terms "the Zionist reconstruction of the Jewish past" (1995, 30).

. . . They take a historic leap to the point of breaking their necks, from the destruction of the Second Temple [70 C.E.] to the founding of Rishon le-Tziyon [1882] and totally obliterate the long period in between these two events" (1914, cols. 1–2).[15] The tendency to idealize the pre-exilic Near East found its most extreme expression in the "Canaanite" political and cultural movement of the Yishuv in the early 1940s; the ideologists and artists of this movement dissociated from any form of late biblical or rabbinic Judaism and attached themselves to premonotheistic regional traditions, buttressed by the archaeological discoveries of the previous half-century. The derogatory name was given the group by the poet Avraham Shlonsky (1900–1973), who was not a member; the disparaging tone derives from the fact that the biblical Canaanites were traditional enemies of the people of Israel. The group termed itself Ivrim Tze'irim (Young Hebrews). Although the movement never gained widespread popularity, the nativist values it espoused while categorically negating all exilic values had a disproportionate impact on Yishuv culture. The "Canaanites," whom I discuss later in greater detail, became a major force in the Israeli art and Hebrew literature of the Statehood Generation (1950–60) and beyond.[16]

The Jewish national movement was not unique in the extraordinary value it placed on the past. It is instructive to examine its analogies with the mid-nineteenth-century Greek national movement.[17] Like the emerging Jewish national movement several decades later, Greek nationalism redefined the

15. Chashin's life was typical of many young Jewish intellectuals of the time. A brilliant writer, Alexander Chashin (Averbukh) was a major leader of Po'alei Zion before the First World War, began distancing himself from Zionism in the 1920s, and joined communist circles. He moved to the USSR in the late 1920s and worked for the Soviet Yiddish newspaper *Der Emes*. However, his Zionist past was apparently deemed unsuitable there, and he was executed in 1937; his name was cleared in 1950 (Berger-Barzilai 1968, 62–89).

16. For a detailed presentation of "Canaanite" ideology, politics, and history, see Y. Shavit 1984; for an overview of the group's impact on Israeli society and culture, see Diamond 1986 and Gertz 1985; for the relationship between "Canaanism" and mainstream Zionism, see Shimoni 1995, 316–21. For more specific discussions of the influence of the movement on the Yishuv's visual arts and literature, see Zalmona 1998, esp. 66–67; and see my discussion of the "Canaanizing" Yiddish poetry of Rikuda Potash in chapter 5.

17. Gregory Jusdanis notes several parallels between the Greek national movement and Zionism, such as similar grounds for their appeal to the West: "the Greeks laid claim to the cultural and secular roots of western civilization, while the Zionists exploited the foundational role of the Hebrew Bible in the Judeo-Christian tradition" (1991, 14). However, his choice of language in making this comparison is not impartial. Jusdanis seems to imply that the Greeks had

link to the classical past, a past that was reified in a language. Greek culture over the centuries had traditionally included a modern vernacular (termed *demotic*) and an ancient, sanctified "classic" language, *katharevusa* (albeit in a modified archaistic form rather than in the truly classical Greek). Similarly, European Jewish culture used Yiddish as its vernacular and Hebrew (in its original form) as its sacred language. A cultural war ensued in late-nineteenth-century Greece between supporters of the vernacular and those who strove to revive the purist language. A hybrid of demotic and *katharevusa* was designated as the official language of the state, education, and "serious" writing, but demotic continued to be used in popular culture, including its literature; the Greek cultural struggle has been resolved only rather recently in favor of demotic. Gregory Jusdanis even argues that in Greece the disjunction between the realms of the state and national culture frustrated the formation of a cultural homogeneity (1991, 46). In Zionist Palestine, in contrast, it was Hebrew, the sacred language, that predominated and provided the basis for the culture.

Zionism's selective reconstruction of the past designated Hebrew as the once and future language of the new community. For Christian Europe, whose support was deemed vital for any future Jewish political entity, the biblical connection with the language would substantiate the image of antiquity so crucial to modern nationalism and would legitimize the nation that lacked a recognized territorial base. Yet the correlation of Hebrew with the idealized values of a specific historical period was at least in part artificial. Hebrew was not the only language spoken by the residents of pre-exilic Judah; the Bible itself provides one of the earliest examples of bilingualism among them. Aramaic was a Judahite court language: in the conversation between the commander of the Assyrian army and King Hezekiah's officials during the Assyrian siege of Jerusalem in 729 B.C.E., the Judahite officials emphasize their knowledge of Aramaic (2 Kgs. 18:26).[18] Over the following centuries, Aramaic grew increasingly widespread and became a major component of postbiblical (rabbinic) Hebrew. The ubiquitous Aramaic, the regional lingua franca of the time, was the vernacular of the Jewish residents of Palestine for centuries and apparently was the language that Jesus and the

---

a legitimate "claim" to the roots of Western civilization, whereas the Zionists unfairly "exploited" the Jewish connection to the Bible.

18. The incident is repeated in a slightly different version in Isaiah 36:11 and 2 Chronicles 32.

Jews of his time spoke (the Babylonian Talmud is written predominantly in Aramaic, as are innumerable ancient Jewish inscriptions and documents). Thus, the choice of Hebrew as the language of the revival was an act that involved an adjustment of the perception of the past, or of a particular (imagined) past, to suit the nationalist requirement. Ironically, Aramaic components that had become part of the *leshon-kodesh* (sacred language) over the centuries constituted a significant proportion of modern Hebrew as it was forming in the late nineteenth century. This fact went virtually unremarked by the zealous modern "revivers" of Hebrew, who chose to highlight the biblical components.

By the second decade of the twentieth century, *Hebrew* was being widely used to signify the reinvented Jewish community. In the Yishuv, the adjective *Hebrew* was adopted—rather than, say, *Jewish* or *Zionist*—for the four units of Jewish volunteers (the Zion Mule Corps and the Thirty-eighth, Thirty-ninth, and Fortieth Royal Fusiliers) that were formed in the British army toward the end of the First World War (the "Jewish Legion"). These units were thus known in the Yishuv as the *ha-gedudim ha-ivriyim* (Hebrew battalions); it is worth noting that many, if not most, of the volunteers knew no Hebrew beyond traditional religious usage. The Yishuv's name for the units indicates the Zionist hope—echoing Jabotinsky's vision—that those who served in them would be freed of the stigma that all Jews were cowards. Their new "Hebrew" identity would be synonymous with bravery on the battlefield.

The 1922 volume *Cholmim ve-Lochamim* (Dreamers and warriors), a collection of pieces published in Palestine to praise the founders of the Yishuv, exemplifies some applications of the adjective *Hebrew* in the prevailing cultural climate. The book opens with a description of Yehoshua Shtamper, a proto-Zionist founder of Petach-Tikvah (1879).[19] The writer, Ya'akov Ya'ari-Poleskin, uses mainstream Zionist terminology when he describes Shtamper as "one of the first founders and builders of the first Hebrew settlement [in Eretz-Israel]."[20] Although Hebrew as a spoken language was still a dream in the 1880s, the pioneering settlement with its new ideology is char-

19. Petach-Tikvah is usually considered the first modern Jewish settlement in Palestine.

20. The writer's hybrid last name is composed of his original Russian name (Poleskin, connoting "forest") and its literal translation into the Hebrew, *ya'ar* (forest), with an adjectival ending. The hebraization of personal names in an act of renaming was a hallmark of Zionist practice that, as Amos Elon points out, "reflected the emotional climate of the times [and a] fervor to live the revolution body and soul" (1971, 131).

acterized in hindsight as Hebrew. Ya'ari-Poleskin continues in this vein when he speaks of "Tel-Aviv, the Hebrew quarter of Jaffa" rather than the "Jewish quarter," and of "Hebrew workers" in Galilee rather than of "Jewish workers" (1922, 17, 78). However, in the first decade of the twentieth century, neither the founders of Tel-Aviv nor the Zionist immigrants to Galilee were likely to speak Hebrew. Ya'ari-Poleskin and others concretized in the language all their aspirations and hopes for the future community. This characterization persisted well into the period of Israeli statehood. The third volume of a mid-twentieth-century history textbook, which was a staple of Israel's educational system for decades, differentiates between "the Hebrew Yishuv in the Land and the Jewish people of the world" (Ettinger 1969, 282).

A more recent study gently interrogates the identification of nationalism with Hebrew in Yishuv culture. Elyakim Rubinstein's essay on the history of the Yishuv details the agenda of its first organizational meeting in 1918, which addressed "Hebrew language and culture, the Hebrew *militzyah* [military force] . . . Hebrew civil law . . . and Hebrew labor" (1979, 152). Rubinstein is evidently struck by the aggregation of instances of *Hebrew* used as an adjective rather than as a noun and appends a rare footnote: "The use of the word 'Hebrew' as an attribute of each item in the agenda is interesting. This is characteristic of the prestatehood period, and indicates Jewish institutions or actions, as opposed to government or non-Jewish bodies and actions. 'Hebrew' also indicated the revival of the Hebrew language in Palestine" (152). He is aware that the use of *Hebrew* in this context went far beyond its lexical significance. By separating his observation into two parts, he notes the cultural implications of the 1918 phrasing, according to which every Jewish project in Palestine was defined as Hebrew even if it had nothing to do with the language per se. His remark is an instance, rather unusual in traditional Zionist historiography, of sensitivity to the ideological implications of Zionist terminology.

Rubinstein is also careful with his phraseology when he describes the curriculum of the Yishuv's elementary schools: "About one-third of the curriculum was devoted to Hebrew subjects because the schools regarded themselves as shaping the Eretz-Israeli Jew growing up in the land and his national culture with its new character" (1979, 217). Although he characterizes the curriculum subjects as *Hebrew,* he defines the young Zionist natives of Palestine—the objects of this educational system—as *Eretz-Israeli Jews* rather than as the more conventional *Hebrew,* with its attached valences. He does not detail the Hebrew parts of the curriculum; in the tradition of the time, they probably consisted of subjects with a bearing on Jewish history in Palestine. Rubinstein's distinction between Hebrew subjects and Eretz-Israeli Jews is noteworthy for its tacit questioning of the mainstream's terminology.

The opposition "Hebrew-Jewish" is still resonant today, though *Israeli* gradually replaced *Hebrew* as an adjective after the founding of the state. Shlomo ha-Ramati, writing more recently on the evolution of Hebrew into a national language, perpetuates the mainstream position when he consistently refers to Zionist education in Palestine as *ivri-le'umi* (Hebrew national), opposing it to other modernizing educational projects such as the Alliance Israelite schools for Jewish boys established in Jerusalem in 1883 by the French Jewish aid organization of that name. The Alliance school, says ha-Ramati, "was not a Hebrew-national institution, but a modern Jewish school. . . . [T]he first Hebrew-national school began to operate in Rishon Le-Tziyon in 1888" (1997, 147–48). The clear implication is that Alliance school pupils were members of the Old Yishuv (the Zionist name for the native Palestinian Jews whose culture was considered to be of a negative diasporic nature), not motivated by proto-Zionist ideology—unlike the founders of the Rishon Le-Tziyon school.

Building a Hebrew Nation

The establishment of the new "Hebrew" values did not come easily or naturally to the immigrants who made up the population of the Yishuv. It was necessary to implement a nation-building policy, in the sense applied by Anderson when he speaks of post-Second World War states: "[I]n the new states one sees both a genuine, popular nationalist enthusiasm and a systematic, even Machiavellian, instilling of nationalist ideology through the mass media, the educational system, administrative regulations, and so forth" (1991, 114). The prestatehood Zionist leadership certainly used systematic measures in order to shape the Yishuv as the basis for a future state. Early on, the Seventh Zionist Congress (1905) adopted the majority view that the educational system in Eretz-Israel should be "Hebrew in character" (Ettinger 1969, 189). The Tenth and Eleventh Zionist Congresses (1911 and 1913) affirmed and encouraged the Yishuv's exclusive use of Hebrew. The quasi-official Yishuv press was Hebrew (an attempt in 1908 to publish a Zionist Yiddish newspaper in Palestine ceased after two issues).[21] By 1914, Hebrew

---

21. See the discussion of this attempt in chapter 3.

was the exclusive language of instruction (Wallach 1974, 29). In 1923, the British Mandate authorities named Hebrew as one of the official languages of Palestine, along with English and Arabic. The victory of Hebrew seemed to be complete. Nonmainstream positions in the Yishuv concerning the language choice, such as the position supporting the legitimation of Yiddish, were frowned upon and strongly discouraged. The Yishuv was beginning to construct a mainstream narrative that could not concede the existence of an alternative culture—or even a subculture—marked by language because such an admission would cast doubt on the total success of the project.

The dominance of Hebrew came at a steep price, although public opinion largely concurred in the need to adopt the language. Let us return to Renan's seminal definition of nationhood in "What Is a Nation?" in 1882: "The essence of a nation is that all individuals have many things in common, and also that they have forgotten many things" (1990, 11). What are the "things" that the members of the nation have forgotten and that, if remembered, might endanger the nation's essence? In illustration, Renan referred explicitly to acts of physical brutality that he believed are sometimes necessary in order to achieve national unity. From his late-nineteenth-century position, he mentioned specific acts of violence and massacres carried out in the course of molding the French nation. Renan's emphasis on the imperative of forgetting is intriguing: "[E]very French citizen has to have forgotten the massacre of Saint Bartholomew, or the massacres that took place in the Midi in the thirteenth century" (11). Commenting on Renan, Homi Bhabha takes special note of the rhetoric and syntax of the latter's argument:

It is this forgetting—the signification of a minus in the origin—that constitutes the beginning of the nation's narrative. It is the syntactical and rhetorical arrangement of this argument that is more illuminating than any frankly historical or ideological reading. Listen to the complexity of this form of forgetting which is the moment in which the national will is articulated: 'yet every French citizen has to have forgotten [*is obliged to have forgotten*] Saint Bartholomew's Night's Massacre, or the massacres that took place in the Midi in the thirteenth century.' It is through this syntax of forgetting—or being obliged to forget—that the problematic identification of a national people becomes visible. (1994, 310, square brackets and emphasis in the original)

The nation cannot be articulated until the forgetting is complete; a new beginning to the national narrative is contingent upon forgetting the old one. Bhabha's argument about the centrality and implications of forgetting for the nation's sense of identity is particularly applicable for understanding the development of the Yishuv's culture. The syntax of forgetting was crucial to Zionism, which sought to discard diasporic Jewish culture and to obliterate its very existence from collective memory in order to realize its own ideology and vision. The success of the new creation depended on the suppression of the old one, including its most emblematic element, the Yiddish language.

So total was the act of official forgetting that the prolonged Hebrew-Yiddish conflict, which was of such personal and general cultural significance, is often not even mentioned in the mainstream histories. Thus, Ettinger presents only the Hebrew-German *"riv ha-leshonot"* (language quarrel) of 1913 as the key event leading to the victory of Hebrew in the schools of the Yishuv. The German Jewish philanthropic organization Ezra stipulated that German be the language of instruction in the technical schools it was establishing in Palestine. Says Ettinger: "This decision gave rise to a wave of protest in the Yishuv. Most of the 'Ezra' school students went on strike and the teachers resigned. . . . Since [the resolution of the clash in favor of Hebrew,] the dominance of Hebrew throughout the educational system in the country was assured" (1969, 210). Ettinger subsumes the Hebrew-Yiddish opposition in a brief reference to the "war about the languages of Jewish creativity" (219) in which he takes a long historical and geographic view when he groups Yiddish with Aramaic, Greek, Arabic, and Spanish. By doing so, he minimizes the cultural and political significance of the language dilemma.

Efraim Talmi and Menachem Talmi's popular reference book *Leksikon Tziyoni* (Lexicon of Zionism) gives substantially the same account, using the more militant term *"milchemet ha-safot"* (language war), and ends with the triumphant statement, "The struggle ended with the victory of the Hebrews [*ha-ivrim*]" (1981, 226–27). The authors seem to shift the cultural dispute into the realm of militant physicality, which the Hebrew-Yiddish dispute also inhabited.[22] It is not education in Hebrew that is victorious, but "the Hebrews," conjuring up a David-and-Goliath scenario. In this interpretation, the brave young Hebrews—students, teachers, and workers—are pitted

22. See the discussion of the incident, which included physical violence, in chapter 3.

against a formless bureaucracy that controlled the funding for the proposed schools. Elyakim Rubinstein, too, refers to the German-Hebrew language conflict of 1913 as the decisive event that led to the "victory of national Hebrew education" (1979, 214). But here again he proves more discerning than other historians when he appends a note about the significance of the attribute *Hebrew* in the names of the Yishuv's early educational flagship institutions, the 1905 Hebrew Herzliya High School (known as Gymnazyah Hertzliyah) in Jaffa and the 1909 Hebrew High School (Gymnazyah Ivrit) in Jerusalem: "It is not for nothing that the name 'Hebrew' appears in the names of these institutions. It symbolizes their innovative character" (214).

When these standard histories of the Yishuv mention Yiddish, they carefully circumscribe it within mainstream parameters. They characterize it in terms of the geographic Diaspora, or the Old Yishuv. None of these sources acknowledge the fact that Yiddish was widely used in the Zionist "new" Yishuv. Talmi and Talmi devote their entry on Yiddish to the spread of the language in the European Diaspora. Speaking of the movement known as Yiddishism, their *Leksikon Tziyoni* explains: "From the end of the nineteenth century, a cultural movement developed and grew among the Jews of eastern Europe that aimed to base secular nationalism in the diasporic locations of the nation in exile on the foundation of the Yiddish language, its literature, and press" (1981, 181). In this characterization, Yiddish is located exclusively in the Diaspora (although "the recent center [of Yiddish] in Israel" is noted [181]). Rubinstein, too, situates Yiddish exclusively within the prestatehood Old Yishuv, equating it with the Diaspora community. His appendix on the Old Yishuv notes its members' demand to receive municipal funds for "education in Yiddish, as was formerly the custom, and as was still practiced in the Diaspora at the time" (1979, 203). He identifies Yiddish with anti-Zionism. Describing the Jewish communist factions in Palestine, he says, "These communist groups chose Yiddish names in order to symbolize their negative attitude toward Zionism and their identification with the Jewish communists in the USSR" (278). True to the syntax of forgetting, none of these historians mentions the Yishuv's own intense and changing relationship with Yiddish. Such resounding silence on a vital cultural issue may well express a deep ambivalence on the issue as well as the sense that Yiddish was a continuing threat to Yishuv culture throughout the prestatehood period.

In fact, there were clashes, sometimes violent, within the Yishuv over the role and use of Yiddish. For example, teen-aged students of the Gymnazyah Hertzliyah forcibly prevented Chaim Zhitlovsky, the foremost proponent of

Yiddishism in eastern Europe, from giving the last in a series of talks in Yiddish in Palestine in 1914 (Pilowsky 1986, 17, 70n. 15); they tore his shirt as he was leaving the hotel for his lecture. Decades later, an eyewitness recounted in 1945 that stones were thrown at the hotel and shots were fired (Yatziv 1947, 567). It is significant that the students were incited by their principal, Chaim Bugrashov; this was not simply the impulsive response of hotheaded teenagers, but an act guided by one of the Yishuv's most respected educators and cultural leaders. Although the Zhitlovsky incident was heatedly discussed in the Yishuv's contemporary press,[23] it does not appear in later histories. Nonthreatening issues, however, are openly discussed in these histories. Thus, because German was never a contender for cultural dominance in the Yishuv, the failed 1913 attempt to use it as a language of instruction is considered a banner for the victory of Hebrew. The common and persistent use of Yiddish, in contrast, goes unnoted.

Yiddish was a force to be reckoned with in this period. It provided the name for and was an integral part of the Yiddishist movement that proposed an alternative to Zionism. The Yiddish-Hebrew issue served the different ideological positions of both Bundists and the Zionist participants in the 1908 First Yiddish Language Conference; the left-wing non-Zionists considered Zionism a bourgeois movement and Hebrew the language of a small group of Jewish intellectuals.[24] The language issue became a convenient tool of political conflicts within contemporary Jewish culture.

The strategy that the mainstream Zionist culture of the early Yishuv adopted toward Yiddish can perhaps be best understood through Gellner's notion of a high culture. Rephrasing and expanding Renan's principle about forgetting, Gellner's formulation resonates deeply with the course taken by the Yishuv:

> Nationalism has its own amnesias and selections which, even when they may be severely secular, can be profoundly distorting and deceptive. The basic deception and self-deception practised by nationalism is this: nationalism is, essentially, the general imposition of a high culture on society, where previously low cultures had taken up the lives of the majority, and in

---

23. Such as *ha-Achdut* 5, no. 37 (10 July 1914) and nos. 38–39 (24 July 1914).

24. This view was later echoed by the Palestinian Po'alei Zion Party, whose left-wing members militated in favor of using Yiddish in Palestine. The Yiddish publications in Zionist Palestine were popularly associated with Po'alei Zion in a politicization of a cultural issue.

some cases of the totality, of the population. . . . The nationalism revives, or invents, a local high (literate, specialist-transmitted) culture of its own, though admittedly one which will have some links with the earlier folk-styles and dialects. (1983, 56–57)

At the turn of the twentieth century, the deliberate imposition of a high culture in the interests of ideology seemed a natural corollary of the paternalism that was part of Enlightenment thinking. Referring to the process that shaped the culture of modern Greece, Jusdanis applies the notion of an imposed culture when he states, "The idea of a national culture, the invention of a new identity, was made possible by cultural engineering" (1991, 26). Paradoxically, it was the young Zionists, rebelling against tradition, who imposed this high culture and made Hebrew, the language of the diasporic Jewish cultural elite, its emblem. A concept akin to cultural engineering seems to underlie at least one early discussion on Hebrew and Yiddish in the Yishuv.

In 1910, Po'alei Zion—which, along with ha-Po'el ha-Tza'ir (the Young Worker), was one of Palestine's two main Labor Zionist political parties—was debating the publication of a Yiddish-language newspaper.[25] Countering the arguments in favor of a Yiddish publication, David Ben-Gurion (1886–1973), one of the founding fathers of the Yishuv and later Israel's first prime minister, endorsed a policy of selectivity when he stated: "If in speech and propaganda we are forced to use many languages, we may not use any language but Hebrew in our cultural work. For concerning language, one cannot take into account only temporary and practical observations, because this is an essential issue that bores and descends into the abyss [tehom] of our national existence and our future as a healthy nation, united in its land" (Ben-Gurion 1910, col. 30). Ben-Gurion's remarks, which resonate on more than one level, merit careful reading. In distinguishing between the languages of speech and propaganda, on the one hand, and the language of cultural work, on the other, he was perpetuating the traditional separation between the functions of Yiddish as the language of "low" everyday and utilitarian culture and Hebrew as the language of "high" culture. In fact, according to his categorization, speech and propaganda lie outside the realm of "culture" altogether. Ben-Gurion went a step further when he appropriated Hebrew, the prestigious language of study in diasporic culture, as "ours"—

---

25. This debate is discussed and analyzed in detail in chapter 3; here I focus on a single telling phrase.

in other words, that of the Zionist immigrants who considered themselves the founders and vanguard of the new nation. The Hebrew *chalutz,* used in the Bible to denote those who go ahead of the masses (usually in the context of conquest of the Promised Land), was appropriated to designate "pioneer" in the Zionist lexicon, where it bore both the full biblical connotations of daring and courage in exploring new terrain and the modern sense of avant-gardism. Ben-Gurion's wording conveys the sense of elitism that was pervasive among members of the Second Aliyah (1904–14). "Practical and temporary considerations" were shunted aside, such as the fact that the changeover to Hebrew was difficult and anything but natural for the vast majority of the immigrants.

But then Ben-Gurion's tone underwent an odd change. In a haunting choice of words, he used *tehom* (abyss) to designate "our national existence and our future," intimating a profound sense of unease about the current state of the Yishuv and a fear for its future identity. The biblical *tehom* (Gen. 1:2), usually translated as "the deep," parallels the *tohu va-vohu* (without form and void) in the same verse. The two terms *tehom* and *tohu* in Genesis are linguistically connected and are aspects of pre-Creation formlessness.[26] In other biblical occurrences, *tehom* is the site of lurking premonotheistic danger and chaos. Ezekiel (26:19), for example, describes the future destruction of Jerusalem as the victory of *tehom:* "When I make you a city laid waste . . . when I bring up the deep [*tehom*] over you and the great waters cover you." Ben-Gurion's diction, with its dark overtones, seems to belie his overt confidence in the future of the Yishuv. The highly influential contemporaneous Hebrew poet Chaim Nachman Bialik used the related concept of *tohu* to denote the threatening menace of nonexistence in his 1915 essay "Giluy ve-Khisuy ba-Lashon" (Revealment and concealment in language) when he suggested that language itself, especially poetic language, functions as a defense against the dark void *(ha-tohu ha-afel)* that is an ever-present danger to human consciousness (1965c, 202). When Ben-Gurion used *tehom* in 1910, he perhaps anticipated Bialik's sense of the fundamental importance of lan-

26. Both *tehom* and *tohu* are also linguistically linked with the figure of the female goddess Tiamat in the Babylonian creation epic *Enuma Elish,* possibly composed in the early part of the second millennium B.C.E. In this renowned version of Mesopotamian creation stories (of which there are quite a few), Tiamat, the sea, is the mother of the gods, but she also emblematizes chaos and poses a threat to order. She is eventually slain by her offspring in a fierce battle (Dalley 1989, 228–77). Biblical references to *tehom* seem to echo this ancient local tradition.

guage for the condition of being—in this case, of collective being. Language, specifically Hebrew, is a safeguard against threats to the continued existence of the Jewish people, which in Ben-Gurion's view hinged on the survival of the Yishuv.

From its beginnings, the Yishuv was essentially an immigrant society seeking an identity, unlike the societies of countries where an indigenous population was striving for national legitimation and independence. Yet it was an atypical immigrant society. Even-Zohar notes the difference between the immigration to Palestine and other migrations in modern times and delineates the cultural dilemma faced by the Zionist immigrants. In his analysis, the cultural behavior of immigrants as a rule oscillates between the preservation of the source culture (as in the case of the English migrations abroad) and the adoption of the culture of the target country (as in the case of European migrations to the United States). The latter course often leads to attitudes of contempt toward the "old" as an expression of the hope to begin a "new" life by becoming part of the target country's culture. But, as Even-Zohar points out, in the case of immigration to Palestine a "decision to 'abandon' the source culture . . . could not have led to the adoption of the target culture since the existing culture did not possess the status of an alternative. In order to provide an alternative system to that of the source culture . . . it was necessary to *invent* one" (1981, 170, emphasis in the original). However, the new Zionist culture of Palestine was compiled as much as it was invented; its raw materials came from many sources, including the local culture of the Palestinian Arabs. Guided by romantic European orientalizing notions, the early Zionists selectively appropriated elements of Arab culture, such as dress, food, and customs, which they considered diametrically opposed to Jewish diasporic life or even derived from pre-exilic tradition that had somehow survived in the country.[27] Yiddish, the language that the eastern European immigrants brought with them, had no place in this picture.

This language was also linked in Palestine with the pre-Zionist, mostly religious Old Yishuv, thus further delegitimizing it for Zionists. In the mid-nineteenth century, most Palestinian Jews were Yiddish speakers of European origin living mainly in Jerusalem, Safed, Tiberias, and Hebron; they

---

27. For a fascinating account of the first Zionist settlers' attraction to Arabic culture, see Berlowitz 1996. Oz Almog (2000) provides details and examples of the ambivalent attitude toward Arabs that developed in the Yishuv. For an analysis of the far-reaching effect of the Orient on culture in the Yishuv and in Israel, see Zalmona 1998 and chapter 3 in this volume.

subsisted on *chalukah,* an intricate system of donations from Jewish communities abroad (see, for example, Kosover 1966, 3–93). The Zionist pioneers of the Second Aliyah, young people in an ideological climate that idealized youth, had only contempt for anything marked as "old." They disapproved of the Old Yishuv's way of life, equating its economic basis with the "nonproductive" economy of diasporic Jews, which Zionism aimed to change through "productivizing" the people. Yet by the time of the Second Aliyah, members of the Old Yishuv had actually broken away from the charity system that the young pioneers so disparaged. In 1879, a group of native Jerusalemites founded Petach-Tikvah; members of the Old Yishuv, joined by proto-Zionists of the First Aliyah, established other farming villages in the 1880s. By the turn of the century, however, circumstances had led many of these villages to become dependent on the aid of Jewish philanthropists such as Baron Edmond de Rothschild. Zionists perceived this aid as no different from *chalukah* and viewed all segments of the pre-Zionist community—including the First Aliyah villages—as a totality. Thus construed, the Yiddish-speaking Old Yishuv posed a sharp negative contrast to the self-image of independence and initiative that the Zionists considered superior and were striving to create.

Class, ideological, and generational differences were enlisted in the Zionists' struggle against this culture. The Jewish farmers of the First Aliyah preferred to employ Arab laborers, who were more familiar with the physical conditions and had no socialist ideals such as equality of employers and employees. Paradoxically, the socialist Zionists of the Second Aliyah perceived the farmers simultaneously as beggars because of their dependence on philanthropy and as rich capitalists devoid of national consciousness, ignoring the impulse that had brought many of them to Palestine. The animosity between the older, nonsocialist, and better-established farmers and the young, revolutionary, and penniless laborers was firmly entrenched. Yiddish, which many First Aliyah farmers spoke, was a convenient signifier for the culture that the Zionists negated, and the inevitable clashes often focused on the language issue. But members of the First Aliyah, who had mostly immigrated from eastern Europe, used Yiddish as a matter of practicality rather than out of an anti-Hebraic principle (Sadan 1978, 68).[28] Although Hebrew culture was one of their ideals, the Hebrew of the time, being a "deficient" polysystem in Even-Zohar's formulation, was poorly suited to quotidian

28. See my discussion of Esther Raab's first language later in this chapter.

needs. Interestingly, however, Kosover's summary of the history of Yiddish in Palestine extends from the late fifteenth century to 1880, the eve of the First Aliyah (1966, 3–94). This time frame clearly marks off the Yiddish of the Old Yishuv as the language of diasporic values and implies that members of the First Aliyah spoke only Hebrew.[29]

The mobilization of language as emblem and instrument is perhaps most striking in Yosef Chaim Brenner's important early modernist Hebrew novel *Shekhol ve-Khishalon* (Breakdown and bereavement [1978]).[30] Set in the second decade of the twentieth century, the novel sharply criticizes many aspects of the Yishuv and also castigates the Old Yishuv's way of life. One of Brenner's poetic devices is the representation of Yiddish speech and Yiddish linguistic conventions in his novelistic Hebrew. The first Old Yishuv characters in the novel are two women who carry on a *"sicha-genicha"* (conversation-whining [1465]), a neologistic phrase that in its rhyming reproduces a Yiddish device of mockery as the second element of the rhyme degrades the first.[31] This very first reference to their conversation marks it as Yiddish, the language of feminine weakness, sickness, and passivity—all stereotypical diasporic values. The conversation takes place in the courtyard of a mental hospital in Jerusalem, the stronghold of the Old Yishuv. As they speak, the women punctuate their discourse liberally with the conventional Yiddish exclamations *"oy-oy-oy!"* and *"vey-vey-vey!"* Even more interesting are Brenner's Hebrew representations of Yiddish idioms. *"Eyn klal mah le-daber"* (there's nothing more to say [1465]) is a literal translation of the Yiddish *nishto mer vos tsu zogn; "mah at medaberet"* (what are you saying [1466]) reproduces the Yiddish *vos redstu;*[32] and *"lech ve-shave'ah chai ve-kayam"* (protest in vain [1468]) represents the Yiddish *gey shray khay ve-kayem* (go scream to the one who lives and exists—a euphemism for God).

Chefetz, the pioneer protagonist of the novel, has just arrived from a

---

29. Yet Kosover himself breaks out of this time frame, without acknowledging the fact, when he includes examples of Yiddish in the speech of pioneers as late as the 1920s; see the discussion of a pioneer song later in this chapter.

30. The novel was written in stages during 1913–14 and 1917–18 and was finally published in its entirety in 1920.

31. For a discussion of the structure and function of Yiddish collocations, see Harshav 1990, 27–40, and Matisoff 2000.

32. These two idioms, like many others, have become an accepted part of Hebrew discourse, though their origin is popularly unacknowledged.

new settlement to seek treatment for a mysterious general malaise. As he eavesdrops on the Yiddish conversation, he is overwhelmed by the grim realization that "I am in Jerusalem," an internal exclamation that frames the women's conversation (1465, 1467). Yiddish is inherently linked with the inability to function "normally." The setting of a mental hospital in Jerusalem, with its women inmates, seems to embody the worst aspects of diasporic life. For Chefetz, the Yiddish conversation foreshadows the inevitable breakdown of his life and his bereavement from any hope of normality. When Brenner positions the sick Zionist in a Yiddish-speaking location in Palestine, he is using the conventional metonymies of Hebrew for Zionism and Yiddish for diasporic culture to express his own profound skepticism about the validity of the Zionist ideal, or perhaps about its very possibility. By implying the use of Yiddish to signify diasporic elements both in the Old Yishuv and, as we shall see, among the pioneers, he reveals his apparent conviction that the features of diasporic life would be perpetuated even in Palestine.

Cultural Ambivalence and Narrative Creation

Hayden White characterizes historical narratives as "verbal fictions, the contents of which are as much *invented* as *found* and the forms of which have more in common with their counterparts in literature than they have with those in the sciences" (1985, 82, emphases in the original). He considers the narrativity of historical discourse to be a value arising out of "a desire to have real events display the coherence, integrity, fullness and closure of an image of life that is and can only be imaginary" (24). It is this desire for coherence, fullness, and closure that fed the rise of Zionism's mainstream national narrative. According to this narrative, the uniformly idealistic Yishuv developed through the efforts of a single-minded group of pioneers who never doubted the successful outcome of their project and never wavered in a single tenet of their ideology. True to the logic of a moralistic fable, they were eventually rewarded for their efforts by the establishment of a Jewish state.

Like any narrative, the Zionist one needed to gloss over the incoherence, partial nature, and open-endedness that characterize actual events as opposed to a fictional narrative. Small wonder, then, that the mainstream Zionist narrative neglects the ambivalent aspects of Yishuv culture, such as the continued use of Yiddish. Yiddish and Hebrew had traditionally coexisted in the Jewish community of Europe within a taxonomy that classified the application and usage of each language in European Jewish practice.[33] However, in Zionist Palestine, the old taxonomic order was radically transformed: Hebrew was designated as the language for everyday use as well as of high culture, and Yiddish was totally delegitimized. Yiddish officially became an anomaly, although it was the de facto language of much, if not most of the community well into the 1930s. "Anomalies," observes Bruce Lincoln, "can be ignored, ridiculed, distorted, or suppressed, these all being means by which they are relegated to the margins and interstices of both a given classificatory system and of lived experience" (1989, 165). Several historical and anecdotal examples illustrate the mechanisms by which the anomaly of Yishuv Yiddish was dealt with in scholarly as well as popular perceptions of the culture.

In the 1976 foreword to their handbook, Talmi and Talmi describe their goal as "an attempt to present, as briefly as possible, a book of information and knowledge about the revival movement of the Jewish people, about the 'ingathering of the exiles and the return to Zion,' about the settlement of Eretz-Israel, etc., processes whose supreme expression was the establishment of the State of Israel" (1981, 4).[34] The book does in fact deal mainly with Zionism's concrete achievements, such as settlements and community institutions. Zionism itself is defined as "the modern national movement that supports the return of the people to Zion, to its historical homeland of Eretz-Israel, the establishment of a free, independent Jewish state, and the renewal of the spiritual, cultural, political, and economic life of the Jewish people." The writers continue, "from its inception, Zionism was an inclusive national movement, with different spiritual and social trends" (312), and they go on to present brief descriptions of various political factions and parties within the movement. Yet they construe the revival of the "spiritual" life of the people exclusively as a return to pre-exilic values (which, as we have seen, were at least in part an artificial construct) and thus suppress dissonant tones in the national culture.

33. For a detailed description of the roles of Yiddish and Hebrew in traditional European Jewish society, see Shmeruk 1978 and Harshav 1990; for an analysis of some changes in these roles in the nineteenth and twentieth centuries, see Seidman 1997.

34. The phrases "ingathering of the exiles" and "the return to Zion" are derived from biblical prophecies of national redemption; in the context of Zionism, they refer to the mass immigration to Israel during its first years and to earlier immigration to Palestine.

An illuminating example of a possible narrative variant are the anecdotes recounted in 1917 by Yehoyesh (1872–1927),[35] the renowned American Yiddish poet who lived in the First Aliyah settlement of Rechovot in 1914–15. The mainstream histories imply that by 1914 Hebrew was prevalent, if not exclusive, throughout the Yishuv. It is therefore intriguing to read Yehoyesh's report of the eagerness with which the town's residents read the American Yiddish newspapers that he received by mail: "People waited for them impatiently, and they would be passed from hand to hand. Some people made me promise, for God's sake, that I would give them the papers first" (1917, 56). Yet though Yehoyesh was a major figure of Yiddish culture, his Palestine memoirs make it clear that he was also a sympathizer with Hebrew and Zionism. His classic Yiddish translation of the Hebrew Bible (1927) is suffused with the geography, flora, and fauna of the Land of Israel, concretizing what were traditionally construed as metaphoric statements.[36] More pointedly for our purposes, he notes in his memoir that children in Palestine used Hebrew for quotidian purposes such as the names of wildflowers (1917, 29). This description of considerable language heterogeneity in Zionist Palestine seems closer to what the actual situation might have been and evokes a picture that is probably more realistic than the unisonant national narrative. His own ambivalence on the language issue is clear from this duality of attitudes: enthusiasm for the revival of Hebrew in the Yishuv but also a yearning for Yiddish in the community. If conflicting loyalties can be discerned in this Yiddishist writer's view of the Yishuv's developing culture, we can only imagine how much stronger the psychological conflict was among those who were ideologically committed to completely renouncing their mother tongue.

Yishuv natives' memories, which provided raw material for the national narrative, often reflect a language ambivalence that was minimized in later accounts. Let us look at accounts of Hebrew usage in the farming villages founded during the First Aliyah. A study by Shlomo ha-Ramati unintentionally provides an instructive example of the "incoherence" that a national narrative must avoid in order to function properly according to White's model. Ha-Ramati exposes the intricacy of the language changeover process

35. The pseudonym of Solomon Bloomgarden.
36. During his stay, Yehoyesh consulted with Yisra'el Aharoni (the self-styled "first Hebrew zoologist") about biblical fauna (Yehoyesh 1917, 50–63).

and its oppositionality to the "closure" required by the Zionist narrative when he introduces and quotes Yehudit Harari's reminiscence about Rechovot at the turn of the twentieth century:

> [There was] a large number of foreign words in the Hebrew speech of the first teachers. It is therefore not surprising that such "mixed" speech was also common among the students, as reported [in 1956] by Yehudit Harari, who was a student in the Rechovot school: "We students spoke Hebrew diluted with Yiddish: *di shvartse parah shlogt zikh mit di karnayim* [the black cow is hitting itself with the horns]." (ha-Ramati 1981, 433)

A close examination of the proportions of the languages in Harari's example is illuminating: of the eight words, only the two nouns are Hebrew *(parah,* "cow," and *karnayim,* "horns"), whereas the other six and the syntax itself are Yiddish.[37] Yet Harari herself presents this as an example of "Hebrew diluted with Yiddish," elevating Hebrew to dominant status despite the evidence of her own memory. Thus, she stays in line with the mainstream national narrative that was almost fully formed in 1956. Even more intriguing, however, is ha-Ramati's characterization of Yiddish, the language that underlies this quote: he further distorts the speaker's perception of the past, using her anecdote to prove that turn-of-the-century Hebrew contained a large number of "foreign words." Harari's Yiddish takes on the status of a foreign language, although it was the mother tongue of those natives who spoke it.[38] Natives wanting to join the mainstream were thus alienated from their original culture in a manifestation of nationalist cultural engineering.

A narrative of great cultural significance that, because of its difference, is not included in normative accounts of the Yishuv's culture is that of Esther

---

37. Kronfeld (1999) notes that in the acquisition of a second language that is considered more prestigious, it is often the nouns that are learned and used first.

38. Yiddish was not the only "foreign language" used in the early settlements. A dream sequence in Brenner's 1911 Hebrew story "Atsabim" (Nerves) strikingly conveys linguistic practice in that society by presenting both Arabic and Yiddish within the Hebrew frame language, in translation and transliteration. A voice shouts, *"Rukh, rukh min hon!* (Go, go away!) *S'tezikh tsugetshepet?!"* (Why are you being a nuisance? [Brenner 1978, 1253]). Whereas the Arabic first sentence is given a parenthetical translation in the text (here given in English), the very colloquial Yiddish is presented in Yiddish spelling, with which Brenner's readers were familiar. The linguistic melange was a key component of Yishuv culture, as is clear in the example later from Brenner's Hebrew *Shekhol ve-Khishalon* (Breakdown and bereavement [1978, 1443–1688]) and in the Yiddish works discussed in chapters 2–5.

Raab, the first native Hebrew and female poet of the Yishuv, born in Petach-Tikvah in 1899; Raab's parents were members of the First Aliyah. On more than one occasion, Raab spoke freely about Yiddish as her first language: "Speech was not in Hebrew, it was in Yiddish. There was no Hebrew" (1978, 14). In a 1981 interview, Raab was asked specifically, "Was Hebrew your first spoken language?" She responded, with considerable affection for her mother tongue: "No, we spoke Yiddish, Hungarian Yiddish. I am from Hungary. Then the Lithuanian Jews came, and the whole household adopted Yiddish, that nice Yiddish that the Bialystokers spoke. . . . Yiddish is a beautiful language" (1981, 109).[39] In Raab's recollection, Yiddish was not only the language of the First Aliyah settlements in the first decade of the century; it was a rich, vibrant language, spoken in a variety of regional dialects. It is worth noting here that Raab was considered an outsider and a maverick in the Hebrew literary establishment in her lifetime. Chana Kronfeld posits that a major reason for Raab's marginal status was the fact that in the immigrant society of the Yishuv Raab wrote as a native, presenting both the land and the Hebrew language of early-twentieth-century Palestine as models (1996, 71–78). Raab uses Hebrew innovatively, employing "a jarringly new and ideologically charged rhetoric of ungrammaticality, the likes of which mainstream Hebrew modernism has never seen" (73). It is a measure of Raab's independent mind that, besides speaking freely about her childhood culture, she was also proud of her multilingualism—she was fluent in French and read German—and of her poetic links with European modernism (Raab 1981, 102–3, 106, 108).[40] Her outspokenness on the predominance of Yiddish in Petach-Tikvah, although perhaps characteristic of her particular sensibility, is a dissenting voice unusual in the Zionist narrative.

The Zionist pioneers could not do without Yiddish. That the use of Yiddish in Palestine was more prevalent than the use of Hebrew among the members of the Second Aliyah is clear from careful readings of contemporary literature and memoirs. In Brenner's *Shekhol ve-Khishalon,* which in-

39. "I am from Hungary" is an interesting remark, considering that Raab was born in Palestine after her family immigrated from Hungary in the late nineteenth century.

40. In the same interview, Raab also provided details of her connections with Jewish and non-Jewish European writers such as the Hebrew modernists David Fogel and Avraham Ben-Yitzchak (Sonne), the French poet Germaine Beaumont, and the German poets Stefan George and Walter Cale. She translated work by several European poets into Hebrew (Raab 2001, 454–57).

cludes representations of Yiddish in Old Yishuv speech, some conversations among the young Zionists are also marked as Yiddish. In these cases, Brenner transposes Yiddish syntax and collocations into Hebrew, mocking the pioneers' fumbling attempts to speak the language. When members of the group say of the sickly Chefetz, *"gam gibor gadol eynenu"* (he is not physically powerful either; *gibor gadol,* literally "a great hero" [1978, 1446]), they are translating from the Yiddish *keyn groyser giber iz er oykhet nisht.* The subject pronoun *eynenu* (he isn't) follows the two adjectives *gibor gadol* (great hero), echoing the respective positions of the equivalent Yiddish pronoun *er* and adjectives *groyser giber,* which, in normative Yiddish, precede the subject in such emphatic sentence structures. In normative Hebrew syntax, the adjective follows the subject, and the word order would be *eynenu gibor gadol.* It is clear from the syntax of the represented Hebrew that the characters are speaking Yiddish.

A different case, equally influential but perhaps less representative because of its unique nature, is the extraordinary one of Shmuel Yosef Agnon (1888–1970), the other towering figure of Yishuv Hebrew literature in the early decades of the century. Agnon is considered, along with Brenner and Uri Nissan Gnessin,[41] one of the fathers of modern Hebrew literature (Shaked 2000, 112) and even its major formative voice (Hever 2002, 46); he was the first Hebrew writer to win a Nobel Prize for Literature (in 1966). Agnon was a protégé of Brenner, who recognized and encouraged his genius and facilitated his first publication in Palestine, the story "Agunot" (Forsaken wives) in 1908. Yet Agnon, more so than Brenner, refused to affiliate himself explicitly with Zionist ideology; he immigrated to Palestine in 1908, went to Germany in 1912, and returned to Palestine in 1924. His political and aesthetic positions were singular: as Arnold Band notes, his stance was marginal, fraught with ambiguities and possessing no easily definable commitment (1994, 29). Although Agnon accepted the ideological values of the Second Aliyah, he did not dramatize their realization (Shaked 2000, 82). This is particularly evident in his novel of the Second Aliyah, *Temol Shilshom* (Only yesterday), in which the doomed protagonist fails in his at-

---

41. The works of Gnessin, a remarkable writer who produced only four novellas and a few short stories before his early death, have been described as "the earliest instance of fully achieved modernist prose in Hebrew" (Alter 1988, 51–52). Although Gnessin was a close personal friend of Brenner, he was not a Zionist and returned to Europe after only a brief visit to Palestine.

tempts first to realize his pioneering ideals and then to return to the traditional culture; in Jerusalem's Old Yishuv, he meets with a horrific death by
rabies. *Only Yesterday* was published in its entirety in 1945, decades after
the Second Aliyah was over, and it reflects the temporal distancing as well as
Agnon's studied detachment and ironic attitude concerning ideologies.

Whereas Brenner's uneven style was often perceived as awkward, Agnon
was immediately recognized as an inimitable master of Hebrew, able to
weave the various registers and historical strata of the language into a seam-
less stylistic fabric. Yet his mother tongue, like that of Brenner, was Yiddish,
and the represented speech of his characters is underlain by "vast layers of
Yiddish subtext" (Harshav 1993a, 169). The early story "Giv'at ha-Chol"
(The sand hill), published in 1919, contains such loan translations from Yiddish as *"mah li le-daber"* (literally, "what have I to say," implying "I have
nothing to say," reproducing the Yiddish *vos hob ikh tsu zogn*) and *"be-
chaiai"* ("By my life," Yiddish *kh'lebn*) to denote surprise (Agnon 1960,
381, 384). Such usage may serve to underscore the linguistic confusion of the
characters, recent young immigrants who have left their families behind in
Europe and are trying to adjust to a culture in which Hebrew is required. In
fact, the protagonist makes his living by teaching Hebrew in Jaffa, where the
story is set.

However, even a relatively late novella such as "Iddo ve-Eynam" (Iddo
and Eynam), initially published in 1950—in which the action oscillates between post-Second World War Jerusalem and an archaizing imaginary Jewish past that combines the magical and mythical with pagan elements—is
replete with versions of Yiddish collocations and syntactical structures that
had entered modern Hebrew and function as a poetic device in the novella.
In a conversation about a shortage of housing in the city, one character begins his description of the situation as follows: "A young man comes back
from the war and seeks a roof over his head" (Hebrew: *chozer bachur min
hamilchamah u-mevakesh lo korat gag le-rosho;* Yiddish: *kumt a bocher
tsurik fun milchome un zukht zikh a dakh ibern kop* [Agnon 1967, 349]). In
normal Hebrew syntax, the noun *bachur* (young man) would be in first position and the verb *chozer* (returns) in second position; yet the sentence reproduces a specific syntax used in Yiddish to refer to a topic introduced earlier
(the housing situation). The speaker is a well-to-do immigrant from Germany with a name that is stereotypically German (Gerhard Greifenbach) and
worldly airs: he and his wife, Gerda (an equally stereotypical feminine German name), are going on a trip abroad "to rest a bit from the toil in the land

[Palestine]" (343).[42] Greifenbach probably considers himself remote from the Yiddish culture of his forefathers, who, like the ancestors of many German Jews, most likely came from eastern Europe. The descendants of such immigrants disparaged Yiddish and its culture as low. Thus, the inclusion of Yiddish turns of phrase in Greifenbach's "cultivated" conversation may be an example of Agnon's particular brand of oblique sarcasm rather than a representation of actual speech.

On the eve of the Third Aliyah (1919–23), however, Yiddish was still functioning widely in everyday use. In a fascinating but little-noted article on the revival of Hebrew in Palestine, Roberto Bachi presents data on the use of Yiddish collected in the 1916–18 Palestine census. According to these data, approximately 60 percent of the Jewish population in 1917 did not report Hebrew as their main language. Yiddish was the language that most of these people spoke, followed by Arabic. Bachi appends a footnote: "Nearly 70 percent of 'parents' of Ashkenazi background and about one-third of 'children' of this background spoke Yiddish" (1956, 74n. 11; there is no age specification for the designation of "children"). "Thus, the position of Hebrew," Bachi states, "was extremely weak" (74n. 11). This observation, made by a prominent government statistician less than a decade after Israel's establishment, is a rare admission that the designated language was in a highly precarious position at this crucial stage of the culture's formation.

The situation was not much different in the 1920s. The Third Aliyah was as Hebraist in ideology as the preceding wave of immigration. In a 1923 speech, David Ben-Gurion proudly referred to the new Zionist immigrants as "Hebrew workers in the land" (1964, 96), and H. Frumkin, summarizing the Yishuv's economy on the eve of the Third Aliyah, uses *Hebrew* overwhelmingly as an adjective for the community (1964, 74–75). Yet a later account by Moshe Palmon, a rank-and-file immigrant of the Third Aliyah, reflects some of the difficulty and ambivalence that accompanied the use of the language. Palmon recounts his language experience while he was working in a Tel-Aviv factory:

42. Agnon often makes punning references in character names—here, a bilingual play on the literal meaning of the German verb *greifen* (to grab). It may be an allusion to the pretentious affectations of Greifenbach and Gerda, concerned for the security of their house while they are gone rather than for the safety of the narrator, who remains in a Jerusalem where Arab rioters and British-imposed curfews are common.

Most of the workers were immigrants from Russia who did not know Hebrew, and one heard mainly Russian. When more workers came, the numbers of those who knew Hebrew rose slightly, yet the situation did not change much. Out of habit and exhaustion from work, no attention was paid to speaking Hebrew. When the workers became more numerous, they tended to overcome habit, and the number of Hebrew speakers increased. Even those who did not know the language did not treat it with such alienation [*lo hitnakru lah kol kakh*], and some of them tried to overcome the difficulty. . . . The craftsmen did not know Hebrew either and did not treat it seriously and spoke Russian or Yiddish. (1964, 577)

Palmon's choice of phrase is telling. The *hitnakru* form of the verb root *n'k'r'* is a reflexive that implies a deliberate estrangement. When the biblical Joseph, for example, decides to punish his brothers who have come to Egypt begging for food, he treats them "like strangers" *(va-yitnaker eleyhem,* literally "estranged himself from them" [Gen. 42:7]). Though the word occurs in the context of a lessening alienation, Palmon spells out the immigrants' unwillingness to grapple with Hebrew; depending on their backgrounds, they preferred Russian or Yiddish, their mother tongues. His account vividly conveys their sense of being burdened with a linguistic requirement for which they were not equipped and that they may not have chosen.

As noted earlier, Kosover's study of Palestinian Yiddish also includes some Yiddish spoken by the Third Aliyah pioneers. He quotes a stanza from "a popular *'chalutzim'* song of the twenties (heard from Meir Roytman in [the new town of] Migdal in May 1927): *'Un dernokh hob ikh tsu zukhn / gelt farn binyan oder kvish— / azoy krig ikh glaykh an entfer / az: 'masari iz mafish!'"* (And later I need to seek / money for a building or a paved road— / and I get the answer right away: / "there is no money!") (1966, 139). The song is mostly in Yiddish. Of its twenty-one words, only two are Hebrew (again, nouns: *binyan,* "building," and *kvish,* "paved road," both highly significant in the Zionist context of "building the land"), and two are Arabic (the noun *masari,* "money," and *mafish,* an expression negating the existence of something). Yiddish songs were certainly popular in Zionist Palestine well into the 1930s and beyond. A personal collection of favorite songs that Zev Segal, a founder of Ra'anana, compiled and copied out in the course of thirty-five years attests to this popularity: of the 108 songs in his notebook, 32, or almost one-third, are in Yiddish (Segal 1934–69).[43] The Yiddish songs were often sung in the home of this Hebraist Zionist, who was totally at home in both languages, saw no real conflict between them, and never relinquished Yiddish in his personal and family culture. The persistence of Yiddish songs in the Yishuv is particularly telling given the ideological engagement of popular song in the Zionist project (Almog 2000, 235–41; Shachar 1999, 495).

The view that by the late 1920s Yiddish had disappeared is an example of a Zionist myth of the type to which Nurith Gertz alludes in her important study of Yishuv literature in the 1930s. Gertz states that the ideological use of "the Zionist myths that were taken for granted by the Yishuv . . . was in line with the tendency to avoid confrontation with complicated real-life conflicts and conferred the appearance of an accepted value even upon positions that were specific and unilateral" (1988, 58). However, Gertz does not apply this insight to the myth of the disappearance of Yiddish. Paradoxically, it was in the late 1920s that Yiddish culture in the Yishuv began to thrive and find expression in print. The years 1928 and 1929 saw the appearance of the first four of the nineteen Yiddish literary magazines that were published through the 1930s; three of these magazines were published in the new "Hebrew" city of Tel-Aviv. The flourishing of Yiddish in the Yishuv was problematic, an anomaly that needed to be integrated into the national narrative.

The old-timers who had come with the Second and Third Aliyahs and who had a socialist and agricultural orientation perceived the eighty thousand members of the Fourth Aliyah (1924–28) (known as the "Grabski" Aliyah, after the Polish prime minister who initiated the stringent anti-Jewish fiscal legislation that led to the emigration of many Jews) as petit-bourgeois and lacking in Zionist zeal because many of them preferred to start businesses in the towns.[44] They were construed as less Zionist because they had arrived out of economic necessity. Bezalel Amikam's historical survey of the Yishuv suggests that the ideological failings of the Fourth Aliyah were at least in part responsible for the economic depression in Palestine during the late 1920s. He quotes a contemporaneous evaluation of the Fourth Aliyah by the prominent Labor movement leader Moshe Beilinson, who regarded the ethics of this wave of immigrants as an evil influence that was corrupting

43. The collection also includes songs transliterated from English, Arabic, and Russian.

44. A popular, Yiddish-inflected pejorative term for Fourth Aliyah immigrants was *grabskalakh*, "little Grabskis."

the purity of the Zionist movement: "Speculation creates a poisonous atmosphere in the country and in the entire Zionist movement. It deprives the movement of its purity of character [*tohar ofya*] and causes many among us to stray from the [right] path and to turn to a path of profit without work" (Amikam 1979, 321). Beilinson accused the Fourth Aliyah of transplanting negative (i.e., nonsocialist) exilic values. Although these immigrants were only following established, though unacknowledged, custom when they continued to use Yiddish in Palestine, this easily identifiable fact was used against them for political and economic reasons as it was against no other group.

Gertz spells out this conventional disapproval in cultural terms when she presents the reasons for the continued stagnation in the numbers of Hebrew literature readers in Palestine in the early 1930s: "A large part of the [recent] immigrants were refugees from European anti-Semitism, and their motives for immigrating were not national or pioneering. They therefore did not feel any obligation toward Zionist values and the [Hebrew] literature that expressed these values" (1988, 34–35).

For an impartial perspective on the conventional belief that Hebrew was uniformly adopted in the Yishuv by the late 1920s, let me return to Bachi's 1956 essay on the revival of Hebrew in Palestine. Presenting the data of three censuses of Jewish workers in Palestine (1922, 1926, and 1937), he appends an intriguing footnote: "The data of the two official censuses of 1922 and 1931 cannot be used because these were damaged by inaccurate statements as a result of intentional political propaganda that was conducted, to have all the Jews declare 'Hebrew' in response to the question about languages" (1956, 69n. 8). He implies that during the official censuses members of the Yishuv were pressured to deny their use of other languages. Without offering specific sources for this information, he indicates that the ostensibly impartial censuses had a clear political cast. When he uses passive and agentless constructions such as "*nifge'u*" (were damaged) and "*hitnahalah*" (was conducted), he seems unwilling to assign blame or responsibility for the falsification of facts.

Perhaps the most revealing bit of information about Yishuv culture in the 1920s is included incidentally in Zohar Shavit's encompassing and detailed survey of the development of the Hebrew culture of Palestine. In 1927, Hebrew and Yiddish newspapers were being read in roughly equal numbers in one public library of Tel-Aviv. On one day in June of that year at the Barzilai Library, 121 people read Hebrew newspapers, whereas 107 read the Yiddish press, published in Warsaw and New York (1999, 386). Shavit does not elaborate on this astonishing statistic, which contradicts the mainstream's denial that Yiddish culture even existed, let alone was sought after, in the Yishuv. Clearly, consumers of Hebrew and Yiddish cultures in the Yishuv were close in numbers. The myth of Hebrew's early dominance in the Yishuv was used to essentialize the sense of a new national identity and to "avoid confrontation with complicated real-life conflicts," according to Gertz's model (1988, 58).

The Fifth Aliyah (1929–39) was the largest, with numbers estimated at 235,000. The *Leksikon Tziyoni* notes, "the Fifth Aliyah was notable for its varied composition. In addition to a young labor force, people with capital as well as professionals and others knowledgeable in economics, commerce, and industry arrived. The population of the cities and towns increased greatly" (Talmi and Talmi 1981, 271). The Yishuv's culture was altered in a way that the ideologists of Labor Zionism found hard to accept in spite of the welcome increase in the population. Their socialist-agrarian ethic construed the growing popularity and rapid development of the cities, which had begun during the Fourth Aliyah, as a degradation of Zionism, a threat to all that had been accomplished, and a regression to undesirable diasporic values. Labor Zionist ideologists also disapproved of the small towns, where agriculture was based on private land ownership and where the laborer-landowner conflict of the Second Aliyah had flared up at the turn of the century. This disparaging view of a changing ideological climate masks the perception of a threat to the dominance of Labor in the Yishuv.

The language issue continued to be of crucial importance, with *Hebrew* now functioning as an oppositional code word in the struggle between Labor and non-Labor factions. Writing in *Moznayim*, one of the two major literary magazines of the Yishuv, writer and critic Shlomo Tzemach expressed disappointment at the direction he saw Yishuv culture taking: "Instead of the villages of Hebrews [*kfarey ha-ivrim*] spread over hill and dale, 'quarters' and 'suburbs' have come, bearing the names of all the middlemen [*sarsurim*] and criminals. . . . What we are creating in the Jewish small town in the land is a nest of spiritual provincialism of the most sterile and empty kind, with all its disgraceful characteristics" (1934, 529–30, quotation marks in the original). In this description, the agrarian "villages of Hebrews" are presented as part of a bucolic landscape, an organic part of the countryside as they spread over the hills and dales (the collocation *"har va-gai"* [hill and dale] was part of the idealized geography of Zionist Palestine and denoted a pastoral existence).

Residential urban neighborhoods, in contrast, had "come" like some unnatural manifestation. Although *sarsur* basically means "middleman," the word has taken on highly negative connotations in modern Hebrew and is used today for pimp; in Tzemach's description, it is equated with criminals. Tzemach used the Hebrew *ayarah* ("small town," a diminutive of *ir,* "city," and the Hebrew equivalent for the Yiddish Jewish term *shtetl,* itself never used in a Hebrew context) in conjunction with the adjective *Jewish,* thus distinguishing it pejoratively from the "villages of Hebrews" that he admires. Tzemach was arguing that the diasporic shtetl had been transplanted. The cultures of Tel Aviv and the towns (as distinct from the agrarian "Hebrew" villages), which were gaining in significance as a result of the Fifth Aliyah's size and composition, now emblematized all that Labor deplored.

The Tongue-Tied Soul

The development of Hebrew culture in Palestine has been studied fairly extensively.[45] However, mainstream Zionist narratives mostly gloss over the personal toll in individual cultural adjustment exacted by the imposition of Hebrew over Yiddish. The process that led to the dominance of Hebrew is usually described in the abstract and through collective rhetoric, as though individuals were not involved. This is true even of relatively recent studies. Yael Zerubavel's innovative and compelling analysis of Israeli collective memory effectively interrogates and exposes the process by which myths adopted by Zionism (such as that of Masada) became unquestioned fundamentals of Israeli culture. Yet, speaking of the revival of Hebrew and its adoption as part of the national renaissance, she notes briefly only that "the emergence of Hebrew as the Yishuv's national language was a complex process that entailed a struggle on both ideological and practical grounds" (1995, 30). Because she does not mention the Zionist immigrants' integral link with Yiddish, she diminishes the personal conflict inherent in the "ideological and practical" struggle to the point of nonexistence. The only language struggle she mentions explicitly is the 1913 German-Hebrew dispute

45. See, for example, Berlowitz 1996, Elboim-Dror 1996, Even-Zohar 1981, Harshav 1993, Karmi 1997, ha-Ramati 1997, Yael Zerubavel 1995, and especially Z. Shavit 1999, whose survey is the most ambitious and comprehensive, though not complete. Almog 2000 provides a multifaceted historical overview of the native Hebrew culture.

(80). This dismissal of a key component of a process recognized as complex is significant in a major study that interrogates mainstream values.

Although some modern mainstream histories of the Second Aliyah do include examples of the pioneers' ambivalence toward Hebrew and the problematics of their cultural adjustment, they often do not analyze or place these examples in proper context. Thus, Michael Greenzweig's essay on the status of Hebrew during the Second Aliyah deals mainly with the "practical" difficulties of using a language that was inadequate (as Ben-Gurion put it in 1910) and details the educational steps taken to increase the vocabulary and the spread of Hebrew in the Yishuv. Greenzweig ostensibly mentions Yiddish only in connection with the Old Yishuv: "Another segment of the Yishuv spoke Yiddish at the time [1904–14] and consciously shunned Hebrew speech. These were mainly members of the Old Yishuv in Jerusalem, and in other cities as well, such as Jaffa" (1985, 199). The nature of the other Yiddish speakers (besides the "main" speakers) is elided, possibly because of the character of the volume that contains the essay: it is part of a series that reflects the consensus and presents mainstream Zionist and Israeli history in a somewhat popularized fashion.

However, a dissonant tone emerges within Greenzweig's essay in the reminiscences of Second Aliyah immigrant and ideologue Shlomo Lavee. Recalling the language situation in the early communal settlement of Kinneret in 1905, Lavee described it as "one of the settlements that was totally Hebrew in its language. The cost cannot be assessed. It is totally impossible to estimate what it costs a person to switch over from one language of speech to another, and especially to a language that is not yet one of speech, and how great the spiritual torment [*inuyey ha-nefesh*] is of a soul that wants to speak, and has something to say, and is dumb and tongue-tied" (quoted in Greenzweig 1985, 207). This pained description comprises a rare attempt to convey a common personal dilemma. Underlying the practical difficulties—expressing oneself in a language inadequate for daily use—is the profound emotional issue of abandoning the mother tongue. The date of Lavee's reminiscence is not given, but it was most likely long after the events. His reference to "spiritual torment"—the same language as in the biblical injunction to fast on Yom Kippur, the Day of Atonement (Lev. 16:31 and elsewhere)—evokes the ambivalence that had to be suppressed concerning the obligation to forget Yiddish. Lavee spoke for the pioneers of the Second Aliyah who were frustrated at being "dumb and tongue-tied." Greenzweig's summary, though, ignores the issues that Lavee's account reveals: "On the eve of the

First World War, it was absolutely clear that in this struggle between Hebrew and foreign languages, the Hebrews and their supporters were ahead" (1985, 211). As in ha-Ramati's study, the mother tongue takes on the status of a delegitimized foreign language.

Perhaps the most revealing contemporaneous articulation of the individual's dilemma is Rachel Katznelson's 1918 essay, suggestively titled "Nedudey Lashon" (Language wanderings).[46] The essay's Hebrew title is ambiguously worded; *nedudey* is a construct form of the plural noun *nedudim* (wanderings). Katznelson's use of this particular noun for the construct form resonates on several levels: it evokes the construct *nedudey sheynah* (literally, "sleep wanderings" or insomnia) and is in dialogue with Bialik's seminal 1905 essay "Chevley Lashon" (Language pangs), which deals with problems of expression in the modern Hebrew of the time (Bialik 1965b). In 1918, Katznelson spelled out the personal conflict involved in the need to choose between languages. She confessed to the hardship involved in the imposition of Hebrew, in anguished terms that few pioneers would admit to in print:

> [In the Diaspora] it never occurred to us to speak Hebrew. Would we abandon what was natural and choose what was artificial? And these were the strong connections we betrayed when we came to Eretz-Israel. For here, we no longer feel like children of Yiddish. . . . We had to betray Yiddish, even though we paid for this as for any betrayal. And we feel the need to justify and explain to ourselves how we so quickly abandoned what was the content of our lives. (1918, 69)

46. My translations of excerpts from this essay are based on the translation in Harshav 1993a, 183–94. Interestingly, a later version of this essay, published in a 1966 collection of Katznelson's writings, contains many significant changes: "jargon," for example, is replaced by "Yiddish," and the key exclamation "we had to betray Yiddish, even though we paid for this as for any betrayal" is omitted (Katznelson 1966, 231–41). Katznelson's decision to follow the consensus here seems to echo some of her other choices, such as the subordination of her own public and literary career to that of her husband, Zalman Rubashov, who became the third president of Israel. When she married, she appended "Rubashov" to her name; when Zalman Rubashov was elected president in 1963, they hebraized their Russian last name to Shazar. For a fascinating self-revelation of this complex modern woman, see her diaries and journals in Katznelson 1989. The title of this work, *Adam Kemo Shehu* (A person as he/she is), which was compiled posthumously, expresses an emphatic refusal to present it as a woman's "confessional" writing.

Elsewhere in the essay she used the extreme military term *"milchemet ha-safot"* (war of languages), perhaps as an indication of her own inner struggle. She stated, "This language was a substitute homeland for us in the Diaspora" (68), a phrase that perhaps foreshadowed Chaim Zhitlovsky's famous 1937 definition of "Yiddishland." How, then, did Katznelson and her comrades rationalize the cultural and emotional dislocation that the language decision involved? "In Yiddish," she said, "we were loved as we were" (73). The choice of Hebrew was derived from the perceived revolutionary nature of Zionism, which called for total change. In her formulation, "There is a trend of thought, which for us was revolutionary, that expresses itself in Hebrew, whereas Yiddish literature—apparently naturally and necessarily— was ruled by narrow-mindedness, mostly inert and reactionary in our eyes. At best it was only a weak echo of what was revealed in Hebrew. And any person, especially we, in our situation and in the situation of our people, yearned for revolutionary thought" (69). For Katznelson, Hebrew satisfied the need for personal as well as national revolution against what Zionism considered reactionary.

A measure of Katznelson's deliberate dedication to Hebrew is the fact that although she was an astute literary critic, her characterization of Yiddish literature as "inert and reactionary" is a stereotypically negative evaluation of a literature that in 1918 was enjoying one of its most vibrant moments. "The Hebrew writer will always be more a citizen of the world than the Yiddish writer," she declared (1918, 74); but Yiddish literature in Europe was then explosively joining contemporary revolutionary and modernist movements in a way that the nascent Hebrew literature could not because of the expressive limitations of the language or did not because of the nationalist bent of Zionism. The Yiddish expressionist poet Perets Markish (1895–1952) had begun publishing his poems in Yiddish journals the previous year and was about to publish his first book of poetry. The Yung-Yidish group, formed in Poland in 1919, marked "the beginning of Yiddish modernist poetry" in Europe (Wolitz 1991, 28). In the early 1920s, Yiddish groups such as Di Khalyastre (the Gang) and individual poets such as Uri Tsvi Grinberg were conscious participants in European modernism. In the United States, Yiddish literature had evolved through several modernist trends.[47] It is difficult to believe that the well-read Katznelson, whose diaries

47. For detailed discussions of European Yiddish modernisms, see Wolitz 1979, 1981, and 1988; and Tilo Alt 1987, 1991. For a detailed survey of the New York Yiddish literary scene, see

indicate the breadth and depth of her literary interests, was not aware of this innovative, multifaceted Yiddish modernism.

What underlies Katznelson's subscription to the Zionist mainstream narrative that identifies "revolutionary" with "Zionist," both emblematized by Hebrew? Could what seems to be a studied refusal to mention contemporary Yiddish literature, in the same diary entries that note her readings in German and Russian, have been a strategy to justify her own language choice? It would certainly have been easier to abandon a language that was stigmatized as undeveloped and reactionary rather than one that was the instrument of modern, revolutionary literature and politics. Katznelson made explicit her internalization of the stereotypes concerning Yiddish when in "Language Wanderings" she discussed the proposal of the 1908 First Yiddish Language Conference to translate the Bible into Yiddish: "You can translate the Bible into the languages of all cultured peoples. . . . But how can the Bible be translated into Yiddish? The Bible can be translated into German or English because there is equality between these languages and the language of the Bible, an equality that does not exist between that language and Yiddish" (1918, 76–77). Underlying this passage is the conventional, Haskalah-derived, Zionist opposition between Yiddish and culture. By equating Yiddish with "noncultured," Katznelson was stifling the ambivalence she expressed earlier in the essay.

Perhaps the most clear-eyed view of the process by which Hebrew came to dominance in the early Yishuv, and one of the boldest for its time, was that of Yosef Chaim Brenner, whose compromising stance toward Yiddish was unique. Although Brenner was a Zionist and a supporter of Hebrew as the language for the Yishuv, he was eminently aware of practicalities. Brenner condemned the imposition of Hebrew by the Zionist establishment; in 1908 he wrote: "The Holy Tongue [*leshon ha-kodesh*] is not a fetish for us; we are free persons and will accept no fetish [*sic*]" (1985, 188). He openly legitimized Yiddish as a Zionist language and appreciated its value and power as a living language that could not be eliminated by sheer force of will. In the first, programmatic issue of *ha-Me'orer* (The arouser), the journal he founded in London in 1906, when the very future of Hebrew letters was in doubt, he declared: "Hebrew we write because we cannot but write Hebrew, because the divine spark within us emerges only in this flame . . . not even in

---

Harshav 1990. For an illumination of some nuances of the Yiddish modernisms, see Kronfeld 1996.

the blended, beloved language, the language of our mothers, that is in our mouths [*ha-safah ha-belula, ha-chaviva, sefat imoteynu, asher be-finu*—i.e., Yiddish]" (1985, 107–8). Brenner's choice of phrase is highly resonant. Through use of *"ha-safah ha-belulah"* (the blended language), he enters into direct debate with *safa berurah* (clear language [Zeph. 3:9]), used as the name of the pre-Zionist movement founded in Jerusalem in 1889 by Eliezer Ben-Yehuda (considered the father of the impulse to revive Hebrew as a spoken language) with the aim of eliminating the use of other languages by the Jews of Palestine. Brenner then expressed his affection for "the language of our mothers" (*"sefat-imoteynu,"* a translation of the common Yiddish term for the language, *mame-loshn,* which incorporates the maternal figure) and ended by locating the language intimately "in our mouths." Like Katznelson, Brenner was struggling with his own personal language dilemma. The dichotomy between the ascribed cultural values of the languages is manifest in his imagery. The comforting, familiar, oral aspects of the mother tongue are opposed to the disembodied elitism of Hebrew—a divine flame, an inherently dangerous element emanating from a distant authoritative entity.

Brenner repeatedly affirmed that the use of Yiddish must continue as a counterforce to the Hebrew elitism that he identified and perceived as dangerous. In 1912, for example, he wrote: "In our world there is no room for the laws laid down by and the assurance of the supposed 'elite.' . . . On the contrary! Let them speak, let the Jews in all their varied locations speak the Yiddish/Jewish [*yehudit*] language, the language that is in their mouths, let them respect themselves and respect their language. . . . Enough of absolute requirements and of the world of the abstract" (1985, 649–51). Brenner uses *yehudit* for Yiddish, one of several Hebrew names for the language. The fact that the Hebrew culture never succeeded in coining a stable Hebrew term for Yiddish—using the transliterations *yidish, idish,* and the euphemisms *idit, yehudit,* and even *ashkenazit* (incorporating *Ashkenaz,* the European Jewish term for Germany, where Yiddish originated)—may be another symptom of its pervasive ambivalence toward Yiddish language and culture (Seidman 2000).[48] Ever the realist and acutely aware of the ideological weight of terminology, Brenner wrote of Yiddish in 1914, "A popular language spoken

---

48. Names for Yiddish also seem to have been ideologically influenced in the scholarly community. In his section on names for Old Yiddish, Jerold Frakes remarks on "the magnitude of potential ideological power manifested in projects such as the naming of a language" (1989, 102–3).

by tens of thousands of people can never be *zhargon*" (1978, 1240), challenging the continued Zionist internalization of the negative "jargon" stereotype for Yiddish. In the years until his death, he continued to review Yiddish publications in Hebrew periodicals. He expressed his linguistic and ideological ambivalence toward both Hebrew and Zionism in his heartfelt exclamation of 1908: *"I do so still enjoy a new, well-printed collection in my Jewish language [bi-leshoni ha-yehudit]"* (1978, 180, emphasis in the original). Yiddish evidently was an integral part of his intellectual sensibility and his reading practice. A year before his death, Brenner was strongly moved by a plaintive Yiddish folksong sung by a Zionist pioneer in Palestine about a poor, lonely Jewish shopkeeper in the Diaspora (Barlev 1964, 328).

Brenner's reputation as an activist and a writer who applied the same absolute and often ruthless honesty to himself as he did to others seems to have sanctioned for the public his continued affirmation of "unofficial" views, such as the admittance of Yiddish into Yishuv culture.[49] The general affection and esteem for him grew even stronger after he was murdered by rioting Arabs in 1921; in hindsight at least, he was "forgiven" for expressing unpopular views. Yitzchak Tabenkin, a contemporary who was a major ideologue of the activist wing in the Yishuv's Labor Party for decades, wrote in the 1960s: "Brenner is the prosecutor of Jewish history. And even though he has an element of exaggeration and sometimes he goes over the line, his words contain a great educational power that influenced many of us" (1977, 14). Tabenkin's notion of Brenner as "going over the line" can perhaps point us in the direction of a possible alternative to the mainstream narrative of the Yishuv and of Israeli culture. What was the "line" that Brenner crossed? Tabenkin seems to refer to Brenner's refusal to be bound by any kind of dogmatic ideology, which essentializes a community's identity.

Benedict Anderson's concept of national unisonance leaves no room for the dissenting or minority voices that are part of any mass movement. To account for the necessarily more heterogeneous linguistic practices of an immigrant community in a newly formed national center, I would propose the notion of "multisonance." This notion is derived in part from Homi Bhabha's suggestion that an "in-between" temporality or space is the actual location of a nation's culture. Bhabha identifies "a liminal signifying space

---

49. Hannan Hever attributes Brenner's tolerance of Yiddish to his universalistic tendency, which incorporated an aversion to any particularism or local patriotism, including the Zionist view that the Land of Israel was the only possible home for the Jews (1994, 70).

. . . marked by the discourses of minorities, heterogeneous histories of contending peoples, antagonistic authorities and tense locations of cultural difference" (1994, 148). In the Yishuv, this liminal space, marked by ambivalence, was the location of such Hebrew literary figures as Brenner and Agnon, the major voices of difference in the cultural consensus. It was also the location of a vigorous, though unacknowledged Yiddish culture that expressed itself in a rich array of unique literary work, several of whose writers I address in the following chapters.

CHAPTER TWO

Meeting Expectations?

The Palestinian Fiction of Zalmen Brokhes

> *We are strangers, Jews, who have strayed into your land.*
>
> —Zalmen Brokhes, "The Jordan Roars," 1937

Defusing the Subversive

Cultural engineering, crucial for the formation of a new national identity, can manifest itself through the production of a body of literature that conforms to nationalist ideology. This canon will then supply the frame as well as the materials for the national narrative. "The canon," says Gregory Jusdanis, "not only represents national identity but also participates in its production by instilling in people the values of nationalism" (1991, 49). The Hebrew literature produced in Palestine from the beginnings of proto-Zionist Jewish immigration in the 1880s and especially after the founding of political Zionism in 1897 was mobilized toward creating a new national identity according to the Zionist ideal. The New Jew would speak Hebrew, be totally dedicated to the Zionist ideal, and possess traits considered typically non-Jewish, such as courage and initiative.

This ideal incorporated an internalization of European anti-Semitic stereotypes, many of which attributed to diasporic Jews negative traits usually viewed as feminine. This view of the New Jew as supermasculine dates back to Max Nordau's concept of *Muskeljudentum* (muscle Jewry), which he presented at the Second Zionist Congress in 1898. Nordau noted the stereotypical characterization of Jewish males as physically underdeveloped, feeble, and inferior and maintained that the condition could be rectified by heightening their athletic prowess (1909, 379–81). "Zionism," says David Biale, "promised . . . the creation of a virile New Hebrew Man" (1992,

176). In the imagery used by Vladimir Jabotinsky, the "Hebrew" is endowed with hypermasculinity. Because Yiddish, the diasporic language of "the Zhid," was associated with the deficient masculinity that Zionism sought to redress, it could not be a legitimate vehicle of Zionist ideology. Yet Zionists whose mother tongue was Yiddish immigrated to Palestine and began producing Yiddish literature there as early as 1910, well within the time frame of the seminal Second Aliyah. In that year, Zalmen Brokhes (1886–1977) published the short story "Di Borvese" (The barefoot ones)—which, in the Jewish cultural context of the time, was a code word for Zionists—subtitled "A Skitse fun Yidishn Lebn in Erets-Yisro'el" (A sketch from Jewish life in Palestine), in the Warsaw Yiddish newspaper *Der Fraynd* (Brokhes 1910). His first Yiddish collection of Yishuv stories, *Untern Shotn fun Chermn* (In the shadow of the Hermon) appeared in 1918 (Brokhes 1918), and the second, *Der Yardn Roysht* (The Jordan roars) in 1937 (Brokhes 1937).[1] A first collection of stories in Hebrew translation, *be-Tzel ha-Chermon* (In the shadow of the Hermon) appeared in 1954 (Brokhes 1954), and a second, *ha-Yarden So'en* (The Jordan roars) twenty years later, in 1974 (Brokhes 1974).

For the most part, cultural historians of the Yishuv have ignored the existence of Yiddish literature in the Yishuv.[2] A major case in point is Zohar Shavit's (1982) important survey on literary activity in Eretz-Israel between 1910 and 1933. The chronological framework of the survey and its inclusive title, *ha-Chayim ha-Sifrutiyim be-Eretz-yisra'el 1910–1933* (Literary life in Palestine 1910–1933), imply that it discusses the Yishuv's total literary production in the decades so crucial for the formation of its culture. Indeed, Shavit's introduction begins with the promising announcement that "this book is the result of a theoretical and descriptive study of 'literary life,' that is, the sociohistorical existence of literature" (10). Yet the book does not acknowledge the sociohistorical existence of Yiddish culture in the Yishuv. Like other Israeli cultural historians, Shavit mentions Yiddish only in connection with the 1927 "Yiddish Affair."

---

1. All references henceforth to *In the Shadow of the Hermon* and to *The Jordan Roars* are to the original Yiddish collections of 1918 and 1937, respectively. References to the Hebrew versions of these books are made explicit. The individual stories are not dated.

2. Among the few who have mentioned this literature are Pilowsky (1980, 1986), Sadan (1966, 1972a, 1972b, 1979), and Shmeruk (1999). Govrin's (1981, 1989) references to Yiddish literature in the early Yishuv are addressed later in this chapter.

Considerably more complex is Nurit Govrin's (1981) appropriation of Zalmen Brokhes into the mainstream of Yishuv literature in her pioneering study of the imprint of the First Aliyah on Hebrew literature. The first chapter of her book, "The Shock of Meeting," deals with the attitude of Second Aliyah writers toward the First Aliyah. To the extent that the Yishuv and Israeli culture addressed the first wave of immigration, it has traditionally been overshadowed and minimized by its successor, the Second Aliyah.[3] Govrin posits that the First Aliyah is actually central to the Second Aliyah writers, but only insofar as they present the problematics of the relationship between the two groups from within the collective psyche of the Second Aliyah. Among the ten fiction writers she surveys, whose work deals with this relationship and its antagonisms, is "Z. Brokhes." However, she ignores the fact that Brokhes wrote in Yiddish, although she first cites Dov Sadan's introduction to the second volume of Brokhes's stories in Hebrew translation (Brokhes 1974)[4] and then addresses two of the translated stories (Govrin 1981, 37–39). As Sadan's introduction explicitly notes that Brokhes wrote exclusively in Yiddish, one of the ten "Hebrew" writers was obviously nothing of the sort. Govrin does not mention this crucial fact, selectively appropriating Brokhes to suit a particular ideological goal. Hebrew literary

3. Yaffa Berlowitz argues that the Second Aliyah set the tone when its historiographers and literary critics minimized the impact of the First Aliyah to the point of denying its very presence (1996, 11).

4. It is worth noting the peculiar composition of the books that present Brokhes's work in Hebrew translations. Translated stories from his first Yiddish volume (1918) were published in the Hebrew *be-Tzel ha-Chermon* (In the shadow of the Hermon [1954]), which is described on the book jacket as "one of the first manifestations of new Eretz-Israeli literature." The only link with Yiddish in this Hebrew book is the cursory remark on the obverse of the title page, "From Yiddish: M. Goldenson." Three of the Hebrew stories are translations of stories from Brokhes 1937. Five of the twelve stories included in the Hebrew *ha-Yarden So'en* (The Jordan roars [1974]), which purports to be a translation of the 1937 Yiddish volume, did not appear in the original Yiddish book. Three of these five stories were published in Israeli anthologies of local Yiddish writing, and two, for which I have found no published Yiddish original, make their first appearance in the 1974 Hebrew version of *The Jordan Roars*: "be-Harim u-va-Sadot" (In hills and fields) and "Nifgeshu" (They met); the latter story is discussed later. One story from the 1937 Yiddish volume, "Untern Sikamor" (Under the sycamore), also discussed later, appears in differing versions as "Tachat ha-Shikma" (Under the sycamore) in both Hebrew volumes. I have not been able to ascertain the reasons—technical, political, or economic—for these discrepancies.

activity in Palestine was sparse during much of the Second Aliyah period, so Govrin may have claimed Brokhes's work for Hebrew literature in order to present a broader literary scene.[5]

Govrin (1989) also appropriates Brokhes in a more nuanced way in her later collection of essays devoted to early Yishuv literature. The section on the " 'Moledet' affair" (288–343) analyzes the reception history and internal politics of the early Palestinian Hebrew children's magazine Moledet (Home- land), which appeared during 1911–29, with some interruptions, and in 1947. According to Govrin, the entire small Hebrew journalistic establish- ment in the country criticized Moledet from its inception, for various rea- sons. The contents of the first issue (April 1911) were considered too "diasporic" and depressing, and hence unsuitable for a youthful audience in a community that saw itself as beginning to realize the optimistic Zionist dream in Palestine. This critique was based mainly on two stories (one by the magazine's editor, the writer Simcha Ben-Tziyon, and the other by Dvora Baron) in which diasporic life is depicted in great detail. Govrin rightly points out that both stories indicate Palestine as the only hope for their protago- nists, but that contemporary critics disregarded this aspect. She then relates:

> Ben-Tziyon in fact obeyed the critique, and opened the second issue with Z. Brokhes's story "I Removed the Shame!" ["Galoti et ha-Cherpa!" (Brokhes 1911a)], an Eretz-Israeli story in the strictest sense about the adventures of a Jewish *hunter* in the country. The second review [*ha-Or,* 2 July 1911] is in- deed more encouraging: "Its first piece, from the memoirs of a Jewish hunter, well befits the Eretz-Israeli *Moledet.* A spirit of revival, of nature em- anates from it, and the moment you see it, you say, this has come from Eretz-Israel!" The editor should have been satisfied because the attitude is one of fulfilled expectations, a typical tale of new life in the Eretz-Israel community. (1989, 303, emphasis in the original)

Ironically, the story that "fulfilled expectations" and satisfied the critics in its romantic presentation of a New Hebrew protagonist in a rousing Pales- tinian adventure was Brokhes's Yiddish story "Nokh Vilde Chazeyrim"

---

5. When Brenner arrived in 1909, there were in the Yishuv "no regular secular publication activity, no regular literary journals . . . and almost no reading public" (Z. Shavit 1982, 29). With his arrival, at the same time as Agnon and the poet Rachel, the foundation for a thriving literary center was laid.

(Tracking wild boars) in Ben-Tziyon's Hebrew translation.[6] This publication was facilitated only by suppressing the fact that the story was originally written in Yiddish. Neither Ben-Tziyon, who translated the story, nor the contemporaneous critic quoted by Govrin acknowledged this fact. Apparently capitalizing on this success, Ben-Tziyon included four more stories by Brokhes in later issues of *Moledet,* never mentioning their original language.[7] The single note acknowledging translation does not name the source language either: the footnote to "ha-Kabarnit ha-Zaken" (The old captain), part of the cycle "The Sailor on the Dead Sea" (Brokhes 1918, 177–242), reads *"turgam mi-ktav-yad"* (translated from a manuscript [Brokhes 1913, 390]).[8]

In this case, the Hebrew establishment internalized the content presented in a vehicle it considered anomalous. The content of Brokhes's *Moledet* stories—which conformed to the emphasis of Zionist ideology on "nondiasporic" aspects of the New Jew such as physical prowess and typically non-Jewish occupations (hunting and sailing) that were part of an exoticizing idealization of and admiration for the "noble Arab"—was divorced from the diasporic linguistic vessel, Yiddish. In a culture that elevated physical pursuits and knowledge of the land to ideological values, Brokhes's close acquaintance with the physical aspects of the country such as climate, landscapes, plants, and wildlife was appreciated.[9] His work was co-opted to the

6. It is intriguing that the Hebrew translation of the story appeared in 1911, before the Yiddish original was published in Brokhes 1918. Brokhes apparently knew little, if any, Hebrew; the correspondence in his archives at the Jewish National and University Library, Jerusalem, is exclusively in Yiddish.

7. "ha-Matmon" (The treasure), subtitled "mi-Zikhronotav shel Tzayad Ivri" (Reminiscences of a Hebrew hunter [1911b]); the two-part "Malach be-Yam ha-Melach" (A sailor on the Dead Sea [1912]); and "ha-Kabarnit ha-Zaken" (The old captain [1913]).

8. Brenner seems to be the only critic who referred to the fact that the stories were translated when he wrote about *Moledet* and Ben-Tziyon in 1912: "Anyone who has had the chance to read the sketches by the beginning writer Z. Brokhes in the Warsaw *Fraynd* or the New York *Dos Yudishe Folk,* and then saw the really nice work, both in content and in form, that appeared in the double issue [*Moledet* 5–6] and had been adapted by the editor from a foreign-language manuscript [*ktav-yad lo'azi*], knows how hard S. Ben-Tziyon worked to prepare it for publication" (1985, 3: 709). He does not mention Yiddish as the original language because this detail would have been obvious from the Yiddish names of the foreign periodicals that published other work by Brokhes.

9. During the prestatehood period, fostering the physical link with the land and its features became a cardinal component of Yishuv culture. Liebman and Don-Yehiya term the Yishuv's re-

point where it was set up as a paradigm for the young "Hebrews" of the Yishuv. The paradox posed by the subversiveness of the use of Yiddish was defused by classifying it in the editor's note as a nameless language.

The selectivity of the appropriation becomes clear when we discover, elsewhere in Govrin's 1989 volume, an acknowledgment that some Yiddish writers in the Yishuv were adopted into the Hebrew culture. A different essay discusses Leo Kenig, a Yiddish writer and art critic of the Second Aliyah, who used the Hebrew name "Aryeh Yaffe" in Hebrew translations of his work (Govrin 1989, 240–56). Govrin notes that Kenig's Yiddish stories were translated for publication in the Hebrew press and that "the translators did everything to create a Hebrew style that would preserve the spirit of the original and would conceal their original style" (246). This statement seems to imply an attempt to suppress the fact that Kenig actually wrote in Yiddish. Perhaps the most intriguing part of this essay is what it leaves unsaid, as in the following footnote: "The contribution of Yiddish writers to the literature of the Second Aliyah has as yet not been fully revealed. Some examples of this literature are in the anthology *mi-Karov u-me-Rachok* [From near and far], edited by Mordechai Chalamish, 'an anthology of Yiddish stories in Eretz-Israel from the beginning of the century to the present.' It may not be a coincidence that all these writers left the country" (244). Two inaccurate and misleading statements in this note create the impression that the Yiddish writers of the Second Aliyah were, en bloc, not committed to Zionism, thus perpetuating the Zionism-Yiddish dichotomy. First, the title of Chalamish's anthology of Yiddish literature in Hebrew translation is misrepresented in what seems to be a telling way; it is actually titled *mi-Kan u-mi-Karov* (From here and from close by). The difference in implication between *From Near and Far* and *From Here and from Close By* is obvious. In Zionist ideology, emigrating from Palestine amounted to a betrayal of the ideal. Govrin's incorrect version of the title signifies a double perspective that incorporates both identification with and distance from Palestine. Of course,

---

lationship with the land "the cult of the land" (1983, 33). Yael Zerubavel notes that "trekking on foot throughout the land was particularly considered a major educational experience, essential for the development of the New Hebrews" (1995, 28). This practice is illustrated in innumerable accounts; Meron Benvenisti, for example, remarks about himself and his contemporaries in the 1940s, "We wanted to turn the sacred, spiritual map of the Land of Israel into a real, physical map" (1988, 135).

the title *From Here and from Close By* is also intended to convey an ideological message: it implies a close emotional and physical link between the writers and Eretz-Israel. The last sentence of Govrin's footnote has the most negative valence. In actual fact, of the seven Second Aliyah Yiddish writers in Chalamish's anthology (Z. Brokhes, A. Talush, Aharon Re'uveni, Z. Y. Anokhi, Ephraim Auerbach, Yehoyesh, and Moshe Stavi), Re'uveni and Stavi never left the country, and Anokhi left but returned to live in Palestine in 1924; Yehoyesh never considered settling in Palestine permanently and thus can hardly be considered a Second Aliyah writer. The group reference—"all these writers"—implicitly brands them as traitors to the Zionist cause, but the well-documented fact that there was widespread emigration of Second Aliyah pioneers (including Hebrew writers) from Palestine is not mentioned. Both Brokhes's language and his 1913 emigration to Europe and America go unmentioned in the context of Govrin's *Moledet* essay because there he is being placed positively within the canon of early Zionist Palestinian literature.

I have addressed Govrin's studies at some length because they have become standard references on the early literature of the Yishuv. The techniques she applies are typical of the national narrative dominant in the 1980s: by selectively arrogating the content of Brokhes's fiction while suppressing the ideological significance of the language he used, the mainstream was able to include him in its canon. Yet when the exclusion of dissonant voices is necessary, Brokhes is grouped with those who are construed as disloyal to Zionism. Perhaps the ultimate appropriation of Brokhes is the fact that he, alone among the Yiddish writers of the Second Aliyah, eventually had a considerable body of his work translated and published in Hebrew.[10] The major Israeli literary critic and academic Yiddish scholar Dov Sadan wrote the introduction to the 1974 Hebrew version of *The Jordan Roars,* thus legitimizing the introduction of Brokhes into the Hebrew canon and completing the process begun almost sixty years earlier when his stories were published in translation in *Moledet.*

10. Re'uveni and Stavi eventually began writing exclusively in Hebrew, after having their work translated for several years by such major Hebrew writers as Brenner (Re'uveni) and Shlonsky (Stavi). The fascinating issues of Hebrew-Yiddish bilingual literary production in Palestine and the related processes of Hebrew translation and self-translation are beyond the scope of this study.

The Stranger: Hunters and Wanderers

The rabbi who gave the graveside eulogy for Zalmen Brokhes noted that one of his pseudonyms was *a Fremder*, "a Stranger" (Tavori 1977, 220). This self-description is borne out by the pervasive sense of alienation that infuses most of Brokhes's writing on Palestinian themes. His work expresses an ideological estrangement from the land and from its inhabitants, native Arabs and Jewish newcomers alike, and from the Zionist ideal that motivated the Jewish settlers; the narrators and protagonists seem committed to no ideal in particular. His fictional characters, though they are physically in the ancestral homeland, for the most part exhibit no sense of homecoming or of feeling at home. It is therefore all the more interesting that he was considered a Zionist writer. I have already noted that critics divorced the content of Brokhes's stories, which they perceived as positive, from the proscribed Yiddish language, but even an initial examination of most of his Palestine stories reveals a thematics and ideological content at variance with mainstream Zionism. Although, as also noted, some Hebrew literature of the period displays varying degrees of alienation from and critique of Zionism (thus indicating the shortcomings of referring to a single mainstream Zionist narrative), the romantic aspects of Brokhes's adventure stories made it easy to group him with the exoticizing writers of the early Yishuv, such as Meir Vilkansky (Shaked 1983, 127–78), rather than with the critics of this style, such as Yosef Chaim Brenner. "With the open heart of a lover and a clear eye, the romanticist Z. Brokhes set out to conquer the landscape of the homeland, attractive in its magic," states the jacket copy of the Hebrew version of *In the Shadow of the Hermon* (Brokhes 1954).

On its face, Brokhes's Palestinian experience seems typical of members of the Second Aliyah. Born in Chuvas, in the Mogilev Province of Belorussia in 1886, he immigrated to Palestine as a teenager in 1903. He left the country in 1913, returning for a time toward the end of the First World War with the Jewish units of the British army. Brokhes later lived for decades in Paris, Argentina, and the United States and eventually settled in Israel some years before his death in 1977. Like other Second Aliyah immigrants, many of whom were also in their teens, he worked at various manual occupations all over the country: stone-cutting in Jerusalem, construction work in Tel-Aviv, guard work in vineyards and granaries in farming settlements. At the same time, he did not subscribe to that portion of the Zionist paradigm that sought to settle on the land and (re)create a pastoral culture. Rooted nowhere, he worked as a sailor on a boat that plied the surface of the Dead

1. Zalmen Brokhes; courtesy of the Department of Manuscripts and Archives, Jewish National and University Library, Jerusalem.

Sea (a lake that is too saline to support any life within it) and hunted with no-madic Bedouins on its desolate shores. These pursuits and locations resonate profoundly in his work. Maintaining the position of outsider, even to his own biographers, seemed to be a constant for Brokhes.[11] By situating himself on the ideological margin, a position reified in his language, he perpetuated the stereotypical diasporic Jewish condition of dislocation. Brokhes's two books of fiction on Palestinian themes were published outside Palestine, the first in New York and the second in Warsaw. His work was spatially re-

11. Literary historiographers present different accounts of Brokhes's life and literary work, perhaps reflecting the difficulty of fitting him into established parameters. Reyzen does not note Brokhes's 1903–13 stay in Palestine, mentioning only that he visited the country with the "Jew-ish Legion" (1928, cols. 440–41). The entry on Brokhes in Niger and Shatsky 1956 states that he "began his literary work in 1907" but provides no publication details; it also notes that he went to Palestine several times and stayed for long periods (cols. 478–79). Kohen reports that Brokhes moved to Israel in 1974 (1986, col. 121), whereas Chalamish says that he moved there ten years before his death in 1977 (1990, 41). A highly skewed entry in a Hebrew encyclopedia of Yishuv personalities (Tidhar 1966) is presented and analyzed at the end of this chapter.

stored, as it were, decades later, when the Hebrew versions of *In the Shadow of the Hermon* and *The Jordan Roars* were published in Israel.

The thematics and central motifs of Brokhes's stories convey an essential feature of modern sensibility: a complex sense of estrangement that goes beyond its implications for Zionist ideology. In its Jewish manifestation, this sensibility of alienation and despair was embodied in the literary trope of the *talush*—literally, "one who has been uprooted." [12] Dan Miron notes that Hebrew prose writers at the turn of the twentieth century "focused on the character of the *talush* and obsessively examined the world of this character, whose every endeavor was futile" (1987, 130). The tradition of the *talush* continued in the Hebrew work of some Palestinian writers of the Second and Third Aliyahs (Miron 1987; Shaked 1983, 1988). In this literature, the turn-of-the-century European Jewish *talush,* usually a young man, has cut himself off from Jewish tradition in search of self-fulfillment as part of the creed of individualism, yet has also become disaffected from modern European social and cultural pursuits (Govrin 1985, 20). This sense of alienation extends to his personal relationships: the *talush* is estranged from his family, cannot form meaningful connections with women, and typically ends up in a social vacuum. Brokhes's characters exhibit many features that conform to this trope: his masculine narrator or protagonist is alienated from traditional Jewish culture and does not observe Orthodox ritual or any other practices identifiably Jewish (if anything, he is enthralled by Muslim customs in the context of Palestine). He has no family, nor is he an active participant in any society, including that of the Zionist Yishuv. Located outside the community spatially and ideologically, he is a lone itinerant observer.

Unlike those characters in Second Aliyah Hebrew literature who are portrayed as turning the traditional Jewish link with the Land of Israel into a profound personal attachment that seems to compensate them for their physical and emotional difficulties, Brokhes's protagonists are not consoled by the Promised Land. The *talush* often turns to nature for solace in a version of the romantic zeitgeist (Miron 1987, 478), yet this refuge is not necessarily linked with nationalist ideology. A Russian pasture will do just as well as a valley in Galilee—better, in fact, because it is a familiar locus of nostalgia.

---

12. The term is derived from the title of Y. D. Berkovitch's 1904 story "Talush." Paradigmatic Hebrew fiction featuring the *talush* includes that of M. Y. Berdichevsky, M. Z. Fayerberg (the title of whose turn-of-the-century novella *Le'an?* [Whither?] became the emblem of the *talush* predicament), Uri Nissan Gnessin, and the early Brenner.

Similarly, Brokhes's protagonist—hunter, sailor—is only superficially connected to the land, sometimes through a premonotheistic biblical association that may perhaps be characterized as "proto-Canaanism" (predating the "Canaanite" cultural movement of the Yishuv by several decades).[13] His link to nature has a much more personal and nonideological basis: he prefers the solitude and independence that the natural setting offers, in addition to the aesthetic pleasure it gives him. The Zionist thrill of settling and recultivating the ancestral homeland, which the ideology construed as a barren wilderness, is conspicuously absent.

It is telling that the greater part of *In the Shadow of the Hermon* (181 out of 258 pages) is devoted to two groups of adventure stories: "Der Yidisher Yeger" (The Jewish hunter [Brokhes 1918, 60–171]) and "Der Matros oyfn Yam ha-Melach" (The sailor on the Dead Sea [177–242]). The titles indicate the thematics: none of these stories focuses on the key Zionist ideal of settling the land. *The Jordan Roars* (Brokhes 1937) includes six stories in this vein, grouped under the title "Vanderungen" (Wanderings). The very title of the cycle expresses the disjunction between the Jewish protagonists of the stories, on the one hand, and the values and culture of the forming Yishuv in which they are nominal participants, on the other. All of these stories are set in forbidding, hostile areas on or beyond the margins of the Promised Land—on the banks of the Jordan River, in the Dead Sea area, in the mountains of Moab east of the Dead Sea, or on the western edge of the Negev Desert. These locations lie outside "civilization": the Jordan River is a boundary that Moses himself could not cross; the Dead Sea region is the site of the iniquities of Sodom and Gomorrah (Gen. 19); Moab is enemy territory; and Gerar was a major city of the Philistines, another remorseless foe of the biblical Israelites, who survived there only by resorting to trickery (Gen. 20; 26).

The sense of being an alien in the Promised Land suffuses all of Brokhes's fiction; even the titles of the volumes connote venturing beyond established borders. Mount Hermon lies outside the area of biblical Israel, and the Jordan River is a crucial geographic and ethnic border. In the title novella of *In the Shadow of the Hermon,* the mountain is not represented as the benevolent "grandfather" usual for the period—a simile beloved in the Yishuv, derived from the mountain's snowy top.[14] Rather, the action is set "in the

---

13. See the discussion of "Canaanism" in chapter 5.

14. This sobriquet is perhaps best known to the Hebrew reader from the poem "Kinneret" written in 1927 by Rachel, in which she describes the *"chermon ha-saba"* (grandfather Her-

shadow" of Mount Hermon, and indeed all the stories in this volume are dark in tone. The mountain is deceptively introduced as *"der alter zeyde"* (the old grandfather [Brokhes 1918, 7]), but this comforting appellation soon proves sarcastic. The narrator watches the fireflies and observes, "It seemed to him that the old grandfather, the Hermon, was lovingly blessing the seated colonists and Arabs by raining millions of stars down on them" (7). The apparent blessing by a benign "grandfatherly" entity is revealed as false. The unfolding story, a tale of forbidden, intense erotic attraction between an Arab man and a Jewish woman, is one of ultimately irreconcilable intergenerational and interethnic conflicts. A similar effect is produced by the title novella of *The Jordan Roars,* the story of a young Yemenite Jew in a colony of First Aliyah European Jews. This protagonist is an outsider in the community who prefers the liminal space represented by the Jordan River and its banks. Far from being the biblical gateway into the fulfillment implied by the term *Promised Land,* here the bank of the Jordan serves as the locus of the ultimate tragedy. The plots of both title novellas culminate in disaster, their grim aspects undercutting the idylls that the titles seem to promise: in one there is a total breach between the girl and her community identity, and in the other the young man dies in mysterious circumstances.

Brokhes seems to doubt the validity of the Zionist dream even as he sets the stage in ostensibly conventional Zionist terms. As the nameless narrator of "Der Oytser" (The treasure) rests on the eastern shore of the Dead Sea, outside the traditional Promised Land, he ruminates, "I myself, a wandering child [*vander-kind*], was dragged here from a distant cold land, and like a silent witness I sit here, on Moab's land" (Brokhes 1918, 67). Not only did he come to Palestine with little enthusiasm, but his current location, in an area traditionally identified with one of the ancient Israelites' most implacable enemies, offers little comfort. The Dead Sea region is fraught with significance. In the wake of the Sodom and Gomorrah episode, in which God "overthrew all those cities and all the plain and all the inhabitants of the cities and what grew in the soil" (Gen. 19:25), biblical tradition has established this geographical region as a virtual synonym for a wilderness eter-

---

mon). The poem was set to music by Naomi Shemer decades later and widely sung; it is usually referred to by its first words, *"sham harey golan"* (there are the Golan mountains). The inclusion of this appellation in a Yiddish story nine years earlier indicates the fluidity between Hebrew and Yiddish cultures in the Yishuv during that decade.

nally cursed with death. It is also identified with the Sodom code of ethics that lies beyond the civilized pale. Brokhes's Jewish drifter is simultaneously enchanted and threatened by the landscape. The narrator searching for gold in "The Treasure" looks west across the Dead Sea into the Promised Land (the perspective of an outsider) and identifies the sites of the biblical catastrophe: "There is Jebel Usdum [Arabic for Mount Sodom], once the place of noisy, licentious Sodom. Now no human voice is heard from there, not even the shadow of a human creature is visible" (Brokhes 1918, 67). The Dead Sea, which cannot tolerate life, itself becomes a malevolent living entity: it "looked at me like a fearfully enormous eye of a mysterious animal," says the narrator of "Nokhn Tiger" (Tracking the tiger [Brokhes 1918, 121]). In the wanderer's consciousness in "Untern Sikamor" (Under the sycamore), the inhuman sounds made by scavenging animals fuse with the thudding of the inanimate waves: "Only sometimes the distorted laugh of the hyena wafts in, accompanied by the wailing of jackals; the Dead Sea's waves slap loudly" (Brokhes 1937, 207). Yet these narrators, outsiders all, are attracted to the very outlandishness of the surroundings they have chosen.

Unless we understand that a selective cultural appropriation was at work, the publication of four of the "Jewish Hunter" tales in *Moledet* in Hebrew translation is indeed surprising, given their thematics. Simcha Ben-Tziyon, the writer and editor of *Moledet,* has been described as a faithful Zionist who was opposed to the fashionable "isms" of the turn of the century (Miron 1987, 250–52). For him, symbolism, Nietszcheanism, vitalism, and above all individualism were indications of the inward-turning *talush* sensibility, dissociating from the community and social responsibility (Miron 1987, 252). Ben-Tziyon thus seems to have missed, or repressed, the liminal, alienated, and highly fraught position of the narrator and characters of Brokhes's "hunter" stories. In fact, he changed the entire personal tone of the first *Moledet* story to suit the new national norm. First, he obscured the non-Jewish nature of the protagonist's quarry—wild boar, which, like all varieties of pig, is forbidden by Jewish dietary law—by an extraordinary title change from the Yiddish original and by the addition of an unattributed prologue linking the narrator with the restoration of Jewish national honor that was part of the Zionist project. The Yiddish title "Nokh Vilde Chazeyrim" (Tracking wild boars) is transformed in the Hebrew version to "Galoti et ha-Cherpa!" (I removed the shame!). The prologue of the Hebrew version explains the title: the narrator relates that he had once failed to kill a wild boar because he had been terrified of it. In his perception, fear is a mark of shame; by overcoming fear, he will redeem his honor. It is more than his own personal good name that he is anxious to reclaim: "Why should the gentiles say, 'A Jew is a hunter only if the fox is a shopkeeper'—No! My national pride cannot endure this!" (Brokhes 1911a, 82). His is a distinctly secularist national project: hunting the forbidden, impure "other."

In the added prologue, however, the figure of the hunter is glorified in high-flown literary Hebrew that is almost *melitsah,* complete with biblical allusions and direct quotations. In a vision that is missing from Brokhes's Yiddish story, a parallelism is set up between the biblical Nimrod and the male "beloved" of the Song of Songs, combining the two masculine ideals in a perfect realization of the Zionist dream of the New Jew: "Indeed, how handsome a man is when he sets forth bedecked with the hunter's jewels [*takhshitey ha-tzayadim*]: the rifle, that tube of heroism [*tzinor ha-gevura*] on his shoulder, a cartridge belt glistening on his thigh, the hunter's pouch, where animals and fowl are swallowed, hanging down from his shoulder . . . —off you march, a mighty hunter before the Lord . . . chasing in the dales, leaping over the mountains, bounding over the hills . . . the voice of the rifle still answers from between the ridges and strikes terror—lizards will scurry, mosquitoes will start, fox and hyena in their dens will shiver—Man has ventured into the mountains!" (1911a, 81).

First, the Hebrew version invokes the biblical characterization of Nimrod, the "mighty hunter," in a direct quote from the Bible (Gen. 10:10), followed by a quote from the Song of Songs recontextualizing the male lover who "bounds over the mountains and leaps over the hills" (Song of Songs 2:8). "The voice of the rifle" is a parodying reference to "the voice of my beloved" (Song of Songs 2:8), at the same time evoking the significance of firearms for the New Jew: its effect on the wildlife also echoes the impact of the divine voice.[15] Then, at the close of the prologue, Nimrod is explicitly mentioned as a model: "I adopted the craft of Nimrod" (82). This telling reference repositions the protagonist in an originary, premonotheistic temporal locus that predates all Jewish stereotypes. Early Zionists construed the biblical Nimrod, the "first mighty man on earth . . . a mighty hunter before the Lord" (Gen. 10:8–10), as the antithesis of everything about Jewish diasporic

15. "The voice of the Lord shakes the wilderness . . . makes hinds to calve and strips the forests bare" (Ps. 29:9).

existence that Zionism sought to change.[16] Ironically, the boar—the wild variety of the pig and thus the emblem of everything that is traditionally alien to Jewishness—is here transformed into an instrument of secular national pride. The honor of all Jews will be restored through an achievement that is opposed to traditional Jewish values. This "ideological" prelude is quite different from the Yiddish version of the story, which mentions the element of "Jewish honor" only briefly and focuses more on the personal challenge.[17]

The very title of the cycle, "The Jewish Hunter," is—as far as cultural stereotypes go—somewhat of a contradiction in terms, revealing another set of tensions reified in the figure of the narrator: he is simultaneously situated in two mutually exclusive categories. Following the biblical Isaac's preference for Jacob over Esau in the blessing scene (Gen. 27), Jewish tradition has always considered Jacob, the shepherd who became the progenitor of the Jewish people, as embodying values that are morally and culturally desirable. By definition, therefore, Esau the hunter has come to symbolize non-Jews and their undesirable values such as the use of power (in Yiddish, "Eysov" [Esau] is a synonym for "non-Jew" [Harkavy 1928, 354]). The Jews of Europe were stereotyped as cowards who did not use weapons, either because they were forbidden to do so or because of a cultural conditioning in the wake of this prohibition, valorizing nonviolence.[18]

In political Zionism, two contradictory views of the Jewish use of force developed. One view called to perpetuate a nonviolent humanistic culture in

16. "Nimrod" became a popular name for boys in the Yishuv during the 1930s and 1940s, signifying the hopes for a new, nondiasporic Hebrew ethos. It was also the title of a seminal 1939 sculpture by Yitzchak Danziger, which became an icon of the "Canaanite" movement; see, for example, discussions of Danziger's *Nimrod* in Zalmona 1998, 66–67, and in Y. Shavit 1984, 154–55.

17. The later Hebrew version of "be-Ikvot Chazirey ha-Bar" (Tracking wild boars) in Brokhes 1954 is much more faithful to the Yiddish original. Although full comparative close readings of the original Yiddish and the translated Hebrew versions of this story and others are illuminating, they are outside the scope of this study; some localized comparisons are presented later in this chapter.

18. David Biale exposes this stereotype when he notes that Jews in western and central Europe were allowed to bear arms during part of the Middle Ages (1984, 72–77). For a premodern view of a Jew who relies on brawn instead of on brains, see Chaim Nachman Bialik's 1898 story "Aryeh Ba'al-guf" (Aryeh the muscle-man [1965a]), in which the protagonist is a caricature of the "Jews with muscles." Bialik's "Muscle Jew" is eventually left with neither property nor social standing.

any future Jewish state, whereas the other espoused militancy as a means to make the Jews a "normal" people.[19] As Anita Shapira remarks, "there was an incredible magic about carrying weapons: after all, what was a more eloquent expression of the change that had taken place in the position of the Jew than such an instrument, symbolizing the independence of its owner" (1992, 71). Both these conflicting views were expressed in the development of Yishuv culture. Mainstream Zionist ideology aimed to (re)create an idyllic pastoral existence that would be closely linked with the agricultural rhythms identified with "Jacobite" values and simultaneously enriched through the introduction of Western ethical and humanistic concepts. The opposition between the two sets of cultural values—those of Jacob and those of Esau— produced a tension in the Yishuv that was perpetuated, though transmuted, in the State of Israel and is still far from resolution today.

However, believers in Jewish militancy found a different "Esau" to serve as a role model of sorts: the tradition of the local Bedouin groups construed violence as a significant positive element.[20] Members of the Second Aliyah who encountered Bedouin Arab hunters in Palestine sought to emulate them, to a degree that went beyond the romantic Orientalism common among newcomers to the region. Attempting to break free of the diasporic stereotype of the powerless Jew, they considered the nomadic Bedouin with their roving bands and warrior tradition to be descendants of the ancient Jewish inhabitants of the country, who could be their "guides to the right way of life upon the land" (A. Rubinstein 1997, 82). As late as 1936, for example, Yitzhak Ben-Zvi identified the Bedouins of Petra in Transjordan as "remnants of a Jewish tribe" and stated with "national" pride that of their total five thousand warriors, seven hundred bore rifles (1960, 115). "Let us live like Bedouins!" exclaimed the Second Aliyah writer Meir Vilkansky (quoted

19. For an exploration of the connection between Zionist ideology and the use of force, see Shapira 1992; for the significance of concepts of power in the statehood period, see A. Rubinstein 1997 and Zerubavel 1995.

20. On the whole, Zionists held a patronizing attitude toward the local Arab peasants (Arabic plural *falacheen,* usually represented in English as *fellahs* and in Hebrew as *falachim*). They perceived them as a poor and backward population, "Esaus" longing for modernization, which would be bestowed upon them thanks to Zionist goodwill and enterprise. This line of thought was reinforced by the socialist ideology of the Second and Third Aliyahs. For a discussion of the ideological dilemma concerning the local Arab population, see A. Rubinstein 1997, esp. 77–103. A contemporary view of the local Arab proletariat is presented in *ha-Achdut* 2, nos. 2–3 (1910); and see my discussion in chapter 3.

in Rubinstein 1997, 82). This is the element of Zionist ideology that Brokhes adopted.

Patchwork Identity, Patchwork Language

Ha-Shomer (the Watchman/Guard), a Palestinian Zionist self-defense group, formed in 1909 and adopted Arab customs, including the prominent display of weapons (daggers and rifles) as well as a nomadic lifestyle, "a special way of life of warriors" (Shapira 1992, 72). Ya'akov Ya'ari-Poleskin's 1922 *Cholmim ve-Lochamim* (Dreamers and warriors) admiringly describes Abu-Yusif, a certain real-life "Jewish Bedouin" known (like several of Brokhes's characters) only by an Arab nickname. In his paradigmatic exploit, Abu-Yusif fended off Bedouin robbers by brandishing his sword and spear: "In this way Abu-Yusif guarded the honor of the Jews" (22).

A comparison of photographs of ha-Shomer members (ills. 2 and 3) and the illustrations fronting Brokhes's "Jewish Hunter" stories (ills. 4 and 5) reveals the extent to which the image of the "Arab Jew," as embodying the New "Muscle" Jew, entered the popular imagination as an ideal.[21] The ha-Shomer men in the group portrait (ill. 2) are wearing the Arab *kefiyeh* headdress, and many sport mustaches, which signify hypermasculinity in Arab culture. Bandoliers and rifle straps crisscross their chests, daggers are displayed, and the rifles of the men in the two bottom rows are prominent. In the second photograph (ill. 3) riders wearing *kefiyehs* strike a classic pose in single file against a stark landscape.

The Arabian horses, decked out with traditional woolen saddlebags and ornaments, were an integral part of the image being projected. Not surprisingly, the illustrations in Brokhes's book lie squarely within this convention. They are almost identical with the ha-Shomer photographs, with an essential difference: they also convey the basic solitariness of Brokhes's characters. The "hunter" scene (ill. 4) has a single gigantic figure casting the only shadow over the land, both feet planted firmly on the ground as he shoots at wild ducks overhead. Like the ha-Shomer men, he is wearing the Arab *kefiyeh* and bears a dagger in his belt. The landscape is forbidding, its only veg-

21. The resonance of these particular photographic images is such that they became public property and continued to be used for decades in popularized histories, without attribution, as representations of ha-Shomer; see for example, Talmi and Talmi 1981, 130, and Na'or 1985b, 101. I have not been able to find any information about the illustrators in Brokhes 1918.

2. Members of ha-Shomer; Ya'ari-Poleskin 1922, 138.

etation a few prickly pears and some sparse clumps of grass. The tiny figures of people and sheep in the background are dwarfed by a formation of jagged rocks. It is the hunter who rules the land. The second illustration (ill. 5) depicts a line of riders silhouetted in black against the sky, with the obligatory palm tree locating the scene in the desert. The composition is dominated by a single white rider in the foreground, who, significantly, is detached from the group, with his attention directed elsewhere to an invisible point.

It was these romanticized aspects of Bedouin tradition that captured the collective imagination of Second Aliyah culture. Like Brokhes's narrator-hunters, the members of ha-Shomer were essentially loners who preferred the solitary life of the armed watchman to the tedious routine of farming and family; it is indicative of the ambivalence toward this particular vision of the New Jew that ha-Shomer was disbanded after the First World War, when the Zionist organization supported and emphasized the strategy of collective agricultural settlements.[22] One of the legendary men of ha-Shomer was Yechezkel Chankin, who was totally captivated by the Bedouin mystique and

22. Some groups in ha-Shomer emphasized other, traditionally less violent aspects of Bedouin life, such as herding sheep. For example, three members of ha-Shomer lived with a tribe of Bedouin for months in order to learn sheep raising (Charit 1937, 227).

3. A group of Jewish mounted watchmen in Palestine. Ya'ari-Poleskin 1922, 142.

would go off into the desert on his own for long periods of time. According to one account, Chankin planned to leave his family, once the organization was disbanded, for a trek around the world (Ya'ari-Poleskin 1922, 47).[23] Ya'ari-Poleskin describes Chankin in language uncannily reminiscent of the way in which Brokhes characterizes his narrator-hunter: "He was an unusual man, a new type among Jews. . . . He could not bear the ordinary, the ongoing around him. He always sought the extraordinary, wandering on foot with his rifle across his shoulder to the farthest places across the Jordan. . . . There he became a hunter, the first hunter among the Jews" (42). The culture selectively appropriated the exploits of people such as Chankin and made them a trope. A Chankin-like figure, perhaps Chankin himself thinly disguised by the similar name of Chanani, actually appears in the Hebrew "I Removed the Shame!" and is described in the following admiring terms: "I was very envious of my friend Chanani, who had already made a name for himself in all the Jewish settlements and was welcomed affectionately from Dan to Beersheba, Jews and Arabs together—and I wanted to be like him" (Brokhes 1911a, 81).

Echoing values of individuality and the solitary life that mainstream Zionism disavowed, the narrator of Brokhes's "Nokh Vilde Entlekh"

23. However, Chankin's wife, Chaya-Sarah, reported that at that time her husband decided to stop roaming and settle down (Chankin 1937, 116).

(Tracking wild ducks) waxes lyrical about the pleasures of hunting alone on the edge of the desert:

> No one knows how beautiful the hunt for wild birds is on the shore of the Dead Sea! No one who has ever tried this will ever forget it. Especially in the last days of the [lunar] month, when the moon is on the verge of disappearing. You go out after midnight to the mouth of the Jordan. The sea whispers secrets to the river that empties into it. As if entrusting a secret to the hills that thrust upwards to it, the distant sky looks down. You walk, listening intently. Each separate twig tugs at you, detains you, as if it wants to tell you that it has been standing here all summer, withering, fainting away without a drop of water; or they tell you who rested in their shadows, which birds hid among them. Who knows what they are saying? . . . It is quiet. Straining, you peer into the pale darkness. A shadow slinks through. It is a wild boar. (Brokhes 1918, 147–48)

4. The Jewish hunter; Brokhes 1918, 61.

The nameless hunter is happiest on his own, without human companionship. Nothing in this description is specific to Palestine or to Zionism; it is the solitude of the desert that touches him most profoundly. The Zionist project, with the Second Aliyah's emphasis on collective commitment and effort, seems far removed from this protagonist.

Brokhes's vision of the native Arabs in these hunting stories seems to conform to one strand of Second Aliyah romanticism. However, a closer examination of the stories reveals that it is not Arabs proper who embody the romantic ideal. The focus of the narrator's admiration is actually Jews who, in their rejection of stereotypical Jewish attributes, have become indistinguishable from their Arab neighbors. These Jews, who have totally assimilated into their surrounding culture and are respected by their Arab neighbors, are introduced only by their Arabic appellations (transliterated into Yiddish). Their "Arab" features are expressed in their appearance and mannerisms. Thus, the "exalted sheikh" in "Der Shtekn" (The stick), who rides in on his "golden, richly decorated noble mare, himself, as the saying goes, 'dressed in vinegar and honey,' " is revealed in the next paragraph as a Jewish colonist (Brokhes 1973, 100). The Yiddish collocation *ongeton in essik un in honik* denotes "dressed in finery." The narrator himself has adopted the trappings of the Circassians, an ethnic Muslim group whose

5. Riders and hunter; Brokhes 1918, 63.

men were renowned for their bravery: he describes himself as "dressed like a Circassian, in gray trousers, a dark shirt, with a large knife stuck into my wide leather belt, and the stick over my shoulder" (98). Such descriptions became something of a trope in the Hebrew literature of the First Aliyah: the appearance of a Jewish settler in Arab guise is proof of his "fitting in like a native" (Berlowitz 1996, 113).

The linguistic medium of Brokhes's stories, however, reifies the cultural confusion of immigrants striving to forge a new identity. Abu-Shawareb (Father of the Mustache), the Arabic nickname of the main character in the story by that name, is the acknowledged expert on local wildlife whom the narrator consults about hunting crows. Repeating the pattern of Jews who appear to be Arabs, Abu-Shawareb, too, is revealed as a Jewish colonist. His "Arab" attributes are reified in the huge mustaches that express his masculinity: "He had mustaches that all Jews [*ale yidishe kinder*] would wish for. What mustaches! When he would proudly take hold of one mustache and place it behind his ear, there was no doubt that the man had mustaches" (Brokhes 1918, 84). This Jew has achieved an ideal "that all Jews would wish for," a common turn of phrase. The Yiddish expression, however, enhances this achievement while ironizing it: the term *yidishe kinder* (Jewish children) stands in opposition to the paradigmatic, hypermasculine non-Jewish figure. Like the "sheikh" in "The Stick," Abu-Shawareb wears expensive Arab clothes, decks out his horse in Arab style, and carries a rich array of weapons: two revolvers, a silver-hilted sword, a "good English rifle" *(a gutn Englishn biks)*, and a long spear. Based on his appearance, he cannot possibly be construed as a Jew: "He looked like a great Arab sheikh or efendi who rules over a large region with many Arab tribes, and not like a colonist [settler] from a Jewish colony" (96). His physical prowess is carried a step further: not only is his own safety ensured, but he lords it over others. Thus, the ideology of Jewish power shifts its emphasis—from self-defense to the domination of the others in the land.

The same pattern is repeated in "Tracking Wild Boars," the story that in its Hebrew form in *Moledet* was hailed as suitable for Zionist youth. In a gesture of modernist alienation, it is the narrator himself who disavows his Jewish identity; rather than flaunting his Jewishness in this new guise, he reveals it only to the "Arabized" Jew whom he meets (Brokhes 1918, 129). Interestingly, his Arab companions are aware that he is Jewish, even though he has not told them: "I wondered that the sailors know who I am, although this is the first time I have ever been at the Dead Sea" (128). His identity apparently is indelible. When the narrator of "Tracking the Tiger" encounters two traditional Jews from Jerusalem who are seeking palm fronds for the Sukkot holiday ritual, he conceals his face with a scarf and begs Chemdan, their Arab guide, "Don't tell them that I am a Jew" (126). Nothing in his new persona is traditionally or identifiably Jewish; although this absence intensifies the character's mystique and attraction, it still falls short of this particular variation of the New Jew ideal.

Brokhes's critique of the Zionist vision gains force through the use of Yiddish. His Jewish characters, situated on the borders of the homeland, use the paradigmatic European Jewish language to disclaim their Jewishness, and the speech of non-Jewish characters—Arabic and Greek—is inserted into *mame-loshn*. These inclusions create a subtly rich and ironic representation of social heterogeneity in the Promised Land, limning an alternative vision of the Yishuv. The characters' displacement and ethnic ambiguity is manifested in the representation of their mixed speech. The sailor-narrator in the "Sailor on the Dead Sea" cycle (Brokhes 1918, 177–242) is surrounded by a motley assortment of dislocated wanderers. The vessel on which he works is jointly owned by a Jew and a Turk. Although Palestine was part of the Turkish Ottoman Empire, no Turks except low-ranking government officials lived in the country; the Turkish owner of the boat is thus an absent, vaguely authoritative figure. The captain is a Greek Christian who is bedeviled by visions when drunk and claims to be a descendant of both the Jewish Abraham and the non-Jewish Lot. The watchman is a North African Muslim who escaped from a prison island. Finally, the Jewish narrator, whom the others call "Solomon," identifies himself—in Arabic inserted into the Yiddish frame language—as a *"walad-moskob,"* a native of Moscow (the term used by local Arabs for the Jewish newcomers of the Second Aliyah, who were mostly of Russian origin), rather than as a Jew (Arabic *yahud*). This near disavowal of traditional Jewish identity is a device that helps him to escape the Jewish stigma of cowardice and weakness. The narrator looks up at the mountain traditionally identified as Mount Nebo, from which Moses saw the Promised Land, and is gripped by a sense of general discontent: "All his life Moses aspired, aspired to enter the land, fought tremendously, scattered an entire generation along his way, and remained standing on that mountain. He could only see. . . . And I see, how he stands there, the world-hero, and looks at me, his descendant, shaking his head at me tearfully. . . . I am in the land. I am here. So what? It's a sailor on the Dead Sea that I am" (185). He projects a keen sense of disappointment at his own shortcomings: located as he is on the fringes of the Promised Land, he can never provide Moses with the satisfaction of seeing his curtailed ambitions realized by a descendant.

The state of being rootless in the homeland is perhaps most powerfully represented in "Untern Sikamor" (Under the sycamore [Brokhes 1937, 207–10]). This story, the first in the "Wanderings" cycle, thematizes the alienation and dislocation so ubiquitous in Brokhes's poetic world. The opening scene conforms to a desert trope: the lone narrator, sitting under an isolated tree as night falls. The firelight from the camp of his Arab acquaintance, Abu-Abbas, attracts him to the other side of the Jordan River. Though Abu-Abbas offers him traditional desert hospitality, the story he tells soon departs from the conventions of campfire conversation, which often consists of tall tales. Abu-Abbas is now a fisherman in Palestine, but he is not a native; he is an exile from his home in Africa. His cliff-top home in the Watutsi (represented in Yiddish as *vasusi*) Mountains was demolished by a band of marauding *"Frendzh"* (an Arabicized version of "French," implying Europeans): "they destroyed our homes and took all our possessions" (209). Abu-Abbas and his niece, Zarifa, the sole survivors, are living a borderline existence (figuratively as well as literally) in the Dead Sea region to which they fled. Zarifa and the narrator are drawn to each other, an attraction with overtones of an anticolonial mutual identification as victims; but the romantic "plot" ends inconclusively at the close of the story, when Zarifa dives into the river as a distant caravan is heard approaching.

The complex liminality of the setting is highly significant. The point at which the Jordan River flows into the Dead Sea is perhaps the ultimate threshold, at once separating and joining life and death: although the freshwater river is the location of life and provides Abu-Abbas's livelihood, it is the chief source of the extremely saline Dead Sea. The Jordan is also a traditional political and geographic boundary line between the residents of Palestine and their enemies. Those who travel freely across this boundary proclaim nonallegiance to any and all of the communities beyond it. Conventional cultural and ethnic affiliations lose validity in this space, where even the distinctions between human and animal are obscured. A plaintive song that the narrator hears in the distance "filled the air like the dying scream of a mortally wounded animal, embracing me like an iron net and pressing upon my heart" (207). It is the wanderer himself, fitfully resting under the old sycamore tree in the dark, who feels like a trapped animal.

The characters who inhabit this forbidding locale are a geographical and cultural patchwork. As Abu-Abbas's story unfolds, we become aware of an implied kinship between the Jewish narrator and the Arab character. The narrator, as we know from other stories in this cycle, left Russia at least partly in the wake of the turn-of-the-century pogroms. Yet here, on the edge of the Promised Land, the Muslim Abu-Abbas is also a refugee from a "pogrom," an event usually linked with Jews. The narrator, though Jewish, is not characterized as such in this porous borderline region where ethnic origins and all cultural values are placed in doubt.

The patchwork nature of the community is reified in Brokhes's Yiddish representations of conversations. Language is no longer valid as a key to identity. Arabic, the apparent lingua franca of all the characters in these tales, is manifested both as Yiddish translation and as transliterated Arabic. Hebrew and Arabic are represented via Yiddish in a single typical scene, enabled by the openness of the frame language. *"Barukh ha-ba* [blessed is he who comes]," says Abu-Abbas, using the biblical and modern Hebrew phrase for perfect hospitality that functions in Yiddish discourse as well (in which it is pronounced *borkhabe*). As he invites his guest to join him by the fire and smoke the *nargileh*, he uses the Arabic *tfadal* (please [207]). His represented speech then shifts to Yiddish, when he calls out through the darkness to his niece, *"Makh kaveh"* (make coffee [208]).

In the "A Sailor on the Dead Sea" stories, the representation of polyglotism expands to include other members of Palestinian society. A stranger who approaches the boat's crew on the shore greets the Jewish narrator in what is represented as a normative Yiddish salutation: *"Vos makhstu, Solomon?"* (How are you, Solomon? [224]). The narrator replies with an idiosyncratic Yiddish transliteration of the conventional Arabic rejoinder: *"Khamdalailai, kif inti?"* (Thanks be to God, how are you?). This transliteration of Arabic is then given a parenthetical translation into Yiddish: *"Dank, vos makhstu?"* (Thanks, how are you?). It is the Greek captain who identifies the approaching stranger by the Arabic name Abu-Yakub, a Jewish guide: " 'Abu-Yakub, what are you doing here?!' cried the captain. . . . Now I recognized him. This is a Jew, a guide in the mountains." The interchangeability of languages palpably reflects the nonspecific fluidity of ethnic and cultural affiliations in Brokhes's nomadic characters.

A related sequence in one of the "Jewish Hunter" tales further illustrates the ambiguity of cultural identity within the Jewish community of Palestine, questioning Zionism's fundamental concept of nationalism. This sequence includes the meeting and subsequent interchange between the European Jewish narrator-hunter and Abu-Yusif, a non-European Jew from Kerak in "Tracking Wild Boars" (Brokhes 1918, 128–39). The Jewish identity of both characters is effectively obscured by all the features that might place them: location, dress, and language are not stereotypically Jewish. Abu-Yusif, who identifies himself by an Arabic nickname, lives in Kerak, considered to be the biblical Kir-Moab, the main city of biblical Moab, Israel's enemy (Is. 15:1), high in the mountains east of the Dead Sea. This region has a traditionally Arab population, with no historical record of a Jewish community. Abu-Yusif's residence there is thus an incongruity. The narrator, as we have come to expect, drifts noncommittally through the region. Abu-Yusif's appearance is not typically Jewish; he is dressed in a motley assortment of Turkish and European clothes, complete with the obligatory firearm: "Over the long Turkish *chalat* he wore a short jacket, a *pidzhak,* as though he were a *yevropeyer* ["European," in Russian pronunciation]. The handle of a revolver stuck out from under his wide sash" (128). The distinctions between European and different strains of the local are further blurred when Abu-Yusif's long garment is described as a "Turkish *chalat.*" *Chalat* is the term for the traditional long coat of Orthodox European Jews; by being qualified as "Turkish" and placed in the desert context, it is doubly exoticized because no Turks resided in the desert. The narrator assumes an Arab identity by wearing an *abaya,* the ubiquitous Arabian cloak.

It is in these characters' Arabic nicknames that their indeterminate ethnicity is most clearly indicated. The Arabic names "Abu-Yakub" and "Abu-Yusif," which denote the two Jewish guides in the wilderness, translate as "father of Jacob" and "father of Joseph," respectively—sobriquets of Hebrew origin used by Arab men. The construct form "Abu-(son's name)" has no parallel in Hebrew, nor does the custom of denoting the father by his son's name. On the contrary, in European Jewish culture the son is often identified by his father's name. The issue of identity is further confused by the detail that Isaac, the father of the biblical Jacob, is also the father of Esau, the paradigmatic "other," and the father of the biblical Joseph is Jacob, Esau's brother. The allusion to Jacob, set in the geographic context of the country's traditional eastern border, is particularly resonant. It is after Jacob crosses the Jabbok tributary of the Jordan in this area, just north of Moab, that he has his momentous encounter with the angel, with whom he wrestles for his life (Gen. 32:23–31). Jacob's very identity is changed by the outcome of this decisive night; his name is altered to Israel. The Abu-Yusif—Jacob—of "Tracking Wild Boars," whose ethnic affiliation is unclear, can be construed allegorically as another manifestation of Jacob-Israel. Affiliations accepted as basic are thus placed in question once again in a modernist version of the biblical tale.

The ambiguity of allegiances surfaces most clearly in the conversation between the two Jews in "Tracking Wild Boars," a conversation that is revealing in its linguistic pluralism. At first, they do not speak to each other, although each is aware that the other is Jewish. Abu-Yusif asks the sailors whether the narrator is English: "*Inglizi?*" (an Englishman?). "*Yahudi sayad*" (a Jew, a hunter), they reply. This exchange is in Arabic, represented in Yiddish and parenthetically translated. Then, says the narrator,

> Abu-Yusif took a few steps toward me, but stopped himself and started to amble nearby, throwing glances sideways. Finally he came up, twisting his hands inside his sash, and asked in Arabic:
>
> "An Englishman [*inglizi*]?"
>
> "A Jew [*yid*]," I replied in Arabic.
>
> "A hunter [*yeger*]?"
>
> "A hunter," I echoed back.
>
> "Of which animals [*chayes*]?"
>
> "Of boars [*chazeyrim*]."
>
> "Of boars?" he screamed, "What will you do with them?"
>
> "Sell to the Greeks."
>
> "Ah," he breathed in relief, and we became good friends. He told me that he was from Kerak, where he had a store, and that his name was Abu-Yusif. (Brokhes 1918, 128–29)

This dialogue goes to the heart of the characters' dilemma. They are two Jews floating in a boat—a liminal location in itself—on the edge of life, between cultures, and on the fringes of civilization. Their conversation, too, straddles several linguistic and cultural worlds. As signaled by the narrator, it most realistically is in Arabic. Although Abu-Yusif already knows that the narrator is Jewish, he approaches him and asks whether he is an Englishman, using the Arabic form *inglizi*. The narrator responds "a Jew, a hunter," using the Yiddish nouns *yid* and *yeger*. The conversation continues, with no explicit reference to the language. The representing medium remains Yiddish, complete with the conventional use of its Hebraic lexical components such as *chayes* (animals) and *chazeyrim* (boars/pigs); yet it is highly unlikely that an Arabized Jew from Kerak would be communicating in the language of European Jews. One of the rationales for the Zionist decision to choose Hebrew as the Jewish language of Palestine was its reputation as the common language of Jews everywhere. The representation in Yiddish of this Arabic dialogue between two Jews in a fictional text highlights the surrealism of the situation: the two, on the edge of the Promised Land, can communicate only in Arabic, the language of the dominant ethnic group.

Incongruously, Abu Yusif, the Jew who has effaced all outward sign of his ethnicity, is the most concerned with the religious implications of hunting boar, the emblem of the unclean. The fact that these two Jews converse in Arabic about a typical religious concern, identified in the Second Aliyah context with the Diaspora, reflects the incompleteness of the mainstream Zionist narrative.[24] At the end of the story, after the Jewish hunter finally shoots a wild boar, it is he who handles the carcass and cuts out one of the boar's tusks as a souvenir. Selim, the local Arab Muslim guide, keeps his distance from the *nagas* (unclean) animal because Muslims are not allowed to eat pork either (1918, 139). Neither of the two Jews in this tale is committed to any Jewish values, but, rather, both are concerned not to upset local customs. The Muslim is the one who is worried about preserving the boundaries of his religious identity.

In the "Hunter" and "Wanderer" story cycles, Brokhes sets forth a vision of the New Jew that perpetuates a modern Jewish dilemma rather than proposing a solution through Zionism. The narrator is not recognizable as Jewish in the traditional sense, yet he does not really subscribe to the modern Zionist creed. His is a culture of negation, which offers nothing positive as an alternative. Situated between cultures, this version of the *talush* continues to be represented in Yiddish, the language of the Old Jew of Europe.

Ethnic and religious identities are first made explicit and then obscured in the story "In di Berg fun Moyev" (In the mountains of Moab [Brokhes 1937, 211–15]). As night falls, the nameless narrator finds himself in the Arab town of Madaba, a few miles east of the Jordan River. Reversing the direction of the biblical Israelites' itinerary, he has walked that day from Jericho, crossing the river out of the Promised Land and into Moab—a territory identified in the Bible with Israel's archenemies. The conversational exchanges, represented in Yiddish, are "actually" in Arabic and mask considerable ethnic uncertainty. The narrator's attempts to find lodging for the

24. The intricate plurality of cultural values conveyed in the Yiddish story is lost in its 1911 Hebrew translation, which homogenizes the languages in accepted *nusach* style and obscures the variegated nature of the human mosaic.

night are unsuccessful: when he identifies himself as a Jew to the monk in the Greek Orthodox monastery, the monk sends him to the Franciscan monastery. The Franciscan monk then asks, in Arabic that is both transliterated and translated: *"Min hada?" ver iz es?* (Who is it? [211]). Now the narrator conceals his ethnic affiliation, saying "I am a tourist, a European *(a turist, an eyropeyer)*; later in that interchange he describes himself simply as "a stranger" *(a fremder* [212]).

When he finally finds a place for the night in the town's guesthouse, it is in a room shared with two Arabs. They greet him in a mixture of transliterated idiosyncratic Arabic and idiomatic Yiddish: *"Itfadal, ru zikh op"* (Please, rest yourself [213]). Unable to sleep, he hears a snatch of song from outside, and sees the two Arabs sitting at a small fire, with white *matzas* and an onion laid out on a cloth between them. One of them begins to chant from the Passover Haggadah: *"Shefokh chamoskho al ha-goyim"* (Pour out thy wrath on the nations) and the other continues the verse: *"asher lo yedo'ukho"* (who do not know thee). " 'Jews!' I sat up suddenly" (215), recounts the narrator, yet he takes no immediate action. When he eventually goes outside to talk to them, they are sound asleep and unmoving to his touch. The next morning, they are gone.

The narrator's conversation with the guesthouse servant encapsulates the substance of the story. "Who are you?" the servant asks the narrator, who replies in transliterated Arabic: *"a yahud"* (a Jew). *"Wallah!"* (really!), the Arab's amazed Arabic exclamation, is presented in transliteration only. The narrator goes on: "He [the servant] was surprised to realize that three Jews had slept together last night and did not know who they were" (215). The linguistic medley that includes Arabic (both translated and transliterated) and Hebrew, in the phrases from the Haggadah, within the frame language of Yiddish metonymizes the ambiguous ethnic affiliations of these Jews. The narrator, a Jew from Palestine where a modern Jewish, Hebrew-speaking community is being established, does not know that it is Passover—the defining national event—although as he tosses in the mountains of Moab his thoughts revolve around the biblical Israelites on the border of the Promised Land. The other two Jews, who are observing the essence of Passover by eating *matza* and reciting the Haggadah, pass for Arabs. In this story, where the term *stranger* recurs more than once, none of these Jews is secure in his identity; indeed, they do not know who they are.

Linguistic ambiguity seems to be a metaphor for ideological confusion and social alienation in Brokhes's most explicitly "Zionist" story, "Akht Za-

ynen mir Geven" (We were eight [Brokhes 1918, 247–58]), a vignette that
depicts a brief moment in the difficult Palestinian experience of young Zionist pioneers who are breaking ground for a new neighborhood. The men are
a disparate collection, including European Jews from Lithuania and Poland,
a non-European Jew from Yemen, and a convert to Judaism. They seem to
have nothing in common until a young woman appears among them and creates a group focus as they compete for her attention. The European Jews apparently speak Yiddish, and Nachman, the Yemenite Jew, is introduced
almost as a kind of comic relief, speaking and singing in Arabic. In Nachman, Brokhes illuminates a discrepancy, little remarked at the time, between
Yishuv ideology and practice. Yemenite Jews, who began arriving in Palestine in 1882 out of a traditional *chibat-tziyon* (love for Zion), were often romantically viewed simultaneously as exotics and as long-lost brothers
descended from one of the Ten Lost Tribes of ancient Israel.[25] Yemenite Jewish culture was sometimes construed as more "authentic" than that of European Jews because of its assumed affinity with biblical pre-exilic Judaism.
Ironically, although revivers of Hebrew posited the Yemenite Hebrew accent
as the most "authentic," this Yemenite Jew in Brokhes's story speaks no Hebrew and communicates only in Arabic. In spite of his Jewish and Zionist affiliations, therefore, he is located by language on the side of the hostile Arab
"other." The only one specifically described as using Hebrew is the nameless
"convert," the most utterly displaced character of all. Yet even he does not
actually converse in Hebrew: he chants what seems to be a fragment of Hebrew prayer, transposed into a nationalist key, at the top of his voice: *"Adir
ho, adir ho, adirim amkho yisra'el"* (Great is he, great is he, great is your
people Israel [250, 255]. This is not part of a real prayer but a pastiche composed of different snatches of ritual: *adir hu* is part of the Passover Haggadah, where it refers to God. The convert, who can communicate only
through a fabricated scrap of Hebrew verse, is thus elevating the Jews ("your
people")—whom he has joined, but with whom he cannot communicate—to
divine status. Brokhes foregrounds the group's disjointed allegiances by
framing the cultural locations of its members in Yiddish, while representing
only the ultimate outsider as using Hebrew. The "natural" connection that
Zionism posited between the ancient language and the modern nation is thus
broken.

    25. See Berlowitz's penetrating study of perceptions of Yemenite Jews in early Yishuv fic-
tion (1996, 81–112).

Aliens in the Homeland

"Di Borvese" (The barefoot ones [Brokhes 1910]) is probably the earliest of Brokhes's stories to deal with Zionist thematics.[26] It is unique in the context of contemporaneous accounts of encounters between old and new Jewish communities in Palestine. As noted earlier, such accounts are usually limited to contacts between members of the First Aliyah and those of the Second Aliyah and are depicted from the point of view of the latter. Written in the present tense, "The Barefoot Ones" reverses the perspective by depicting the impact of the Second Aliyah on the Old Yishuv. Chasye, the protagonist, through whose consciousness the story is presented, is the teenage daughter of an Orthodox Jewish family in Safed, a Galilee town in which the Jewish community retained its Old Yishuv, Yiddish-speaking character. A Zionist lodger, known only by his last name, Yofe, rents a separate room in the family's courtyard. In the course of the delicate relationship that develops between herself and Yofe, Chasye becomes attracted to some aspects of the different way of life that he and his "barefoot" Zionist friends embody. At the story's end, her parents inform her that they have arranged her betrothal to a man from within her own community.

The worlds in which Yofe and Chasye live are diametrically, almost schematically opposed. Chasye is a sheltered young girl, her life dictated by her mother and her behavior shaped by her girlfriends. Yofe bursts onto the scene with no family ties, in what Chasye's mother perceives as wild debauchery: his friends, young men and women, mingle freely. The family's disparaging term for Yofe and his friends is *di borvese*—literally, "the barefoot ones," or, idiomatically, "the paupers"—a Yiddish term used for any group that challenges social norms, in this case Zionists, possibly implying a degree of anarchism. Indeed, Yofe and his friends flout convention, and Yofe himself embodies the modern artist's disregard for the establishment. Chasye cannot comprehend the derogatory valence of *borvese* and *tziyonisten*, terms that her parents use, or of *moskob* (Russians), as the local Arabs call the newcomers. At a community celebration, her attention is fixed on the young Zionists. Her internal monologue alternates with the narrator's description:

26. In my discussion, I refer to this earliest version, dated according to the Julian calendar. The story appeared in slightly different form, titled "Di Shtile" (The quiet one) in Brokhes 1937, 238–45. The significance of the differences between the versions is addressed later in this chapter.

"Groups of people stand and look at them. *'Hada moskobi'* [these are Russians], say the Arabs. *'Borvese, tsiyonistn'* [barefoot Zionists], the Safed Jews mock them. Chasye is annoyed: why are they called *'tsiyonistn'*? That must be a very ugly word. . . . She is strongly attracted to approach them" (Brokhes 1910, 3).

Yofe is an art student, and sketches of naked men decorate the walls of his room. Exposure to art, and to such art in particular, breaches several powerful taboos of Chasye's Orthodox Jewish culture (traditional Jews avoid figural artistic representation because of the interpretation of the Second Commandment that forbids the making of "graven images" [Ex. 20:4]; the Torah also prohibits homosexual relationships [Lev. 18:22] and frowns upon nudity). Her powerful attraction to Yofe thus encompasses the lure of the banned and the exotic. As Chasye becomes aware of his dissonant values, she begins to question those of her own society. She is able to reconcile Yofe's values with her own only when, in narrated monologue, she characterizes the artwork in his room as "nude men, stark naked, just like Machmud the crazy man [*der meshugener*] who runs around the streets" (3). By placing the naked figure in a legitimate negative context, that of the "town lunatic," she defuses its danger.

Chasye's glimpse into Yofe's modern version of Jewish culture takes on an additional valence when she witnesses one of the "barefoot" girls, Yofe's "sisters," striking and injuring an Arab who has been harassing her. "This girl," Chasye mulls over the day's events, "how powerful she is, to have absolutely no fear! . . . If something like this should happen to me, would I have thought of cracking his skull?" (3). Chasye admires the girl's physical strength and courage but realizes that she herself would be incapable of such a deed. Her rebellion is limited to more frequent conversations with Yofe: "Chasye becomes bolder, more courageous. Now she has almost no shame. When Yofe passes and says 'shalom,' she answers him" (4). She gradually withdraws from the girlfriends who had been her companions and spends her time alone. Her choice of location is significant: she takes up a liminal position on the threshold of the family apartment, from which she watches Yofe's door intensely. Chasye is pulled back into her native culture when the match is arranged for her at the same time that Yofe gives notice that he is leaving the apartment. So ends her brief attempt to escape from a tradition that she now perceives as confining.

This sketch of the conflict within a member of the Old Yishuv is innovative in its empathetic angle and its feminine point of view. Chasye is on the verge of becoming a female *talush* figure: she is no longer satisfied with her own culture but is unable to adopt the culture of the "barefoot" ones. In a foray, rare for the time, into the cultural dilemma of Old Yishuv individuals faced with the Second Aliyah's value system, Brokhes reverses the emphasis of the quandary by offering a detailed, modernistic presentation of an individual's response from within her own sensibility rather than creating a stereotypical portrait of group reaction. The Old Yishuv is transformed from a monolithic entity into a community of discrete personalities: Chasye, her mother, and her younger sister are distinct from each other, each with her own needs and dreams.

Such a depiction of the Old Yishuv is quite different from that in Brenner's *Shekhol ve-Khishalom,* in which, as we have seen, the Old Yishuv is presented from the more conventional viewpoint of the Second Aliyah and caricatured through the device of the women's "conversation-whining" that is marked as Yiddish. Brokhes ventures into new literary territory and breaks a double taboo: he not only depicts the Second Aliyah from within an Old Yishuv sensibility, but does so from a feminine perspective. By validating this perspective in Yiddish, the paradigmatic feminine language, he deviates from the contemporaneous Yishuv literary convention that glorified the masculine aspects of the Zionist project, but at the same time he reaffirms these aspects through Chasye's attraction to Yofe.

Brokhes's ability to adopt a feminine position enables him to address the area of sexuality, which was largely off-limits in literature and memoirs of the Second Aliyah. Referring to the "sexual utopianism" of the Second Aliyah, David Biale notes the reticence of both male and female members of the Second Aliyah about sexual matters and their puritanical streak (1992, 182—93). Later Yishuv Zionists positioned women primarily in maternal roles. This problematic is reflected in such Hebrew works as Nathan Bistritsky's *Yamim ve-Leylot* (Days and nights), a major expressionist novel of the Second Aliyah originally published in 1926, depicting the experience of an early commune.[27] In one passage in the novel, the small group of pioneers is

---

27. For the 1940 edition, Bistritsky drastically cut his novel to about half the original size, by his own admission doing away with much of the "heart's melody . . . the heart's ferment and foam" (1978, 8). This revision may be symptomatic of the collectivist drive for uniformity and a more "realistic" poetics. For an extensive analysis of the novel's modernist poetics, see Sadan-Loebenstein 1991, esp. 119–60; on the politics underlying the publication of the second edition, see Keshet 1994.

mourning the death of one of its members. The only woman in the commune is the deceased man's girlfriend Adèle (a name that evokes the German-derived Yiddish word *eydl,* "noble, pure"), who functioned as "mother and sister [*em va-achot*] to them all" (Bistritsky 1978, 155). This double characterization alludes to a well-known poem (which was set to music and became a popular song) written in 1905 by the Hebrew "national" poet Chaim Nachman Bialik. The poem is usually known as "Hakhnisini" (Take me in), after the opening word; the first line, addressed in the feminine, begins, *"Hakhnisini tachat kenafekh va-hayi li em va-achot"* (take me in under your wing and be mother and sister to me). Bialik's "Hakhnisini," which echoes his own ambivalent relationships with women, came to emblematize the complex attitude toward female sexuality during the Second Aliyah, whose members were familiar with both the poem and the song.

Bistritsky's character Alexander Tzuri, the ideological mouthpiece of the pioneer group, sounds an impassioned call to enter into a covenant with "the sister": "We have forgotten our sister, forgotten her, forgotten her! We have not yet dared to approach our sisters—the pure, the dear ones, who are dissolving in their loneliness! . . . Woe to us! . . . We do not have even a single child born *to us,* and our community is still childless, still childless!" (1978, 167, emphasis in the original). Woman's identity oscillates between that of sister and that of future mother to the collective's child; in this literature, she is never a sexual being, as, indeed, Bialik's poem itself reflects a surrender of sexuality.

Eroticism was repositioned and focused on the land itself. The discourse of local landscape was given the Hebrew name *yedi'at ha'aretz*—literally, "knowledge of the land." In the Bible, the conjunction of the verb for "to know" with the noun for "a woman" denotes sexual intercourse.[28] In the 1920s, when a Hebrew curriculum for elementary education was being formulated, the term *yedi'at ha'aretz* came to designate the study of Palestinian geography. This choice, made in a cultural climate to which the Bible was integral, highlights the heavy emotional baggage that accompanied the Zionist return to the Jewish ancestral home. Renewed physical contact with the land aroused and displaced emotions that can be described as erotic. In a fascinating study of Zionism considered in psychoanalytical terms, Jay Gonen interprets passionate invocations of the land as indicating a frame of mind in

28. This biblical usage, associated with legitimate possession (Alter 1996, 16), first occurs in Genesis 4:1, "And the human knew Eve his wife, and she conceived and bore Cain."

which "mother Zion was being fertilized and impregnated by the . . . sons" (1975, 18). Esther Fuchs sets this insight in the context of established literary tradition, which elaborates on the biblical trope of the nation as a wife (Jer. 2:2); like other scholars, she notes the fact that all terms for country, land, state, and motherland are feminine gendered, leading to a "gynomorphic representation of the country" (1987, 23).[29] Meir Shalev's best-selling 1988 Hebrew novel *Roman rusi* (Russian novel) is a fictional attempt to deal with the changing problematics of the relationship between Jews and the land, as Zionist ideology evolved. Shalev's character Piness, a member of the Second Aliyah, is aware of the sexual link with the land. He envies prehistoric man, "who came to an innocent land in which no one had left bruises of sexual possession and petty footprints of loyalty and love" (1988, 287).

David Biale remarks on the eroticization of labor on the land as a transformation of the traditional allegory of love between God and Israel (1992, 183). This transformation is remarkably illustrated in a passage from a Hebrew short story of 1930, "ha-Kever ha-Rishon" (The first grave), by Shlomo Tzemach, an especially articulate representative of the Second Aliyah. Here, the male members of a commune are digging a grave for their only woman comrade, who functioned as their asexual "housewife" and has just died of malaria. The process of burying her in the soil of the land is the only erotic relationship with her: "The hoes were raised, glittered in the sunlight, then were brought down, shoved into the thickness of the soft, wet earth. Clods of rich black earth, covered in tangled field grasses, like slices of hair-covered scalp, were thrown aside in quick succession. And the pit grew deeper from moment to moment" (Tzemach 1930, 92). I read this extraordinary passage as depicting an explosive erotic juncture between the men of the group, the land, and the woman they are burying. The erotic experience is realized after her death, through the medium of the land. The tactile aspects of the burial emblematize the pioneers' displaced eroticism.

Given this cultural context, it is surprising to find that eroticism, including some of its less conventional aspects, figures explicitly in several of Brokhes's stories. Contemporaneous Zionist Palestinian writers, to the degree that they deal with sexuality at all, often adopted the European orien-

29. Discussing a crucial variation on this pervasive theme of Yishuv culture, Kronfeld has shown that the unique link with the land of the first native Hebrew poet, Esther Raab, is a gender subversion in addition to a displacement: the erotic feminization of the land by a female voice renders the connection homoerotic (1993, 3–5).

talizing trope of the Arab man or woman as the repository of sensuality (a trope that Brokhes reverses, as we shall see). But Chasye, the protagonist of "The Barefoot Ones," is enthralled by Yofe, the Zionist whom her parents term "the barefoot one." She seems intrigued by this reference to an uncovered body part, which functions synecdochally for all that is forbidden about the newcomers and their culture.[30] Her sensual awareness may be roused by the "Oriental," when an Arab man assaults a female member of Yofe's group, but Arabs are not the focus of her interest in this scene. Rather, it is the power of the secular, modern woman to resist a man's unwanted sexual attention. Chasye is deeply fascinated by Yofe as someone who is "barefoot" and liberated from the Old Yishuv conventions that she now perceives as constricting. The comradeship between men and women in his group draws her powerfully, with its hint of forbidden activities conveyed by the action of feet: "At night they heard sounds of singing and the thump of dancing feet from his room" (Brokhes 1910, 3).

Yofe's box of painting materials, linked as it is with the prohibited occupation of figurative art, comes to signify his appeal. The box, an artifact from a culture ostracized by Chasye's own, is the catalyst for a surprising erotic moment. Toward the end of the story, Chasye finally musters up her courage: "She asks [Yofe] what is in the box. He opens it, shows her, explains: colors, brushes, paste—for painting. She bends over and looks into the box. Yofe strokes her hair. Mirele [Chasye's younger sister] sees and is silent" (4). Yofe immediately signals the end of their intimacy when he says, "It's time to go!" and closes the lid of the box, shutting off Chasye's glimpse of forbidden materials (an allusion to Pandora's Box is perhaps not too far-fetched). The erotic tension that has been building in Chasye is now channeled toward Mirele, who has been watching the scene: "Chasye goes to Mirele, picks her up, kisses her, embraces her. . . . [C]losing her own eyes, she presses her lips to [Mirele's] hair" (4). Chasye's awakening sexuality carries a tinge of incestuous homoeroticism, a theme more fully developed in the later story "In the Shadow of the Hermon." As she places her lips against her sister's hair, they assume the role of Yofe's hand on her own hair. It is now that Chasye begins to sit on the threshold across from Yofe's room. But once her marriage has been arranged, her experienced world, including the brief flicker of eroti-

30. Biblical references to "the feet" are often interpreted as euphemisms for the sexual organs (Ex. 4:25, Is. 7:20, 2 Kgs. 18: 27) or for private parts (Jud. 3:24, I Sam. 24:4).

cism, is reinscribed into the Old Yishuv's conventions. Chasye's barely articulated vision of other options is no longer a possibility.

The trope of the sensual Arab is inverted intriguingly in the novella "Untern Shotn fun Chermn" (In the shadow of the Hermon [Brokhes 1918,
7–59]). The plot, set entirely within the context of First Aliyah culture, revolves around the family of Yankev, a proto-Zionist who left the Old Yishuv
community of Safed with his wife and two daughters, Rochl and Rivke, to
farm the land. Rochl, the older daughter, falls in love with Salim, one of her
father's Arab laborers, and refuses to marry Avimelekh, the son of another
Jewish farmer. When Rochl becomes pregnant with Salim's child, she is cast
out of her family and her village and finds refuge in Salim's village. Salim
himself initially flees in fear but later returns and is arrested. After his arrest,
Rochl declares that she wants to become an Arab and goes off with the local
Turkish governor, followed by Salim. Her father then sells off everything and
returns to Safed with his family.

After a deceptively conventional beginning, this story takes an unexpect-
edly subversive turn. Salim is initially described as the object of Rochl's erotic
impulses, but her unfulfilled sexual desire seeks an outlet elsewhere. Unable
to fall asleep, Rochl hears someone singing outside:

> [Rochl] saw before her the towering figure of tall, slender Salim: the broad
> sash encircles his dry body firmly. The large white teeth are visible under-
> neath the thick lips, his large black eyes look out from under the "agal"
> headdress, his dark face beckons and smiles to her.
>
> "Why does he come close to our window!" . . . she pushes "him" away
> angrily, while at the same time she presses herself more closely against the
> iron grate of the small window. . . . Rivke moans in her sleep. "What's the
> matter with you, Rivke?" She picked her up in her arms and strongly
> pressed the warm body to herself. Rivke flung her bare arms around Rochl's
> neck and lowered her head to Rochl's shoulder. . . . Rochl brought her sister
> to her own bed, caressed her lovingly, and kissed her slightly parted lips.
> (Brokhes 1918, 17–18)

This characterization of the relationship between the two sisters as incestuous lesbianism continues throughout the story, expanding on the theme only
hinted at in "The Barefoot Ones." The "sensual Arab" trope, first applied
conventionally to Salim, is later reversed and reflected in Rochl in a highly
charged scene between the sisters. When Rivke comes to see her in the Arab

village, "Rivke embraces Rochl more tightly; Rochl takes Rivke's head in her hands and clings to her lips, wet with tears, with a long kiss. . . . Rochl is silent, only a paleness covers her large, thick, lustful [*tayvedike*] lips" (48). Salim's lips, the hallmark of his sensuality, are now repositioned in Rochl. In this description of the sisters' meeting, the word *tayvedike* (lustful) separates the Old Yishuv woman from her repressive culture. This time both sisters are active participants in the erotic relationship. Rivke's curiosity about her sister's sexual experience with Salim takes on an additional, sensual dimension after Salim's flight: "Rivke presses up strongly against Rochl, warming her with her own hot flesh, and keeps asking, 'How was it, Rochl? How was it?' " (44).

Brokhes ventures deeply and explicitly into the uncharted thematic area of Old Yishuv women who are beginning to explore and challenge their cultural norms.[31] For women such as Chasye and Rochl, who are exploring and transgressing boundaries, one type of prohibited sexuality is replaced by another. The breakdown of values that is only intimated in Chasye's hesitant sexual gesture and averted by a surrender to social convention is fully realized in Rochl's choices. Her passionate desires and embraces initially breach a basic taboo of familial relations and then an ethnic-religious taboo. Eventually she disavows both family and ethnic affiliation—tellingly, in speech represented as a mixture of Arabic and Yiddish—and allies herself with the seductive "other." The sexual displacement of conventional, heterosexual desire within the social norm signals the ultimate disintegration of established values and the lack of acceptable alternatives.

Brokhes's sensitivity to the problematics of the "other" is acute in his portrayal of an outsider within the First Aliyah context in "Der Yardn Roysht," the title novella of *The Jordan Roars* (Brokhes 1937, 3–32). We first meet the protagonist, Shlomo, a Yemenite Jewish teenager, as a child worker in a First Aliyah farming village; in the course of the story, he attains the prestigious status of an armed watchman *(shomer)* for the village. However, he can never hope to unite with his beloved Yehudit, the daughter of

---

31. The thematics of the Old Yishuv in general and of religiously observant Jewish women in particular, barely acknowledged by the Yishuv, have over the past decade or so become popular in secular Israeli culture; works of fiction and films portraying these social groups have been extremely successful. Among them are novels such as those by Yisra'el Segal (1990) and Yochi Brandes (1997), collections of short stories such as that by Mira Magen (1994), and the 1999 film *Kadosh* (Holy).

one of the farmers, who is apparently attracted to him yet tacitly intended by her parents for Amnon, her relative. This rather formulaic tale of unrequited love ends as Shlomo dies on the bank of the Jordan River in mysterious circumstances.

Although the plot may be stereotypical, it provides unusual insights into the complex cultural and social status of Yemenite Jews in the early Yishuv. Shlomo is ostracized by the settlement. As a young child, he is nameless; the village children, speaking Yiddish, call him *teymener* (Yemenite) derisively, and he is relegated to the lowliest of tasks—watching the donkeys. He physically resembles the stereotype of a diasporic European Jew: "Shlomo was a small, thin child with a pair of black burning eyes that illuminated a pale face with a long crooked nose. Long curly sidelocks hung down on either side of his face" (Brokhes 1937, 3). As the children tease him, the archetypal Jewish plaint reverberates in his thoughts: *"Vuhin geyt men?* (Where can one go?), echoing the displacement of the protomodernist *talush*. Even in this all-Jewish society, located in the ancestral homeland, Shlomo is an outcast who feels most at home in the village cemetery, "where one can look out as far as the mountains" (4). This New Jewish society-in-the-making apparently has its own internal Zhids.

In his imagination, Shlomo turns the tables on his tormenters by renouncing his ethnicity and religion. He dreams that he is the biblical Abimelech, the non-Jewish king of Gerar (Gen. 20 and 26). Amnon and Yehudit take on the personae of the biblical Abraham and Sarah, and Isaac and Rebekah, respectively. In Genesis, the situations are resolved when Abimelech not only grants asylum to the Patriarchs and their wives (whom they have introduced as their sisters) but asks their forgiveness.[32] In Brokhes's variation, the "king" demands that Amnon hand over Yehudit. As the non-Jewish king Abimelech, Shlomo is omnipotent, humiliating and ridiculing the two Jews who beg for his mercy. "We are strangers," says Amnon in Shlomo's dream, "Jews, who have strayed into your land." The king is merciless: "We are far from the Jews. We know nothing of them" (5). Only in his dream, where he is a non-Jew outside the Promised Land, can this ostensibly genuine Jew assume the power that is denied him in real life: " 'Slaves! Cage him [Amnon] until we investigate the matter!' he [Abimelech-Shlomo] commands sternly" (5–6).

---

32. The three "sister-wife" incidents in Genesis, involving Pharaoh (Gen. 11) and Abimelech the king of Gerar have been characterized as type scenes rather than as a representation of actual events; see Alter 1981, 46–62, and 1996, 52.

Like Chasye in "The Barefoot Ones," Shlomo is adrift in a cultural no-man's-land. Though he lives in the farming village, he is not part of its culture, yet is no longer at home in his own value system. When he visits his parents, who maintain their traditional way of life rich in features of Arabic tradition, he is unsettled by his mother's appearance: "He looked at his mother, who sat across from him in her long blue Arab shirt, with the large white metal rings on her hands and in her ears, and for some reason he felt very ill [*zeyer nisht gut iz em gevorn*]. He himself did not know why" (8). The Yiddish *nisht gut vern* (feel ill) can refer to both physical sensations and emotional unease, and its use here eloquently conveys the precariousness of Shlomo's balance between emotional worlds. As a watchman, he prefers the company of his Arab colleagues and is especially drawn to the song of "the crazy Arab" *(der meshugener araber* [13]), perhaps sensing a kindred "other"; as we have seen, the "crazy Arab" trope provides a haven for anomalies within the dominant Jewish community. The villagers' respect is denied Shlomo; as he makes his rounds, he hears Amnon muttering, "There goes the *teymener* [Yemenite]" (20), the same derogatory nickname that plagued his childhood experience. His alien status perpetuated, there seems no way out. The cause of Shlomo's death on the riverbank is ambiguous and is not necessarily linked with the two Arabs who emerge from the shadows as he collapses; but the dilemma of this eternal outsider is magnified by his presence in the Promised Land and by his death on its border. The "promise" of the land proves hollow.

Brokhes's representations of the First Aliyah deviate from the norm set by Second Aliyah literature, in which it is almost always collectively identified with the Old Yishuv and characterized negatively, ignoring important distinctions between the different components of the community. His noncommittal ideological position, for which Yiddish was the ideal vehicle, enabled him to enter the world of First Aliyah values and to illuminate the problematics of its culture in a way that was not available to his contemporaries, who sealed their affirmation of Zionism by writing in Hebrew. In Nurit Govrin's brief reference to Brokhes in her study of the imprint of the First Aliyah on Israeli literature, she schematically defines his unique insight into cultural issues of the First Aliyah and the Old Yishuv as an "attempt to understand the opposite side and its problems" (1981, 33). She positions him with the Second Aliyah ideologically, focusing on his depictions of economic confrontation between the pioneer societies. But "The Barefoot Ones," for example, is not concerned with the character of Yofe, the cause of

Chasye's quandary. We learn nothing about him except through Chasye's sensibility. Significantly, "Di Shtile" (The quiet one), the title of the second Yiddish version of the story, decisively locates its focus on Chasye, daughter of the Old Yishuv, rather than on the Zionist pioneers. The characters of the two novellas "In the Shadow of the Hermon" and "The Jordan Roars" exist entirely within the culture of the First Aliyah and of those Old Yishuv members who took up agriculture. Brokhes was far more interested in the cultural dilemmas of members of the Old Yishuv and the First Aliyah than in the dilemmas of the Second Aliyah's immigrants.

Induction into the Canon

Brokhes's selective induction into the canon of Zionist literature began, as noted, with the approval of a local Hebrew critic in 1911. It resumed more than forty years later, with the 1954 publication of the Hebrew *be-Tzel ha-Chermon* (In the shadow of the Hermon), presented as a collection of adventure stories, and was completed with the 1974 publication of the Hebrew *ha-Yarden So'en* (The Jordan roars), presented as a translation of the 1937 Yiddish *Der Yardn Roysht*. Yet neither of the Hebrew volumes conforms to the Yiddish volume it purports to represent, for reasons that are impossible to determine today.[33] The content and structure of many stories are changed in the translation, leading perhaps most significantly to shifts in thematic emphasis (as in "Tracking Wild Boars"). A close look at the first page of "Tachat ha-Shikma" (Under the sycamore [Brokhes 1974, 66–69]), a second Hebrew version of the original Yiddish story (Brokhes 1937, 207–10), can provide some idea of the political considerations that impelled the Hebrew translation of these stories.[34]

As described earlier, the plot of the Yiddish original begins as the lonely narrator rests on the bank of the Jordan and hears the plaintive tones of a song that evokes the lost home of his acquaintance Abu-Abbas, the African Arab. There is no initial reference to the narrator's history; the scene seems a nocturnal desert idyll, with stars twinkling through the tree's leaves and the

33. For a pertinent analysis of the politics of translation, see chapter 5 in Lefevere 1992, which deals with the " 'construction' of the image of a writer [Anne Frank] who belongs to one culture in—and especially for—another" (59).

34. As noted, a first Hebrew version of the story, closer to the Yiddish original, appeared in Brokhes 1954, 159—61.

river rushing nearby. It is only Abu-Abbas's song that later creates "an iron net pressing upon [the narrator's] heart" (Brokhes 1937, 207). The Hebrew version, in contrast, opens with two short paragraphs absent in the original. The first sets the stage for an exotic tale, reflecting stereotypes of the "Orient": "The Oriental night strings together magical legends and dreams. The sweet tones of the enchanting *vitra* [a musical instrument] combine with the heartbreaking wail of the jackals [*yilelat ha-tanim*] and arouse melancholy [*nugot*] thoughts" (Brokhes 1974, 66). This rather conventional description alludes to the refrain of the popular Hebrew song "Yafim ha-Leilot bi-Khna'an" (Lovely are the nights in Canaan), written by the Hebrew Yiddish poet Yitzchak Katznelson in 1906 and set to a folk melody: "the melancholy wail of the jackals [*yilelat tanim nuga*] cuts through the night's silence." The song became part of the Yishuv's cultural baggage and still resonates in Israeli culture. Evoking this association in the reader instantly locates the protagonist within the mythic realm of the founding fathers.[35]

The second paragraph introduces the narrator as he expresses his "melancholy thoughts" in high-flown *melitsah*-like Hebrew, already outdated in 1911 and jarringly anachronistic by 1974, which thus serves as another temporal marker: "And I see: as if before my eyes, there, far, far away, borne on the wind like a pure white cloud on high sits my heart's beloved. . . . Where, where are you, my soul's desire? Are you, too, wandering through the wide world laden with sorrow and anguish?" (Brokhes 1974, 66). Focusing the narrator's emotional distress on a feminine object at the outset minimizes the effect of the third paragraph (the first one in the original Yiddish version), in which the narrator articulates his sense of being trapped in an iron net and connects this sense with the feeling of being "an eternal wanderer, forlorn and distant from his home and his homeland" (66). The first two paragraphs point the Hebrew reader toward Zarifa, Abu-Abbas's niece, who is the eventual romantic focus of the story. In the Yiddish original, however, Zarifa is merely a tantalizing presence who stays in the shadows and emerges only once, for the domestic purpose of making and serving coffee. In the original, although the erotic tension between the narrator and Zarifa becomes an increasingly important strand of the plot, it remains an accompaniment to the major theme of Abu-Abbas's tale of destruction and exile that begins reverberating in the opening paragraph and occupies a cen-

35. See my discussion of another echo of this song in chapter 4.

tral position throughout the story. In the Hebrew version, however, the erotic dynamic is foregrounded.

In the Yiddish version, the tension between background and fore-grounded eroticism is not resolved. Although at the end of the story Zarifa seems to be beckoning the narrator to follow her into the shade of the tree, she dives into the river and disappears from his sight. The original story concludes with the following passage, reestablishing the sense of isolation that pervades the entire "Wanderings" cycle: "From afar, from the other side of the Jordan, the calls of Arabs to their camels could be heard in the night; a caravan was crossing the Jordan. I looked at the Jordan, where Zarifa had jumped in, but I could see only golden circles, scurrying, spreading over the flat, moonlit surface" (Brokhes 1937, 210). This ending repositions the narrator in ambiguous sensual terrain, echoing his displaced physical location on the banks of the Jordan.

The ending of the Hebrew version is more conventional for a plot that has foregrounded the erotic element and celebrated the physicality of the New Jew. After a paragraph that describes Zarifa's sexual attributes in florid language that incorporates *melitsah*-like turns of phrase ("her form straight and erect like a cedar . . . breast rounded like a pomegranate, full of blood and fire . . . her scarlet-red lips" [Brokhes 1974, 69]), the narrator continues: "Under the low branches of the sycamore my gaze encountered Zarifa, who sat, half-naked, on the ground. As if turned to stone, I stayed where I was. When she saw me, a slight scream escaped her throat. I looked around me and leapt towards her with a stifled shout . . ." (Brokhes 1974, 69, ellipsis in the original). The story ends with this suggestive ellipsis. Although both versions employ the stereotype of the sensual Arab woman, the Hebrew version's emphasis on the erotic deprives the tale of its nationalist dimension. The Hebrew "Under the Sycamore" becomes another hackneyed story of seduction by an Oriental exotic, with an ending implying that the "Hebrew" narrator succeeds in his erotic pursuit, unlike the "Yiddish" narrator.

It is significant that this version was chosen for inclusion in the 1974 Hebrew volume designed to reintroduce Israel's reading public to Brokhes's Palestinian fiction. By turning "Under the Sycamore" into a romanticized tale of sexual attraction rather than retaining the vision of social, cultural, and spatial estrangement presented in the Yiddish version, the Hebrew version mutes the narrator's pervasive skepticism toward the Zionist project. The change in thematic emphasis legitimizes Brokhes through refamiliarizing the thematics of his work: ideological heresy becomes transmuted into romantic convention. An opposite process seems to have been at work regarding "ha-Charishit" (The quiet one [Brokhes 1974, 126–32]), the Hebrew version of the 1910 "The Barefoot Ones." Interestingly, the story's rather sketchy but overt erotic content had already been minimized in the 1937 Yiddish "Di Shtile" (The quiet one [Brokhes 1937, 238–45]) by omission of the crucial moment when Yofe strokes Chasye's hair, thus rendering disproportionate Chasye's burst of physical affection toward her sister. It is perhaps not surprising that this "expurgated" version was the one chosen for translation and inclusion in the 1974 Hebrew volume.

Brokhes's detachment from Zionism is ultimately reconciled with the audience's expectations of a Second Aliyah writer in "Nifgeshu" (They met), included in the Hebrew *The Jordan Roars* (Brokhes 1974, 133–39). This Hebrew story, absent from Brokhes's Yiddish collections,[36] seems to present the writer's own irreconcilable personal dilemma in a revealing, if rather simplistic, fashion. As in the other first-person stories, the narrator is an uncommitted observer, who—significantly—remains nameless. The story begins in an impersonal, detached vein: "When one comes to a *moshava* and wants to stay there for a while, one is forced [*be'al korcho*] to shoulder work tools and go out to the field" (133). This narrator is not impelled by any desire to settle. He will work in exchange for bed and board and joins a group of workers who are preparing the soil for a new orange orchard. The bucolic scene is described as though it were an artificial museum exhibit: "Far, far away beyond the orange orchards very long green strips were visible. Around and above us birds were singing and displaying, and down there in the valley the village herds roamed" (133). As the laborers take a break in the midday heat, an apparition comes into view: "Suddenly there floated in front of us, like a weed [*tzemach ha-sadeh*], a scrawny Jew, his tall frame bent down to the earth, wearing a short orange jacket with the ritual fringes peeking from underneath, black trousers and an old hat. His scrawny face was surrounded by a clipped, round, black beard. His front teeth were missing, and his eyes darted strangely. He came up to one tall, healthy laborer, who came from a distant corner of Lithuania, and asked: 'Aren't you Brukhman? My name is Brukhman too . . . ' " (133, ellipsis in the original). This vision of a stereotypical diasporic Jew is in immediate dramatic juxtaposition with the mod-

---

36. I have not been able to locate any Yiddish version of this story; however, it is very unlikely that Brokhes wrote it in Hebrew. See fn. 6 in this chapter.

ern Palestinian pastoral scene that precedes it. The biblical collocation *tzemach ha-sadeh*, literally "field plant," indicates wild vegetation, in opposition to the Zionist vision of cultivated land. While the laborers are working on the future orange grove, an emblem of early-twentieth-century Zionist agriculture in Palestine, the diasporic Jew materializes like an unwanted, malignant "weed." Appearing as if out of a mirage or a nightmare, he is dissociated from the Zionist project. The clothing and demeanor of this "scrawny Jew" are in conventional opposition to the "tall, healthy" laborers. His posture is bent (implying sickness); against the pioneers' picks and shovels, symbols of a new, "productive" way of life, his attributes are the ritual undergarment, dark trousers, and hat of an Orthodox Jew. The laborers immediately label the newcomer insane: "We knew at once that this was a crazy person" (134).

However, we are soon given a hint that this dichotomy between Diaspora and homeland is not as clear-cut as it seems. The brief diasporic apparition has a profoundly unsettling effect on the laborers: "The sudden appearance of the madman had a harsh, depressing effect on us, we were assaulted by an indistinct feeling, and felt ourselves as weak [*refey-onim*] as children. How strong the contradiction and disharmony between the bent body of the madman and the fields of passion [*sedot ha-ta'avah*] around us, swept by light and warmth that constantly whispered tales of life and love" (134). The "madman," immediately characterized as a Jew (as opposed to a "Hebrew") and therefore non-Zionist, is a manifestation of the repressed diasporic culture that the pioneers believed they had renounced—an unwelcome "return of the repressed." His startling appearance in the midst of the "fields of passion" [37] seems to hint that the Diaspora is ubiquitous and to threaten the vision of the new; the laborers suddenly feel powerless in spite of their work tools. The biblical *onim* signifies robustness and virility; the choice of the Hebrew phrase *refey-onim* to denote the sense of weakness that overcomes the laborers in the "fields of passion," with their promise of fulfillment, is ominous indeed. This is a confrontation with the unacknowledged simultaneous coexistence in Palestine of the two contradictory and mutually threatening cultures, that of the Diaspora and that of the Yishuv.

The two are organically linked, as the very first conversational exchange

---

37. The biblical *ta'avah* in the story of the yearning of the Israelites in the desert for the food of Egypt (Num. 11:4) is translated as "craving"; in modern Hebrew, the word has come to signify any strong desire, especially sexual.

establishes. The diasporic visitor, introducing himself as Brukhman, immediately approaches his namesake, "Palestinian" Brukhman. After the visitor disappears, the Palestinian Brukhman is clearly deeply affected: "He sat unmoving and gazed glassy-eyed in that direction [after the visitor]. His face was pale and his lips moved silently" (134). "Palestinian" Brukhman soon reveals that he once had a brother but does not know his current whereabouts: " 'Yes, I have no relative here . . . Where do I have a relative? I am alone and solitary in the world . . . I had a brother—and where is he?' Brukhman added with a sigh" (135, ellipses in the original). We learn that his brother followed the paradigmatic route of the *talush:* he had aspired to be a university student in Europe but failed the entrance examinations four times and finally vanished in despair "to seek his own road." Since then, "Palestinian" Brukhman has carried around his brother's farewell letter, signed "Zalmen Brukhman" (136). The stranger reappears the next day; although "Palestinian" Brukhman continues to deny the man's identity, he shares his bread with him. "That is Brukhman's brother," comments one of the laborers. "There is no resemblance between them," says another (137).

The final confrontation between the two Brukhmans encapsulates the repression of the narrator's underlying duality. "Diasporic" Brukhman addresses "Palestinian" Brukhman, seeming to offer a partnership: " 'Work! Dig! Dig fast! And why aren't you digging?' he turned to Brukhman, who was standing all that time and looking at his face. 'I'm Brukhman and you're Brukhman too, we'll split it [the work] between us . . . ' 'Brukhman hasn't come yet,' said the other. 'Yes, you are Brukhman,' the madman went on shouting, 'do you want to deny your name?' " (138, ellipsis in the original). In a remarkable expression of disavowal, "Palestinian" Brukhman first renounces his ideological goal as he stands idle in this culture where manual labor is elevated, and then he attempts to efface his own presence from the scene. However, the stranger does not allow him the luxury of dissociation. When he produces a scrap of paper bearing the name "Zalmen Brukhman," "Palestinian" Brukhman is finally forced to admit that the physically repulsive, mentally unbalanced vagrant is indeed his brother: his mirror-image Other. Yet in a telling reversal, when he tries to embrace his long-lost brother a second time, the latter flees. It may be too late for a reconciliation between the two aspects of this Janus-faced figure that serves as a polysemic metaphor for a key conflict of modern Judaism.

This short story seems to express its author's complex ideological position and, possibly, his personal problematics as well. Given Second Aliyah writers' propensity for pen names, "Brukhman" may embody two aspects of Brokhes the writer. This reading is bolstered if we recall that Zalmen, "Diasporic" Brukhman's first name, is also the author's first name. The similarity of "Brukhman" to "Brokhes" is revealing. Indeed, the two words are semantically linked through their common root, the Hebrew letters *b'r'k'* (bless). The connection between "Brukhman" and "Brokhes" is visually obvious in the original orthography: in both Hebrew and Yiddish, the same letter, a soft *kaf,* produces the sound that is transliterated in Yiddish as *kh.* In such a construal, "Palestinian" Brukhman is posited as the realizer of the Zionist ideal, haunted by the dark shadow of "Diasporic" Brukhman: Brokhes himself, who spent ten formative years in a Zionist environment, eventually returned to the Diaspora, in which he lived for most of his long life.

It is significant that this story was chosen for inclusion in the 1974 Hebrew volume, which contains work encompassing more genres (a play and a novella in addition to short fiction) and a wider thematic range than the Hebrew collection published twenty years earlier. As we have seen, Brokhes's work underwent significant and substantive changes in the process of translation. This may have been the case here; the final scene of "They Met," in which "Palestinian" Brukhman acknowledges and embraces his brother, seems to reconcile the ideological tensions evident in Brokhes's other work. In this manner, Brokhes—the self-described stranger and paradigmatic wanderer—was co-opted into an early Palestinian canon that was in need of writers. Although the story has thematic undertones that are disturbing in a culture that upholds uniform ideology, these undertones are defused to the point of legitimation within the mainstream's parameters: first, by being presented in Hebrew and then by providing a positive plot resolution. It is, of course, possible that, for one reason or another, Brokhes himself collaborated in this defusion.

Perhaps the ultimate reinscription of Brokhes into Zionist culture is his inclusion in David Tidhar's popular and massive (nineteen volumes) *Entsiklopediyah le-Chalutzey ha-Yishuv u-Vonav* (Encyclopedia of the pioneers and builders of the Yishuv) and by the wording of this entry (1966, 3866). Almost an entire page is devoted to "Z. Brakhot." Tidhar uses the Hebrew pronunciation of his name, taking the trouble to note the Yiddish pronunciation phonetically: *"brakhes."* The entry makes much of Brokhes's "romantic" occupations in Palestine during his relatively few years there, emphasizing his adventures and travels. The fact that "Brakhot" wrote in Yiddish is elided, if not totally misrepresented. Tidhar goes so far as to state that his "Palestinian hunting stories are unique in Hebrew literature for their content and style" (3866). Although he does note Brokhes's ideological independence and reluctance to settle in the country, his phrasing of the entry completely incorporates Brokhes into the Yishuv's Hebrew culture and effaces his Yiddish aspects. It is only through a close examination of Brokhes's texts that his unique contribution to a more inclusive account of early Zionist culture in Palestine can be better understood and appreciated.

CHAPTER THREE

The Problematics of "Language Wanderings"

We may not use any language except Hebrew in our cultural work.

—David Ben-Gurion, 1910

Although the Yishuv prided itself on creating a new culture in the Land of Israel that would be totally liberated from any links with the Diaspora, the Hebrew-Yiddish ideological dichotomy was carried over from the heated arguments over nationalism and language that divided the European Jewish community at the turn of the century. The language issue reproduced itself within the Zionist community when it was appropriated to serve internal political purposes of Labor Zionism. Especially interesting is the course of the debate over Yiddish within Po'alei Zion, one of the two major factions (with ha-Po'el ha-Tza'ir) that vied for primacy in Labor Zionism between 1906 and 1919. Other ongoing complexities of the internal dilemma were exposed as late as 1927 in the course of two clashes over Yiddish: the "Yiddish Affair," which embroiled Hebrew writers, and the proposal of a chair of Yiddish studies at the Hebrew University. The ambivalence concerning local linguistic practice, now a major characteristic of Yishuv culture, was finally brought to a head with the appearance of Yiddish magazines beginning in 1928. This chapter presents and considers these processes and events as localized manifestations of the same quandary.

The Politics of Yiddish in the Labor Movement, 1907–1914

Po'alei Zion, founded as a socialist Jewish movement in Russia around 1901, was affiliated with other Russian socialist movements and did not initially consider Palestine to be the exclusive solution to the "Jewish problem."

Although the Palestine branch of the party, created in 1906, affirmed its goal as the establishment of political independence for the Jewish nation in Palestine, it continued to maintain strong ties with the bulk of its membership, which was located in Europe and whose culture was Yiddish (Garnczarska-Kadari 1995, 258–98; Gorni 1971). Ber Borokhov (1881–1917), who formulated the ideology of Po'alei Zion, fused Marxism and Zionism when he considered the basis of the Jewish problem to be economic. With a rather unique dualistic ideology, Po'alei Zion originally had a firm commitment to a universalist democratic socialism at the same time that it incorporated Zionism as a solution to the Jewish problem. Although it agreed that Hebrew should be the future language of the Palestinian Jewish community, its traditional socialist concern with the Yiddish-speaking Jewish urban proletariat led it to legitimize the widespread use of Yiddish in the Yishuv, where an urban proletariat was beginning to develop.

The other major Labor faction, ha-Po'el ha-Tza'ir (the Young Worker), was founded as a Jewish socialist party in Palestine in 1905 and had no previous connections with an umbrella organization abroad. Its chief ideologue, Aaron David Gordon (1856–1922), developed a unique type of semisecular nationalism based on agricultural settlement in the homeland. Although Gordon was influenced by socialism, he disapproved of Marxism—and of its Jewish offshoot, the Bund—as a viable alternative to religion. In fact, he viewed socialism as a real danger to the Zionist enterprise in Palestine: although the Gordon-inspired movement adopted and practiced the principle of collective settlement that developed into the kibbutz (commune) and moshav (cooperative agricultural settlement), it was a vehicle for Zionism rather than for socialism. Lacking a European Jewish socialist tradition, ha-Po'el ha-Tza'ir was a major campaigner against Yiddish because it espoused the Zionist aim of "a spiritual revival based on Hebrew as an everyday language as well as the language of cultural creativity" (Ettinger 1969, 207).[1]

These different concepts of the future Yishuv, loosely defined as socialist versus nationalist, caused serious conflict on many levels. Because the easily identifiable marker of language use was construed in this context as an indication of political affiliation, the Hebrew-Yiddish language issue became a

---

1. For a mainstream overview of the Labor politics of the Yishuv in this period, see E. Rubinstein 1979, esp. 242–56. For a different perspective on the unique combination of nationalism and socialism in the early years of the Yishuv, see Sternhell 1998.

tool in the rivalry between the two major parties (Pilowsky 1980, 3).[2] Po'alei Zion was first subordinated to ha-Po'el ha-Tza'ir and later liquidated as an autonomous body when the Achdut ha-Avodah (Labor Unity) Party was founded in 1919. The lingering grievances of the nonsocialist factions toward the socialist components were now transferred to the Po'alei Zion splinter group Left Po'alei Zion, which had not joined Achdut ha-Avodah and whose members formed a distinctive bloc with a Marxist orientation. Left Po'alei Zion, with its strong links to European Jewish socialism, continued to use Yiddish in some of its publications in both Palestine and the Diaspora, and it supported the use of Yiddish as one of the Jewish languages of the Yishuv.[3] Its members were therefore singled out as traitors to Zionism, an accusation that reverberated for decades to come.

The cultural problematics of the Yishuv in the 1920s and 1930s should be analyzed against this background of persistent, considerable, and significant ambivalence about the role of language in the nascent community. The evocative title of Rachel Katznelson's 1918 essay "Nedudey Lashon" (Language wanderings) provides an apt metaphor for the Yishuv's continuing cultural duality as manifested in language. Many Zionist pioneers, although unified in their sense of mission, seemed to be adrift in a linguistic and emotional limbo, unable to commit themselves exclusively to either of their two languages.

The fact that most Second Aliyah immigrants were more at home in Yiddish than in Hebrew was usually obscured in public discussion. However, within Po'alei Zion the role of Yiddish was the subject of much internal debate. There are considerable differences between the language of contemporaneous arguments and that of later accounts, which often present the events in an apologetic tone. For example, the major leader Yitzchak Ben-Zvi (1884–1963, later the second president of Israel) seems to sound a mea culpa when he states in his 1966 memoir: "In those days [the first decade of the century] most of us were influenced by the prevailing spirit of the Jewish communities abroad. We had not yet rooted ourselves deeply in the soil of the homeland" (90). Ben-Zvi here employs the traditional biological

---

2. Whereas Pilowsky (1980) presents a detailed history of the role of language choice in internal Labor politics, here I closely examine the language used in some political debates in order to explore the implicit messages underlying the exchanges.

3. The faction joined other left-wing parties in 1948 to create Mapam, the United Workers' Party.

metaphorics of Zionist programmatic literature, reflecting an ideology that considered diasporic Jews "rootless," with a culture that was weak and doomed. Only the construction of a new, nondiasporic Jewish culture, "re-rooted" in the ancestral homeland, could heal the nation and ensure its future.[4] Sixty years after the events, Ben-Zvi seems to ask the reader's forgiveness for a communal show of weakness when he speaks in the plural.

Reflecting the pragmatic approach of Po'alei Zion, which recognized and accommodated the practice of Yiddish, the party's 1907 platform (the "Ramleh platform") was written in Yiddish.[5] Moreover, in that year Po'alei Zion decided to publish its first Palestinian periodical, *Der Onfang* (The beginning), in Yiddish. It seems clear that both local and general political considerations influenced the party's decision to publish its first party organ in Yiddish. At play were the language needs of the potential reading public in Palestine as well as the wish to avoid conflict with the large numbers of Yiddish-speaking party members in Europe and to gain their support as the largest potential reservoir of pioneers. In his memoirs, Ben-Zvi notes that "the decision to publish a Hebrew newspaper might have led to a split" with the party members abroad (1966, 175). *Der Onfang* began to appear a few months before its rival Hebrew organ *ha-Po'el ha-Tza'ir*. Only two complete issues of *Der Onfang* were published, in July and August 1907; a third, partial issue was published in September of that year. Although both issues were devoted mostly to ideological essays, they also included reports of the pioneers' experiences. By the second issue, *Der Onfang* was trying to reach a wider public both in Palestine and abroad; it included a Hebrew article entitled "me-Chayey ha-Aretz" (Aspects of life in the land) as well as a page in Russian with information on party activities in Poland and Russia. The next party convention (September 1907), however, resolved to publish a Hebrew periodical; it is not clear to what extent this decision was made because of the political conflict with ha-Po'el ha-Tza'ir.

4. One of the Yiddish writers in the Yishuv uses this pervasive imagery as the foundation for an ironic twist on the ideology itself: Avrom Rivess's story "Der Bal-tshuve" (The penitent) of 1932 (Rivess 1947a), discussed in chapter 4.

5. The party convention that produced this platform was held in an old inn in the Arab town of Ramleh. The reason for this unusual choice is not given. In his 1966 memoirs, Ben-Zvi reports that the party chose this markedly non-Jewish, non-Zionist location because they wished "not to be disturbed by curious members" (87).

In his memoirs, Ben-Zvi uses a different rationale, explaining that *Der Onfang* failed because "the Hebrew worker in Eretz-Israel needed a newspaper not in Yiddish but in Hebrew, a newspaper that would unify and link the new immigrants with the natives [*bney ha-makom*] and would respond to the problems faced by the Hebrew worker and laborer in the country" (1966, 90). In this phrasing, the "Hebrew worker" is distinguished not only from the diasporic and Old Yishuv "Jew," but also from the "natives"—the non-Ashkenazi Jews who had been in Palestine for generations and who were thought to be able to communicate with the Zionist pioneers only in Hebrew.[6] Supporters of Hebrew consistently presented the issue of communication as a major reason for establishing it as the language of the community.

Although Po'alei Zion resolved to publish a Hebrew weekly in 1907, *ha-Achdut* (Unity) did not appear until the fall of 1910. It is symptomatic of Yishuv culture at the time that Ya'akov Zerubavel, a member of its first editorial board, was also a strong proponent of Yiddish. In the Yiddish memoirs he published forty-five years later, Zerubavel reports that two speakers at the party's 1910 spring convention favored publication of *ha-Achdut* (as a weekly) in Yiddish because they believed that the paper "was meant mainly for the *members abroad*" (Zerubavel 1956, 66, emphasis in the original). Po'alei Zion expressed its own language ambivalence when, on the one hand, convention delegates denied that Yiddish was widely spoken by Zionists in Palestine (the Yiddish version was ostensibly meant for a readership abroad), while, on the other hand, the official use of Yiddish in Po'alei Zion's local publications was still a major issue and subject of debate at the 1910 fall convention (a debate reported in *ha-Achdut* 2, nos. 2–3 [1910]).

One of the main topics at this convention was the role of the party's planned publishing house, also named ha-Achdut. Zerubavel's address,

6. Of course, Ben-Zvi was discounting and ignoring here the non-Jewish natives, although a year later (1911) he proposed an intriguing alternative involving the Jewish and non-Jewish "masses" in Palestine who were acknowledged as using Arabic: that *ha-Achdut* should also publish an Arabic newspaper. The first installment of his two-part article (*ha-Achdut* 3, no. 4 [1911]: cols. 1–5) called for the expression and protection of the interests of the Arabic-speaking Jews in the Ottoman Empire. In the second part of the article (no. 5: cols. 5–7), he broadened the aim of a projected Arabic newspaper; it would serve the non-Jewish Arab population as well, with an editorial board that would consist of both Jews and Arabs. This unusual proposal, which apparently was never discussed further, indicates considerable sensitivity on the part of this major leader.

"Our Cultural Activity," and the ensuing discussion are particularly interesting.[7] Zerubavel was acutely conscious of the elitist nature of Hebrew and, unlike other party members, expressed his concerns freely. Echoing the traditional position of European Jewish socialist movements, he defined Hebrew as the language of the intellectuals, not suitable for the party's objective of reaching the Jewish "masses" abroad. Zerubavel injected conventional socialist terminology when he distinguished between "intellectuals" and "masses," but his particular choice of words merits close examination: "Our publishing house . . . must publish pamphlets that will explain current affairs, the arts, politics, etc. This will be popular material for propaganda. On the other hand, the publishing house must aspire to create [*livro*] in Hebrew a scientific socialist literature" (1910, col. 12). Zerubavel used *chomer* (literally, "clay"), the most malleable of materials, to refer to the "popular material for propaganda." He did not specify the language of this popular material; it would be Yiddish, the natural language that does not need to be named—and, in the prevailing political climate, was better off not named. Hebrew, in contrast, is the language of Creation, suitable for "literature." Speaking of literature, construed as a higher register of culture than propaganda, he used the infinitive of the verb "to create" *(livro)* that appears in Gen. 1:1 *(bara,* "created"). His choice of language in this passage seems to be influenced by the biblical resonances of the verb that is exclusively reserved in the Bible for divine creation. Like other contemporaneous Zionists, Zerubavel was keenly aware that the Zionist project was unique and considered it to be a re-creation of the Jewish nation (a pervasive feeling that is echoed in the name *Der Onfang,* "the beginning," for the first Palestinian Zionist Yiddish journal). Yet, by implication, only Hebrew-reading intellectuals were then capable of appreciating "scientific socialist literature."

Zerubavel referred to Yiddish explicitly only when he went on to speak of the need to be understood by the majority of Palestinian Jews. Conforming to normative practice, he adopted the Hebrew term *yehudit,* a circumlocution that was considered more appropriate than "Yiddish," the name that its speakers used: "Not only the newcomers, but a large part of those who were born here understand and speak only Yiddish [*yehudit*]. I believe that a large part of them will in future also conduct their lives in *yehudit,* and we must take that into account. Just as we use *yehudit* in our meetings, so that

7. The Yiddish version of Zerubavel's address and the debate that followed it is entitled "Kultur un Shprakh" (Culture and language [1956, 62–76]).

all our members may understand us, so must we do in literature as well" (1910, col. 13, emphasis in the original). Use of *yehudit* to avoid saying the actual word *Yiddish* was consistent with Zionist ideology.[8] Interestingly, although Zerubavel was a member of the editorial board of *ha-Achdut* (which consisted entirely of European Zionists), the board saw fit to append a footnote to his use of the term *yehudit*: "The writer uses *yehudit* for the language spoken by our Ashkenazi brothers" (col. 13). The editors added a second footnote immediately below the first: "This opinion is totally the responsibility of the writer," reaffirming the party's official line that the use of Yiddish in the Yishuv was a temporary measure. Zerubavel, however, seems to have envisioned the future Jewish community in Palestine as bilingual in Hebrew and Yiddish (ignoring the non-Ashkenazi Jews). This future would have been a continuation of the 1910 cultural and linguistic status quo.

On closer examination, an unintentional, ironic implication of Zerubavel's language choice emerges. As noted, in the biblical meeting between the Assyrian army commander and King Hezekiah's court officials (2 Kgs. 18:19–35), the common people's language is named as *yehudit*. In fact, throughout the Jewish Bible, *ivri* (Hebrew) is never used to designate the people's language but only—and rarely at that—as a term of what we might call national affiliation. The language begins to be referred to as *ivrit* only when it ceases to be spoken—in postdestruction, rabbinical texts such as the Mishna (third century C.E.); ironically, at this point the earlier elite language, Aramaic, becomes the vernacular. Yiddish speakers usually termed Hebrew *loshn-koydesh* (the holy tongue) and seldom used *ivrit*. Seen in this biblical and traditional context, the discussion at the Po'alei Zion convention placed modern Hebrew on a par with the elitist, foreign language of the Bible but equated Yiddish with the language of the commoners in the biblical episode. Hebrew became the language of an elite minority at a time when Zionism sought to re-create the people. For all practical purposes, Yiddish, the emblem of orality, was equivalent to the biblical *yehudit* that the people spoke.

Although Zerubavel retained warm feelings for Yiddish, in his 1956 Yiddish memoirs he writes apologetically about his early days on the editorial board of *ha-Achdut*: "Actually, I was still very weak in Hebrew. . . . I still

8. The suffix *-ish* in *Yiddish* is derived from German; the *-it* in *yehudit* is a Hebrew suffix. As late as 1966, Ben-Zvi used *idit* as a more "Hebraic" form of the name of the language (1966, 90).

had to write my articles in Yiddish. Yiddish for me was more natural [than Hebrew] because in *this* language I thought, felt, lived" (8–10, emphasis in the original).[9] He associates Hebrew with his childhood studies of religious texts in the all-male cheder (religious school) or "at my father's knee" (10). The traditional binary characterization of Yiddish as the language of emotion and daily experience and of Hebrew as the patrilineal language of the intellect was thus still valid for him in Israel forty-five years after his early years in *ha-Achdut*. The duality of the language significations obviously continued to hold for those who had not completely repudiated their Yiddish world.[10]

The elitism attached to Hebrew strikes an especially dissonant note in the ideology of a party that espoused ideas of egalitarian socialism. Zerubavel was not the only one to point out this problem. The very first speaker in the 1910 Po'alei Zion debate, Yosef Nachmani, acknowledged this elitism when he suggested that *ha-Achdut* would better achieve its goal if it were published in "the language commonly used by the vast masses"—that is, Yiddish (Nachmani 1910, col. 27). Yitzchak Ben-Zvi observed that "in general in the Land of Israel there is only a small number of developed people who do not understand Hebrew" (1910, col. 28), and therefore the ideological material of the party could continue to be printed in Hebrew. Like the other participants, he distinguished the "developed" intellectual elite from the "masses" by its members' familiarity with Hebrew. The bilingual He-

9. Zerubavel continued to write his articles for *ha-Achdut* in Yiddish for some years; they were translated into Hebrew by other members of the editorial board such as Ben-Zvi and Brenner.

10. But even Zerubavel tailored his writing, half a century later, to his audience. It is instructive to compare the Hebrew original of the Po'alei Zion debate, published in the official party organ *ha-Achdut* in 1910, with Zerubavel's Yiddish version of the discussion in his 1956 memoirs. A small but telling part of the *ha-Achdut* report, discussed later, deals with Ladino, the Judeo-Spanish language of the Sephardic community that had a true status of "other" within Palestinian Jewish society. Zerubavel's 1956 "Culture and Language" ignores those parts of the debate, an omission that reflects the cultural marginalization of Israel's Sephardic community at the time. This marginalization was never officially acknowledged. The choice of a Sephardi Hebrew pronunciation as the ideal for the "new language" seems ironic in light of Ashkenazis' consistent disdain toward Sephardis in the country (Even-Zohar 1981, 172; and see Elboim-Dror 1990, 370–72, for some of the reasoning underlying the choice of Sephardi pronunciation). Yet delegitimation of a rival culture is hardly confined to the mainstream. Ammiel Alcalay's 1993 work is concerned exclusively with Levantine Jewish cultures but does not admit the marginalization of one of these cultures—that of the non-Zionist Ashkenazi Old Yishuv during the Zionist period.

brew-Yiddish writer Aharon Re'uveni, Ben-Zvi's brother,[11] echoed this sentiment when he said that the Hebrew *ha-Achdut* could "influence only the more intelligent workers" (1910, col. 29). The recurring "developed/undeveloped" opposition functions as a synonym for Zionist (metonymized by Hebrew) and non-Zionist (metonymized by Yiddish) cultures, respectively. Language is clearly an indicator of ideological and cultural status. Rachel,[12] however, complicated the position of Hebrew as a social marker when she characterized the readers of *ha-Achdut* as follows: "Concerning the elements for whom our newspaper is designed—we must distinguish between the old-timers and the newcomers. There are many undeveloped readers among the newcomers, and, on the contrary, there are developed readers among the old-timers" (Rachel 1910, col. 28). In other words, many of the Zionist pioneers ("newcomers") could not read Hebrew, whereas some members of the non-Zionist Old Yishuv and the First Aliyah ("old-timers") could read it. This was a rare admission that the practical situation was far from ideal or that knowledge of Hebrew could be strictly associated with a particular generation and ideology.

Ladino entered the discussion in the comments of Yablonkin (identified only by his last name), who voiced the thought, highly unusual for the time and the cultural context, that "literature [*sifrut yafa,* literally "belles-lettres"] in the Land of Israel may eventually be created by the Sephardis. . . . The Land of Israel will never have [a human] element that will be satisfied with Hebrew alone" (1910, col. 27). He was echoed by Re'uveni, who maintained that "the publishing house must publish the most popular, elementary literature in the spoken languages Ashkenazic [Yiddish] and Sephardic [Ladino]. Such pamphlets in Hebrew are currently not necessary" (1910, col. 29). Next, Nachmani added that "as long as we do not teach ourselves Ladino we will not be able to influence the Sephardi workers" (1910, col. 29). Thus, three delegates to the 1910 convention legitimized language pluralism in the future Zionist utopia. Even David Ben-Gurion, who was a radical proponent of Hebrew as a unifying principle, conceded that "in speech and propaganda [as opposed to 'culture'] we must use many languages" (1910, col. 30).[13] At the close of the debate, Zerubavel cobbled together a

11. Members of the Yishuv's political and intellectual elite were often related.

12. Rachel Yana'it, Ben-Zvi's wife.

13. Ben-Gurion's deep-lying conviction about the need for a monolithic society was fully realized when he became Israel's first prime minister and furthered the idea of statism as the

practical compromise when he suggested that Hebrew be used as the language of representation abroad because "undoubtedly and in everyone's opinion, it is our national language. The issue of Yiddish or Ladino is our internal business" (1910, col. 30).

Indeed, the "internal business" of language continued to be problematic. The persistent ambivalence toward Yiddish in the Yishuv was a source of political ammunition. The physical clash during the "Zhitlovsky incident" in 1914, in which the Yiddishist Chaim Zhitlovsky was forcibly prevented from lecturing in Tel-Aviv, served ha-Po'el ha-Tza'ir in its ongoing political struggle against Po'alei Zion (Pilowsky 1980, 5). In the discussion that subsequently developed in *ha-Achdut* over several years, Zerubavel agreed that "the ideal is to have Hebrew the language of the nation that resides in the land [*ha-am ha-yoshev ba-aretz*]" (1914, col. 9). Yet he distinguished this ideal goal from the prevailing situation, employing a traditional tool of Jewish discourse—biblical allusion: "We do not need an official language that will not be our internal language at the same time. . . . The truth is that matters are managed in *yehudit* in almost all settlement committees. And that is understandable. Can the Ethiopian change his skin? Can a nation deny its language, in which it has lived for hundreds of years?" (1914, col. 8). Zerubavel here used a complex biblical metaphor that Jeremiah applies to the sins of the people of Judah, who are figured as a wayward wife:[14] just as the Ethiopian is fated to retain his own distinctive skin, the woman who is Judah is condemned to be exposed and exiled by the conqueror as God's punishment for abandoning his ways (Jer. 13:23–27). "Can the Ethiopian change his skin?" is a common trope in Jewish culture for a situation that is considered immutable, yet the characterization of the nation as feminine and black in the context from which Zerubavel took his phrase is intriguing, given the feminine grammatical gendering of Yiddish and the common per-

---

paramount value at the expense of many ethnic traditions and languages of the numerous different Jewish communities that immigrated to Israel in its first years. See Liebman and Don-Yehiya 1983 for a discussion of processes of cultural homogenization in Israel from the inception of the state.

14. Several biblical prophets employ the trope of the sinning nation as an adulterous wife ("How the faithful city has become a harlot [*zonah*]" [Is. 1:21]; "You have a harlot's brow" [Jer. 3:3]; "But you . . . played the harlot" [Ez. 16:15]). The biblical Hebrew *zonah* usually refers to a wife who has been unfaithful.

ception of European Jews as feminine and swarthy. The feminine association is further strengthened by the fact that Judith (Yehudit) was a common name among Jewish women.[15]

Zerubavel emphasized the importance of addressing the language needs of the entire Jewish population. As in 1910, he evoked class differences and wryly contrasted the proletariat of the Neve-Shalom neighborhood of Jaffa with the Hebrew-speaking "intellectual nobility [*atziley ha-ruach*, literally 'nobles of the spirit']" of Tel-Aviv: "Here [in Neve-Shalom] the Jewish masses spend their days. . . . For the most part, this is a productive element, living by its own labor and not being successful, an element whose life is full of anger and sorrow, a life that is miserable both materially and intellectually" (1914, col. 7). Zerubavel exposed the social tensions within the nascent Yishuv when he said, "Even if you find here [in Tel-Aviv] people who work hard and who are familiar with the travails of life, the 'tone' is still set by others, by those who are well off" (1914, col. 6). Clearly, Hebrew within the socialist-Zionist Yishuv continued to be associated with the economic and intellectual elite—a paradox that perpetuated the traditional positions of both languages. This paradox loomed large in the argumentation of proponents of Yiddish in the Yishuv.

The "Yiddish Affair," 1927

By 1927, the Fourth Aliyah was nearing its end. This was the largest wave of immigration so far: an estimated 80,000 Jews immigrated to Palestine in four years, swelling the total population of the Yishuv to 150,000 (Wallach 1974, 50). As noted in chapter 1, the continued preference of Fourth Aliyah immigrants for Yiddish was an easily recognizable attribute of their supposedly contaminated Zionism, and the mainstream narrative had trouble coping with a culture that continued to exist in the face of official denial. These cultural preferences were perceived as a potential danger. This was the background for the furor over the "Yiddish Affair" *(parashat ha-yidish),* an event usually analyzed in the context of the internal politics of contemporaneous Hebrew literature as the beginning of an overt poetic and generational rebel-

---

15. Although, as Seidman (2000) notes, the Judith of the Hebrew Bible was paradoxically one of Esau's wives (Gen. 26:34)—that is, presumably non-Jewish.

lion within Palestinian Hebrew literature (Z. Shavit 1982, 173–85).[16] However, the episode also illuminates the Yishuv's continuing language ambivalence, more than a decade after the Zhitlovsky incident and, significantly,
among its major Hebrew writers in particular.

The "Yiddish Affair" was triggered by the visit of the major American
Yiddish writers Sholem Asch and Perets Hirschbein, who were the guests of
honor at a reception held on 3 May 1927 by the Association of Hebrew Writers in Tel-Aviv. Interestingly, Asch and Hirschbein, both well-established
writers, evidently did not consider the breach between the cultures irrepara-
ble. Both made it clear that they had no interest in establishing Yiddish as a
language of the Yishuv and expressed their sorrow at the rift between the
languages; the Hebrew writers who spoke at the reception also tried to min-
imize the clash. The older generation of Yishuv intellectuals and cultural
leaders was represented by such established writers as poet Ya'akov Fichman
and Berl Katznelson, the chief ideologue of the Palestine Labor movement—
figures who were thoroughly at home in Yiddish (Fichman had published
rather extensively in the Yiddish press of Europe [Oyerbakh et al. 1968, 7:
361–67]). Uri Tsvi Grinberg, who had begun his remarkable literary career
in Yiddish, spoke for a younger generation of modernist, avant-garde writers. The most notable figure by far at the reception was the national icon of
Hebrew literature, the poet Chaim Nachman Bialik, who initially wrote in
both Hebrew and Yiddish.[17] At the reception, it was Bialik who in fact spoke

16. Zohar Shavit remarks: "Shortly after [the 4 May reception] the argument shifted, from
[a discussion] about the position of Yiddish culture in relation to Hebrew culture to a bitter,
probing debate between the literary generations" (1982, 177). She then delineates the course of
this generational clash in detail. In focusing on the personal rather than on the cultural aspects
of the controversy, Shavit adheres to the linear model of Hebrew literary dynamics posited by
mainstream literary historiographers such as Dan Miron (1987). Pilowsky, in contrast, locates
the "Yiddish Affair" in the context of the extreme sensitivity in *Ketuvim* concerning all Yiddish
topics in general and its militant Hebraism in particular, which was not confined to Yishuv culture (1986, 119–23).

17. In 1904, for example, Bialik published his Hebrew poem "Be'ir ha-Harega" (In the city
of slaughter) in impassioned reaction to the Kishinev pogrom of 1903, and in 1906 he published
his self-translation of the poem into Yiddish, "In Shekhite-shtot." These two *poemas* resonated
widely throughout European Jewish culture. His first Yiddish collection, *Fun Tsar un Tsorn*
(Out of sorrow and anger) was published in Odessa in 1906; three more Yiddish collections
were published during his lifetime, in 1913, 1918, and 1922 (Bialik 2001, 19). He also planned
a Yiddish translation of the Bible (Niger and Shatsky 1956, 1: col. 280). See also Shmeruk's remarks on Bialik's complex attitude toward Yiddish (Bialik 2001, 30–31).

out most strongly against the continued function of Yiddish in the Yishuv and supported the exclusive use of Hebrew.[18] However, his description of the traditional relationship between the two languages until modern times as "a marriage made in heaven, like [the biblical] Ruth and Naomi who could not be separated" (1935a, 212) was construed by a group of young Hebrew writers (headed by the gifted young poet Avraham Shlonsky) as a defense of Yiddish.[19] The image of a divinely ordained relationship was immediately taken as legitimizing the use of Yiddish in the Yishuv. Bialik's perceived defense of Yiddish instigated a series of reactions in the Hebrew literary journals, especially in *Ketuvim,* of which Shlonsky was a founder and an editor.

However, rather than expressing a clear-cut ideological dichotomy, the controversy illuminates the complexity of the cultural processes at play in the Yishuv and the ambivalence that impelled the players. This complexity becomes evident upon a close examination of the language used by both sides in the debate (all of whose participants were writers exceptionally sensitive to nuance and resonance) and of particular details of these writers' personal and cultural milieus. Let us first look at some fine points of Bialik's formulations (omitted in the summary account of his address published in *Ketuvim* [11 May 1927]).[20] A careful reading of his full remarks in 1930 reveals that he considered the emerging culture of the Yishuv to be considerably more intricate than did his detractors: "Language is but the mirror of life, the looking-glass in which reality is reflected. Woe betide a nation that considers language the sole basis for everything. . . . I want to correct the mistake made by the young people [who think that] everything is only language" (1935a, 211). Bialik was chiefly concerned with cultural content and

---

18. In his 1930 speech in Kovno, Lithuania, Bialik explicitly located Hebrew in Palestine: "Hebrew is not planning to depict the Diaspora, life in the ghetto. The Hebrew language will be used to describe the free life in Palestine" (1935c, 155).

19. Bialik used a Hebrew phrase that had become embedded in Yiddish, *zivug min ha-shamayim,* for "a marriage made in heaven." The phrase is derived from a midrash that has God sitting in heaven after completing Creation and arranging matches between men and women (Gen. Rabbah 45). Seidman's finely nuanced interpretation of the complex gender issues implicit in this phrase is set against the changing relationship between the languages (1997, 124–31).

20. It is this summary that Zohar Shavit (1982, 176–77), for example, quotes as the basis for her discussions of the incident; its selectivity apparently suits the mainstream construction of Yishuv cultural history.

was aware of the pitfalls that await ideologues who mistake the means for the end and endow those means with moral significance.[21] Language, the instrument of expression, must not supplant the reality it expresses. He did, however, unequivocally ally himself with the Hebraists in Palestine, blaming Yiddishists for the rift: "In the very moment that Yiddish was preparing to cut itself off from Hebrew, it ceased being ours" (1935a, 212). It was Yiddishism, he intimated, that initiated the split.

Yet both Bialik's view of the role of language and his essential support for Hebrew in Palestine were minimized to the point of nonexistence by his main opponent, Avraham Shlonsky, whose brief response was published several days later among five unfavorable reactions to Bialik's address; the front page of that issue of *Ketuvim* bore the revealing headline "be-Chazit ha-Ivrit" (On the Hebrew front). Shlonsky's language drew on some of the most extreme images prevalent in Zionist ideological expression: "We did not accept the match between the languages as a marriage made in heaven. . . . [W]e view this catastrophe of bilingualism as we would view tuberculosis, gnawing away at the lungs of the nation. We want Israeli [*yisre'elit*] breathing to be *entirely Hebrew,* with both lungs! A Land of Israel that is Hebrew, working and popular, loving its creators and its culture—that is the 'Tuberculosis-Fighting Association' " (Shlonsky 1927a, 1, emphasis in the original). Shlonsky was perpetuating the Zionist view of the diasporic condition as a disease. Using the metaphor of tuberculosis, then widely dreaded as a highly contagious and fatal illness, he presented Yiddish as the conduit through which the Diaspora and its negative values ("tuberculosis") would infiltrate and "infect" the new, "healthy" Hebrew society of the Yishuv—a process that had to be prevented at all costs. Significantly, Shlonsky adopted the notion that the desirable culture must be intentionally created and imposed rather than allowed to develop naturally and without intervention.[22] His inclusion of mandatory love for the "creators" of a Hebrew Land of Israel as an integral part of the prescription for healing the nation indicates his misgivings about the actual chances for eventual success of the Zionist-Hebrew cultural renaissance project.

Given a cultural and ideological climate in which the roles of Hebrew

---

21. This balanced approach recalls Brenner's formulation almost twenty years earlier, "The Holy Tongue [*leshon ha-kodesh,* i.e., Hebrew] is not a fetish for us" (1985, 3, 188), discussed in chapter 1.

22. Evoking Jusdanis's terminology: "cultural engineering" (1991, 26).

and Yiddish were fraught with such emotional baggage, it is not surprising to find that Shlonsky himself was quietly ambiguous about his own language and poetic affiliations. For instance, both before and after his immigration to Palestine in 1921, this fervent Hebraist and linguistic innovator (Kena'ani 1989) maintained a strong poetic and personal relationship with his contemporary, the major Yiddish expressionist poet Perets Markish; both lived in Ekaterinoslav in about 1917.[23] The affinity between the two poets in Europe is reported by Lyova Leviteh, who recalls that in 1921, while still in Europe, Shlonsky told him about Markish and would read from the latter's poetry at literary gatherings (Leviteh 1978, 144). The two met again during Markish's 1923 visit to Palestine (Dor 1974, 18), and the following year Shlonsky published his own translation of a poem by Markish in a leading literary magazine of the Yishuv (Markish 1924).

Shlonsky's silence about Markish's significance in his own work is echoed in the fact that both Hebrew and Yiddish literary critics and chroniclers have generally neglected his poetic link with Markish, though it is clear in his early Palestinian poetry. The reasons for this silence seem to be political; apparently, neither Hebraists nor Yiddishists were able to acknowledge an artistic kinship that bridged the ideological differences implied in the language choice. It was the Soviet Hebraist Avraham Krivorochka, writing in a rare Hebrew publication in the USSR, who astutely noted and characterized the close link between the two high modernists: "The close relationship [zikat ha-dam, blood relationship] between [Shlonsky's poetry] and the poetry of Perets Markish is obvious" (1926, 173).[24] He cited persuasive poetic and linguistic examples of this linkage, which include imagery as well as Yiddish calques (quite common in Hebrew, though unacknowledged at the time). It was almost sixty years after Krivorochka's article that the affinity was finally admitted into Israeli literary historiography. In 1981, the critic Avraham ha-Gorni-Green pointed out that Shlonsky's aesthetic credo "can be understood against the background of contemporaneous modernist Yiddish poets such as Perets Markish" (118).

In what may be considered reverse snobbery, Yiddish critics took even longer to remark on the link. Leyzer Podriatshik wrote in a 1986 essay on

---

23. At public appearances in Israel, Shlonsky recounted their meetings (Podriatshik 1991, 174).

24. After the demise of Soviet Hebrew culture in the late 1920s, Krivorochka left the USSR for Palestine, where he hebraized his name to Kariv and became a prominent literary critic.

Markish: "In spite of the different languages, there is a commonality of image and color between Markish's Yiddish books *Stam* [Randomly, 1920] and *Di Kupe* [The pile, 1922], and Shlonsky's Hebrew book *Devai* [Suffering, 1924] and his poem cycle "Stam" [Randomly, which opens *Ba-galgal* (In the wheel), 1927]" (5). The postbiblical word *stam* (random, indefinite) carries the identical meaning in modern Hebrew and in Yiddish. Shlonsky's choice of this particular word to head his poem cycle resonates in both Hebrew and Yiddish and was an evocative title for the Hebrew readers who were at least equally at home in Yiddish. It is symptomatic of his deep cultural ambivalence that Shlonsky's article railing against Yiddish was published in 1927—the very year that saw the publication of *In the Wheel*, with poems that are closely akin to Markish's work earlier in that decade.[25]

Shlonsky continued to use Yiddish in his personal life, though he wrote exclusively in Hebrew.[26] Yet this facet of his cultural world plays no role in the mainstream view of him as the paradigmatic Hebraist, a view that he himself encouraged. Significantly, many years later, in a 1962 conversation with the editor of the New York Yiddish newspaper *Der Morgn-Zhurnal*, presumably conducted in Yiddish, he sounded a conciliatory note and diminished his own pivotal role in the Asch-Hirschbein incident. In Shmuel Izban's description, "Shlonsky, the former stormy petrel[27] became apologetic and in a calm tone undertook not to repeat the long-gone arguments concerning the language conflict. He did not dwell on that painful episode dur-

25. Shlonsky's second book of poetry that year, *le-Aba-Ima* (To Papa-Mama) is even more closely attuned to Yiddish culture; its very title echoes the Yiddish collocation *tate-mame* (father-mother), which emblematizes family. Indeed, as the title implies, the poems in this book are addressed to his family and express considerable nostalgia for their culture (Kronfeld 1997).

26. Izban notes that Shlonsky was a close friend of the Yiddish novelist Yosef Opatoshu, one of whose works he translated into Hebrew. When Opatoshu visited Palestine in 1934, the two met in a Tel-Aviv café, and Shlonsky "cheerfully carried on a conversation in a hearty Yiddish, with the true 'Lubavitch' [the Hasidic sect in which he had grown up] melody and character" (1988, 127).

27. This is a clear reference to Maxim Gorky's 1901 poem "The Stormy Petrel"; the image of the ocean bird soaring and reveling in the storm became an icon of early-twentieth-century political and cultural European revolutionaries. Shlonsky, a masterful translator, included his Hebrew version, "Shir ha-Yas'ur" (The song of the stormy petrel), in an anthology of Russian poetry that appeared in Palestine during the Second World War (Shlonsky and Goldberg 1942, 32–34). Shlonsky also coined the Hebrew name *yas'ur* for this bird (Kena'ani 1989, 102). By alluding to Gorky, Izban is ranking Shlonsky with him.

ing the visit of Asch and Hirschbein in Palestine. 'This belongs to my period of youthful indiscretions,' he said with a smile" (1988, 128).[28]

Perhaps even more indicative of the personal dilemma and of the way in which the same life is constructed differently according to ideological preference are the contradictions inherent in the figure of Eliezer Shteynman (1892–1970). Shteynman had made his reputation in Yiddish, writing in a variety of genres and venues for at least a dozen years. By the time he immigrated to Palestine in late 1923, he had published widely in Yiddish in Poland and Russia and was very well known.[29] Shteynman and Shlonsky founded *Ketuvim* together in 1926 as an expression of poetic independence from the earlier generation of Hebrew literature, emblematized by Bialik (Z. Shavit 1982, 173–86). The two seem to have been perfectly matched in their zeal for Hebraism and Hebrew literature in Palestine, yet personal differences soon caused a rift between them; by 1933, Shlonsky had led the departure from the magazine, and *Ketuvim* was discontinued that same year. Yet in 1927 the young rebels of *Ketuvim* were still a closely knit group that used the perceived danger of Yiddish in its own interests. Shteynman, one of the five participants in the response to Bialik's address published in *Ketuvim*, employed language that is extremely revealing. Although his article is relatively short, it appears in the key last position in the group. Summarizing all five responses, he wrote:

> These articles will serve as a call to our Hebrew troops [*gyasoteynu*], wherever they are, to gird their might [*le-hit'azer oz*] and increase their force and passion [*cheylam u-teshukatam*] for our Hebrew movement [*tenu'atenu ha-ivrit*] and to mount a new and renewed attack on the ranks of our opponents of all types and classes, on fronts both near and far. We shall convey an eternal gift to every faraway Hebrew soul, our language, the one and only, from times immemorial to the last generation of the Hebrew race . . . the one to which we have betrothed ourselves. (Shteynman 1927, 2)

28. Shlonsky's youthful battles had been won by now, and he was facing his own detractors. Izban quotes him further in the same conversation: "I have my own generation of rebels these days, who are revolting against yesterday's guide" (1988, 127).

29. In contrast, Shlonsky, eight years younger than Shteynman, had spent a year in Palestine as a schoolboy in 1913—a period that cemented his literary allegiance to Hebrew—and began his literary career in the Yishuv after his immigration in 1921.

At its core, his piece is a call to action, in language from the biblical semantic domain of war, which is part of the Zionist metaphorical system. In this trope influenced by medieval European romantic stereotypes, a beloved woman, the Hebrew language, is "won" by knights who swear their eternal fealty.[30] This action reclaims the Hebraists' erotic bond with the language. The fact that Shteynman, of all people, applied such language against Yiddish indicates that he was not only repudiating his mother tongue, but also disavowing his earlier career.

Shteynman's difficult switch of cultural allegiance may have underlain his extreme reaction: he was the respondent who was calling most forcefully to expand the reign of Hebrew beyond the scope of the Yishuv. His imagery of power and warfare against Yiddish is all the more striking if one considers that, although a member of the Yishuv, he continued to publish articles and correspondence in the Warsaw Yiddish newspaper *Moment* up to November 1930. Thus, his reaction seems to be emblematic of the ambivalence at his personal and ideological core: Shteynman was waging war on a culture in whose production he was still actively participating.

The biblical terminology of warfare is also heavily invested with erotic overtones. In the Bible, the verb root '.z.r. (to gird), is often combined with *chalatzayim* (loins), linked with masculinity ("Gird up your loins like a man," Job 38:3) and with the production of male heirs in particular, as in *binkha yotze chalatzekha*, "your son who shall be born to you" or, more literally, "your son who emerges from your loins" (I Kgs. 8:19). The other common biblical combination with "to gird" is *chayil*, translated as "strength" ("For thou didst gird me with strength [*va-ta'azreni chayil*] for the battle" [Ps. 18:39]), but also meaning "military might" or, more plainly, "troops" *(ish chayil sholef cherev*, "valiant men who draw the sword" [2 Sam. 24:9]). In Shteynman's call to arms, the troops *(gyasot*, plural of masculine singular *gayis)* are exhorted to increase their passion *(teshukah)* for "our Hebrew movement" *(tenu'atenu ha-ivrit)*, a construct in which the noun and hence the adjective are gendered feminine. In the first part of his call, Shteynman applies the conventional sexual imagery of Zionism, in which the revolutionary pioneers are males. The object of their masculine

---

30. Seidman (2000) points out that the sexual conservatism in this passage makes its military language less forceful than Shlonsky's rejection of all heterosexual imagery; see also Seidman's rich analysis of visual representations of Hebrew and Yiddish as female figures in the early decades of the twentieth century (1997, 28–39).

passion is the feminine "Hebrew movement," yet the unnamed rivals are also champions of Yiddish, that stereotypically feminine entity. Shteynman's complicated language use here seems to indicate the profound problematics of a writer whose intellectual identity had been shaped in Yiddish and who was still intimately engaged with it. His vehemence on this issue is a measure of the tragic personal fracture inherent in the need to choose linguistic sides.

Finally, let us look at the unique situation of Uri Tsvi Grinberg (1896–1981), who represented a group of different provenance and different poetics. At the time, Grinberg was a major young European Yiddish poet who was affiliated with European expressionism and a founder (with Perets Markish and Melekh Ravitsh) of the Polish Yiddish expressionist group Di Khalyastre, beginning in 1919. He later published his own Yiddish literary magazine, *Albatros,* in Warsaw and Berlin (1922–23) before losing hope for a Jewish national and cultural renaissance in Europe and immigrating to Palestine in late 1923, where he became an important figure in Yishuv culture. It is at this point in accounts of Grinberg that ideology's influence on historiography becomes obvious: most Hebrew literary historiographers state that Grinberg abandoned Yiddish writing after his immigration and resumed it only in the 1950s.[31] This, however, was not the case: Chone Shmeruk documents Grinberg's continued production of Yiddish poetry and activity in the Warsaw Yiddish press in the late 1920s and the 1930s, while he was living in Palestine. This account paints a much more complex picture, exposing the tendentiousness of both Hebrew and Yiddish mainstream literary history. Shmeruk quotes from two authoritative biographical sources: " 'Immigrated to Palestine in 1924 . . . in Palestine returned to Hebrew and did not return to Yiddish until the second half of the 1950s.' . . . 'In 1924 he moved to Palestine . . . where he then vigorously participated in militant Hebraism and distanced himself from Yiddish literary work' " (1999, 177). Shmeruk then points out that in the 1920s and 1930s Grinberg published a number of Yiddish poems in Poland and goes on to comment: "[I]t is hard to understand how in some cases Grinberg's work in Yiddish could be totally ignored and in fact ostracized. After all, he is undoubtedly one of the greatest poets of Yiddish literature in recent generations" (178).

Shmeruk ascribes the significant omissions of this aspect of Grinberg's work to cultural and political differences. Hebraists could not acknowledge

---

31. Some scholars of Yiddish literature agree: Wolitz, for example, notes unequivocally that Grinberg "abandoned Yiddish" in Palestine (1981, 18).

the existence of Yiddish creativity in the Yishuv, even when that Yiddish work was published abroad. The Labor Zionist factions that dominated Yishuv politics boycotted Grinberg because of his switch of allegiance from the Labor movement to the right-wing Zionist Revisionists (for whom he became a prominent spokesman) and his admiration for messianic visionaries such as Sabbetai-Zevi and Shlomo Molcho, who were anathema to Labor Zionism.[32] The local Yiddish culture considered Grinberg a traitor to the cause of Yiddish and ignored both his important literary presence and his Yiddish work because of his right-wing politics.[33] Shmuel Huppert delineates Grinberg's ambivalence toward Yiddish in an interesting examination of the attitude toward Europe in his Palestinian poetry. Huppert notes Grinberg's own distinction between "mother tongue" (Yiddish) and "blood tongue" (Hebrew) and his awareness of the tension between the two languages. In this interpretation, Grinberg's choice of terminology highlights the divide between Yiddish, the personal and intimate language, and Hebrew, the national historic language that incorporates collective archetypes (Huppert 1979, 94).[34] Grinberg was able to separate the two effectively, reserving Yiddish for publications in Europe.

It is therefore hardly surprising that Grinberg spoke out strongly against the perception of a Hebrew-Yiddish dichotomy and gave both languages equal standing as creative media: "It is not true that creation in Yiddish is a surrogate. There is creativity in both languages that use the twenty-two letters of Eretz-Israel. . . . All roads lead to Jerusalem" (1927, 6). In view of his continuing link with Yiddish literature, it is perhaps only natural that he was the one who championed Yiddish as a legitimate literary language and attempted, in his own words, to "build a bridge" between Hebrew and Yiddish (quoted in Shmeruk 1999, 181). Grinberg's marginalization by both

32. Zionism viewed itself as a secular "messianic" movement in that its adherents were determined to take their fate into their own hands rather than wait passively for divine intervention. Labor Zionism, in particular, felt that the Jews should redeem themselves by the diligent work of the community and not by spectacular actions by individuals; traditional religious messianism was considered a dangerous temptation to inaction.

33. Shmeruk argues that Grinberg did not publish in the Palestinian Yiddish periodicals because they were supported by the extreme Left Po'alei Zion group (1999, 184).

34. Noting Grinberg's profound ambivalence toward Yiddish, Shmeruk quotes from his 1937 book of poetry *Sefer ha-Kitrug ve-ha-Emunah* (Book of prosecution and faith): "it is my Jewish mother-tongue, that I cut off / a living limb of the soul" (Shmeruk 1999, 179).

cultures for decades may have been in part fueled by his admission of linguistic ambivalence.[35]

The younger Hebrew writers' violent reaction to the visit of major Yiddish literary figures in 1927 may indeed have been impelled mostly by factional politics. Yet if Shteynman's attack on Yiddish is the most extreme of these reactions, it is also perhaps the most extraordinary manifestation of the cultural and personal dilemma that Rachel Katznelson had so effectively expressed almost ten years earlier in "Language Wanderings" (1918). The passage of a decade had not blunted the acuteness of the issue. Although differences of personality and of social context are certainly factors in the dissimilar registers and tones of both Katznelson's and Shteynman's essays, they do not disguise the essential fact that the essays show two faces of the same problem: establishing a monolingual cultural identity consistent with Zionist ideology.

The Yiddish Chair, 1927

The establishment of a Hebrew University in the Yishuv was considered fundamental to the renaissance of the Jewish people in the Land of Israel; creating a national institute of higher education was part of the nationalist ideology.[36] As early as 1913, the Eleventh Zionist Congress debated the

---

35. The use of Yiddish along with Hebrew served as a pretext for the inclusion or exclusion of writers or portions of their work from the Hebrew literary canon. Gluzman (2002) suggests that a major reason for the exclusion of the poet Avot Yeshurun from the Hebrew literary canon in the 1940s and 1950s was the fact that in more than one way he brought the Yiddish heritage into his writing. Yeshurun incorporated Yiddish and Arabic into his Hebrew poetry, creating a highly idiosyncratic style. This incorporation was construed as a betrayal of Zionist ideology. Thus, even as late as the first decade of statehood (1950s), when the full scope of the destruction of the world's Yiddish-speaking community had become clear, its language was still perceived as a threat to the culture shaped by Zionist ideology.

36. Anderson discusses the significance of "native" universities as centers of national language and culture that nourish developing nationalist movements. He notes, for example, that "in the eighteenth century, Ukrainian was contemptuously tolerated as a language of yokels. . . . In 1804, the University of Kharkov was founded and rapidly became the center for a boom in Ukrainian literature" (1991, 74). This model, of course, may be seen to apply in reverse in the case of Jewish nationalism: Hebrew, the literary language, became a vernacular.

foundation of a Hebrew university in Jerusalem. Zionism exploited the traditional elitist aspects of Hebrew as the language of scholarship to add prestige to its campaign for the vernacularization of the language. This institution would be a secular academy, patterned after the great universities of Europe. Under the pressure of the Zionist Organization, the cornerstone of the Hebrew University was laid in July 1918, while Palestine was still partly in Ottoman hands and Jerusalem itself was under British martial law. The university was officially inaugurated and opened in April 1925 and instantly became an emblem of the ongoing "normalization" of the nation.

Small wonder, therefore, that both intellectuals and popular sentiment strongly opposed a proposal in November 1927 (based on a funding offer initially made two years earlier by the publisher of the New York Yiddish daily *Der Tog*) to establish a chair of Yiddish studies at the Hebrew University. Support for the chair was carefully articulated, based on its function as a venue for the academic study of Yiddish; the plan was confirmed in principle by the university's board of directors in December 1927. Although the language of instruction was to be Hebrew, the plan stood no chance of realization at the time. The Yiddish chair was seen not only as an attempt to legitimize Yiddish in the Yishuv but also as an act of sabotage against the basic concept of a Hebrew University and therefore a direct threat to the Hebrew character of Yishuv culture.[37] It was only in 1951, after the destruction of Yiddish culture and the founding of Israel—when, presumably, Yiddish no longer posed a danger to Hebrew—that a chair of Yiddish studies was finally created at the Hebrew University. An examination of the discourse used in the course of the public debate of 1927–28 illuminates another facet of the ongoing Hebrew-Yiddish conflict.

The harsh tone of the debate indicates the depth of emotion involved. In a telegram (apparently never sent) to Chancellor Judah Magnes, Menachem Ussishkin—a member of the board of trustees and the Executive Committee of the university and an ardent Hebraist—employed extreme terms to describe his concerns: "Huge outburst being organized . . . [w]hoever triumphs University ruin certain" (quoted in Pilowsky 1981, 106). The planned "huge outburst" referred to a demonstration arranged by the Gedud Meginey ha-Safa ha-Ivrit (Brigade of the Defenders of the Hebrew Lan-

---

37. For detailed chronological accounts of the affair, see Myers 1995, 76–81; Pilowsky 1980, 116–53, 1981; and Segev 2001, 263–69.

guage), an organization consisting mostly of teenagers who often used militant tactics to advance the cause of Hebrew.[38] Members of the Brigade piled stones in the university's courtyard to throw at its windows if the Yiddish chair was in fact established (Segev 2001, 266).

However, the Brigade's choice of language for its opposition to the Yiddish chair reveals some lingering basic insecurities concerning the status and prospects of Hebrew. One slogan proposed to the daily newspaper *Do'ar ha-Yom* was "Shylock sold a chunk of his flesh for money; we are selling our entire soul for money" (quoted in Segev 2001, 267). This is another internalization of an anti-Semitic stereotype—that of the avaricious "Jew" who is easily tempted by material things and can be convinced to relinquish his national heritage in exchange for money. Even more telling are the language and typographic layout of two posters printed by the Brigade (ills. 6 and 7). Both posters are framed by the black border typical of Jewish death notices, instantly locating the text in the domain of individual bereavements and thus involving personal emotions in what is presented as a national disaster. The text of one (ill. 6) reads, *"ha-katedrah le-zhargon churban ha-universitah ha-ivrit"* (the Chair of Jargon [Yiddish]—the Destruction of the Hebrew University), with the final word *Hebrew,* printed in larger typeface, occupying the entire bottom line and thus providing a visual anchor; the wide spacing between the letters H E B R E W emphasizes the word and heightens the poster's militant, tendentious tone.[39] The typographic presentation of the word *jargon* provides a striking antithesis: it is squeezed in at the end of the top line, with the letters seeming to run together indistinguishably and creat-

38. The Brigade developed from the early activities of the principal and students of Gymnazyah Hertzliyah, who orchestrated the physical attack on Chaim Zhitlovsky during his 1914 visit to Palestine. Founded in 1923, with the onset of mass immigration from Poland, the Brigade was active until 1936, mainly in Tel-Aviv and Jerusalem (Karmi 1997, 102–3). It became identified in public opinion with the extremist right-wing Zionist Revisionist movement; its tactics, such as eavesdropping on private conversations to determine which language was being spoken, were characterized as "fascist" by its detractors. Its activities were overwhelmingly directed against Yiddish; English posters for cultural events, for example, drew no reaction (Pilowsky 1986, 158–59), possibly because English was the language of the ruler. Pilowsky makes the interesting point that the Brigade is ignored by encyclopedias and has not been seriously researched (157).

39. Because Hebrew does not employ capital letters, words were often emphasized at the time by extra spacing between the letters.

6. "The Chair of Jargon[—]the Destruction of the Hebrew
University": poster of the Brigade of the Defenders of the Hebrew
Language protesting the plan to establish a chair of Yiddish studies at
the Hebrew University, Jerusalem, 1927; courtesy of the Central
Zionist Archives, Jerusalem, File A492/1.8א.

ing a blurred effect, indicating the "unnatural" character of Yiddish compared with the stately appearance of H E B R E W at the bottom.

The second poster (ill. 7) uses language that was even more resonant in a
secular cultural climate that had negated traditional religion and now
revered the Hebrew University as the temple of modern Judaism (Bialik, for
instance, referred to the Hebrew University as "our temple," the temple of
the Zionist religion [1935b, 9]). This poster reads, *"ha-katedrah le-zhargon
tselem ba-heykhal ha-ivri"* (the Chair of Jargon—an Idol in the Hebrew
Temple); the layout is similar to that of the other poster, with *jargon*
squeezed together at the top and the final H E B R E W spaced out at the bottom of the text. The use of the noun *heykhal* (temple) modified by the adjective *ha-ivri* (Hebrew) instantly equates the Hebrew University with the
pre-exilic Temple, the sole residence of God (in the Bible, *heykhal* refers exclusively to the Jerusalem Temple). By inference, it also places the Hebrew
language on a par with divinity. Even more remarkable is the identification
of Yiddish with the image of a pagan god: the young rebels of the secular
Brigade of the Defenders of the Hebrew Language employed the very phrase,
tselem ba-heykhal, used in the rabbinic sources to denote the desecration of
the Temple by pagan rulers who placed images there, such as the Hellenistic

הקתדרה לזדגון

צלם בהיכל

העברי

הנהגת גדוד מגני השפה בארץישראל
סניף ירושלם

7. "The Chair of Jargon[—]an Idol in the Hebrew Temple": poster
of the Brigade of the Defenders of the Hebrew Language protesting
the plan to establish a chair of Yiddish studies at the Hebrew
University; Jerusalem, 1927; courtesy of the Central Zionist
Archives, Jerusalem, File A492/1.8א.

Syrian kings in the second century B.C.E. and the Roman emperors in the first
century C.E. (Megillath Ta'anith 26, 2).[40]

Yiddish, the language of European Jews for a millennium, was now not
only considered illegitimate "jargon," but was further demonized as an
alien, threatening entity. Although the phrase *tselem ba-heykhal* had become
a loose synonym for any kind of desecration, its use here indicates a profound fear of the repressed language and the danger it represented for the integrity of the new Hebrew nation that had become emblematized by the
university, its "temple."

Let us return to Bialik for a final word on this issue, one that eloquently
expresses the complexity of this cultural period. On 13 September 1930, the
national poet—perhaps by now more revered outside the Yishuv than within

40. "Placing the idol in the Temple" is the ultimate item in Ta'anith's list of desecrations
that purportedly occurred on the seventeenth day of Tammuz (along with Moses' breaking of
the tablets, cessation of the daily offering in the Temple, the breaching of Jerusalem's walls, and
the burning of the Temple scrolls). The phrase was apparently first applied in the context of the
Yiddish chair in the Hebrew right-wing daily *Do'ar ha-Yom* (Pilowsky 1981, 111).

it because of the changing poetic and political climate in Palestine—gave a talk at a synagogue in Kovno, Lithuania. At that time, the Brigade of the Defenders of the Hebrew Language was threatening violence upon two Jerusalem movie theaters that were about to screen the Yiddish film *Di yidishe Mame* (The Jewish mother) and was personally intimidating the theater owners.[41] The title of Bialik's talk, "The Question of Jewish Languages," placed the issue on an academic plane of discussion in what seems to be a calculated attempt to defuse the emotions involved (1935c, 142). Most of the address, in fact, presented his theory that the use of other languages actually served to protect Hebrew from foreign influences. However, deep emotions surfaced poignantly near the beginning of his talk, after he noted that over the centuries Jews had used as many as sixteen different languages:

> It is undoubtedly a tragic phenomenon for a nation—to keep changing its languages every so often. All this is in the nature of a real transmigration [*gilgul*]: the soul must be transferred from one body to another. And the relocation of a nation from one language to another is like the transmigration of the soul from one body into another. Such reincarnations do not occur without awful torture. This is a very difficult, malignant process, entailing bitter and awful suffering, and the soul loses much of itself at that time. Such a profound tragic phenomenon should be discussed objectively, only from a historic point of view. (1935c, 143–44)

Bialik's transmigration image is multifaceted, combining a theme of Jewish mysticism with the lexicon of modern nationalism. Let us first examine his image on the level of Jewish mysticism. The doctrine of *gilgul neshamot,* part of mystical Jewish thought from the early twelfth century C.E.,[42] became a major component of Lurianic Kabbalah (the Jewish mysticism developed by Rabbi Yitzhak Luria in Safed in the late sixteenth century) and as such became prevalent in Jewish philosophic works. According to the Kabbalah, transmigration was a very harsh punishment, essentially connected with sexual transgressions, but it also offered an opportunity for restitution (Scholem

---

41. The film eventually had a single showing, under police protection, and a planned second showing was canceled (Pilowsky 1980, 171–72).

42. Its roots lie in the notion of *gilgul mechilot,* transportation through tunnels, which, according to the Palestinian midrash Genesis Rabbah 96, 5, will miraculously translocate righteous Jews who died outside the Holy Land back to it so that they will be resurrected there in messianic times.

1974, 344–47). Transmigration is extremely dangerous: the soul may become lost in a kind of limbo, the no-man's-land between physical bodies. The act of abandoning one body and adopting another one involves excruciating agony and the inevitable loss of some of the soul's essential qualities.

Kabbalah, a familiar area of Jewish thought that was largely marginalized by European Jewish orthodoxy, was then undergoing reevaluation in the wake of Zionism, after being overwhelmingly rejected by nineteenth-century Jewish historians (Scholem 1974, 202–3). The overtones of the earlier negation make Bialik's language all the more striking: he incorporated general nationalist metaphors involving soul and body, at the same time evoking Zionism's particular modification of this imagery. E. J. Hobsbawm notes that for late-nineteenth-century ideologists of nationalism "language was the soul of a nation" (1990, 95). As we have seen, political Zionism privileged the tangible, "bodily" aspects of nationhood over "soul" by aspiring to a spatial relocation of the nation in its homeland and by ranking physical activity over spiritual activity as a way of curing the diasporic state of "physical disease." Bialik, however, seemed to be saying that, for the Jewish nation, "soul" is paramount and that the nation had actually been losing its soul incrementally through repeated transmigrations into different bodies— that is, through changes of languages. Moreover, and perhaps most significant in the context of Zionism, which considered its project of national rebirth to be the ultimate answer to the "Jewish problem," he did not consider the renewed use of Hebrew as the vernacular to be the final stage in the sequence of recurring language switches. His anguished implication here, against Zionism's glorification of the physical, was that the future nation would be nothing but a soul-less body; the existence of the Jewish nation could be assured only by imposing the Hebrew language on its life (1935c, 156). By using the verb *le-hashlit* (to impose), Bialik implied considerable doubt about the future of Hebrew in the Land of Israel: if Hebrew had to be imposed, it could not be a natural outgrowth of Yishuv culture.

The conclusion of Bialik's talk is ambiguous. In the penultimate sentence, he declared his creed in what seems to be a positive statement: "As for me, I believe in a nation that has only one 'spinal cord'—the Hebrew language!" (1935c, 157). This imagery is confined to the realm of the purely physical, with no mention of a "soul." [43] But he followed this statement by an

---

43. Bialik formulated what Kronfeld terms "an organistic account of language" (1996, 85) as early as his 1905 essay "Chevley Lashon" (Language pangs), in which he described a lan-

abrupt change of tone, ending the essay with a brief quote from Ecclesiastes, set off on a line by itself: "What has been is what will be" (Eccl. 1:9). The contemporaneous Hebrew reader, familiar with the Bible, could not help but hear the rest of that verse: "and what has been done is what will be done; and there is nothing new under the sun." We cannot, of course, know how much of this pessimism was owing to Bialik's own sense that the younger generation in the Yishuv perceived him as being hopelessly out of touch. Yet in this powerful utterance he apparently gave voice to the Yishuv's cultural ambivalence as no one else had. This pervasive ambivalence was the background for the appearance of Yiddish literary magazines in Palestine.

The Emergence of the Yiddish Magazines, 1928

By August 1928, the number of people in the Yishuv had increased considerably (150,000 compared with 93,000 five years earlier [Wallach 1974, 45, 50]). Although Hebrew was now an official language, censuses of Jewish workers carried out by the Jewish Labor Federation in 1922 and 1926 showed that the percentage of Jews who reported that they knew Hebrew actually dropped—from 91.6 percent in 1922 to 85 percent in 1926, at the height of the Fourth Aliyah (Bachi 1956, 69). Roberto Bachi attributes this drop to the massive immigration from Europe during those years (1956, 70). Clearly, there was an audience for locally produced Yiddish literature.

Indeed, Yiddish texts were not long in coming. The Yidishn Literatn un Zhurnalistn-klub in Erets-Yisro'el (Yiddish Writers' and Journalists' Club in Palestine) was organized in 1928 to meet the cultural needs of both readers and writers (the Fourth Aliyah included many Yiddish writers, some of whom had already published in the Yiddish press of Europe). The first production of the club was *Onheyb* (Beginning), subtitled "A Collection for the Yiddish Word in Erets-Yisro'el," which included literature and criticism. The title echoes that of the 1907 Palestinian *Der Onfang* while establishing its own separate character.[44] Only a year earlier the poet Yehoyesh (Solomon

---

guage as "a living, organic creature" (1953, 201). In his 1930 talk, he carried this imagery further by applying it to the nation, locating his deep concern for language as soul within the larger context of the nation as body.

44. The word *onheyb* was less obviously linked to German than *onfang* and thus more "authentically" Yiddish for those Yiddish purists who delegitimized the Germanizing tendencies of the Haskalah. *Onheyb* had been used as the one-word title of several Yiddish magazines

Bloomgarden) had completed his masterful Yiddish translation of the Bible; his version of Genesis begins with *"In onheyb."* The Yiddish writers who participated in *Onheyb* were clearly animated by a strong sense of mission, likening their initiative to Creation itself. The editorial "Unzer Onheyb" (Our beginning) strongly conveyed the sense of a new start in the ancestral homeland and reflected the feeling that the Yiddish project was a vital part of the Zionist renewal rather than the opposition that the mainstream construed it to be. This sense of a new beginning persisted in the participants for decades: when Y. Z. Shargel, one of the founders, published a collection of his memoirs and essays in 1977, he titled it *Fun Onheyb On* (From the beginning). Significantly, the Hebrew translation of Shargel's title uses the word *bereshit,* the Hebrew word that opens the Bible.

In his memoirs, Shargel underscores the biblical and national connection by the rather pompous style and the first words of his introductory paragraph: ". . . and it was in the year 1928, in the sunny month of August, that there appeared in the eternal Jerusalem the first collection for the Yiddish word in Palestine, under the name 'Beginning' " (1977, 5, ellipsis in the original). Linking his evocation of Genesis with the traditional ideological significance of Jerusalem in the same sentence, Shargel seems to set the publication of *Onheyb* on a par with Creation itself. This meaning is implied in his use of *dershinen* ("appeared," signifying both a visual appearance and a publication), with its magical or divine connotations. Shargel also explains why the Lithuanian dialect form *onheyb* was chosen over its widely used variant *onhoyb:* the founders wanted to revert to a "purer" Yiddish; *onhoyb,* he says, is too close to the German (26).

Over the next eleven years, nineteen Yiddish literary magazines appeared in Palestine under the auspices of the Yiddish Writers' and Journalists' Club in Palestine.[45] *Onheyb* apparently was published in Jerusalem for symbolic reasons; most of the other magazines were published in Tel-Aviv. In 1929, *Eyns* (One), *Tsvey* (Two), and *Tsvishn Tsvey un Dray* (Between two and three) appeared. The year 1931 saw the publication of *May* (May), *Yuni*

---

and collections following the First World War, signifying the sense of avant-garde innovativeness that animated the writers. It was the name of a collection published by the Di Yunge poets in New York in 1918. Another *Onheyb,* "a collection for literature and science," was published in Berlin in 1922, the same year that Grinberg moved his journal *Albatros* there from Warsaw.

45. The most comprehensive historical accounts of these magazines are in Pilowsky 1980, 1986.

(June), *Dray* (Three), and *Oktober.* In 1932, *Mir* (We) and *Fir* (Four) appeared in Tel-Aviv and *Chayfe* in Haifa. In 1934, the Yiddish biweekly *Nayvelt* (New world), sponsored by Left Po'alei Zion, began publication; its content was political as well as literary.

Later publications were more sporadic, and their titles were less optimistic than those of the first magazines, in which the use of numbers conveyed a hope that the publications would form a series. This shift suggests caution, if not misgivings, about the future of Yiddish culture in the Yishuv. The Yiddish writers were clearly aware that Hebrew was predominating. *Vayter* (Further) appeared in 1935; *Shtamen* (Roots), *Yunge Shtamen* (Young roots), and *Bleter tsum Ondenk fun Leyb Malakh* (Pages in memoriam, Leyb Malakh) were published in 1936; *Erets-yisro'el Shriftn* (Palestine writings) and *Undzere Shtamen* (Our roots) surfaced in 1937. *Naye Shtamen* (New roots) appeared in 1938, another *Shtamen* in 1939, *Undzers* (Ours) in 1940, *November Shtamen* (November roots) in 1942, *Februar Shtamen* (February roots) and *Merts Shtamen* (March roots) in 1943, *Di Brik* (The bridge) in 1944, and *Di Heftn* (The notebooks) in 1945. These Yiddish magazines defined themselves variously as devoted to "literature and art" *(Eyns);* "literature and culture" *(Tsvishn Tsvey un Dray);* "literature and criticism" *(Oktober, Tsvey, Hayfa, Mir);* "literature, art, and criticism" *(May, Yuni).* They were mostly "little" magazines in the literal sense of the word; *Eyns* and *Tsvey* were the largest, at 80 pages each. The other magazines varied in length from 19 to 22 pages; the sole exception is *Erets-yisro'el Shriftn,* with 221 pages, which was published with the aid of organizations in the United States, Canada, Argentina, Uruguay, and Australia that supported the cause of Yiddish in Palestine ("Fun di Aroysgebers" (From the publishers), *Erets-yisro'el Shriftn* [1937], 221).

There is no information about the distribution of these magazines, yet the fact that they continued to appear despite the establishment's disapproval of Yiddish culture is a measure of the vitality of this culture in the Yishuv. The factionalism of Hebrew literary life in the country during the late 1920s and the 1930s (Z. Shavit 1982, 13) was characteristic of Yiddish writers as well: the same small core of writers participated in all the publications, assuming the roles of cultural critics as well as of fiction, poetry, and review writers. One or another of the writers always served as the editor, although this title was not an official one (often the name of "the one responsible," a style current in Russian publishing, was given). *Eyns* seems to have been a group effort; the editors were "a group of colleagues." Name abbre-

8. Cover of Yiddish magazine *Tsvishn Tsvey un Dray*, Tel-Aviv, December 1929.

viations and pseudonyms were widely used to mask the small number of writers.[46]

The mainstream perceived these magazines as being initiated by Left Po'alei Zion solely for political purposes;[47] labeling them as "party organs" may have made it easier to discount their cultural significance. Pilowsky notes that although most of the twelve[48] founders of the Yiddish Writers' and Journalists' Club were members of Left Po'alei Zion, the only two professional journalists in the group had no connection with the party (1980, 175). *Tsvishn Tsvey un Dray* (1929) ends with a declaration signed by the leadership of the Yiddish Writers' and Journalists' Club in Palestine, defining the club as "a nonparty organization of Yiddish writers and journalists, regardless of party affiliation and belief, who have a positive attitude toward the Yiddish language and Yiddish culture in the entire world and in Palestine" ("Derklerung" [Explanation], *Tsvishn Tsvey un Dray*, 36). Probably only a small proportion of Yiddish readers in the Yishuv were actually members of, or even sympathizers with, Left Po'alei Zion. Yiddish readers were a culturally involved community in immediate need of a local milieu in which they could be at home.

The proportions of the different genres represented in these magazines are instructive. Cultural criticism, reviews, and responses to the often hostile reactions in the Hebrew press usually constituted the majority of the material, followed by fiction. Poetry appeared in relatively small proportions. Virtually all the work was original and reflected the concerns of the Yiddish writers who had immigrated to the country and were passionately involved in creating a new community. Interestingly, however, *Eyns* included Abraham Ayssen's translation of Oscar Wilde's poem "By the Arno," a decidedly nonideological work ("Bay dem Taykh Arno," *Eyns* [1929], 34–35).[49]

46. According to Shargel, Leybl Cheyn used no less than five pseudonyms (1977a, 40).

47. Even so careful a scholar as Shmeruk repeats this characterization without being explicit: "The declared tendencies of these publications were definitely left-wing, politically speaking" (1999, 184).

48. Ten, according to Shargel (1977a, 11).

49. This lyrical, pensive poem by a notoriously decadent aesthete of fin-de-siècle Europe strikes an odd note in a left-wing publication devoted to the culture of Palestine's Zionist pioneers. The translation shifts from aestheticism to a more expressionist mode, consistent with the dominant poetics of the Palestinian Yiddish writers. Although a close comparative reading of the Yiddish translation of this poem and a discussion of the editorial choices of the Palestinian Yiddish magazines are outside the scope of this study, it is worth noting that Wilde seems to have been a favorite of Yiddish modernists; for example, the 1922 Berlin Yiddish magazine *Der On-*

This was one of the ways in which the Yiddish writers did not conform to a society that was increasingly becoming more univocal. The appearance of the Yiddish magazines was greeted with great animosity. Avrom Blay responded in *Yuni* to the violent reaction of the Hebrew daily *Do'ar ha-Yom* to the publication of *May*. Blay quoted (in translation) from the *Do'ar ha-Yom* review of 6 May 1931: " 'The specter of "*zhargon*" is back among us in the country! We considered it to be dead, and here it is, stealing back among us like a snake!' " (1931b, 18, quotation marks in the original). Even if we take into consideration the extreme right-wing politics of *Do'ar ha-Yom*, which considered this period a chance to attack socialist Zionism in the Yishuv, the language of this quoted diatribe is striking. The imagery evokes overtones of no less than the first biblical tempter: the snake who beckons Eve to stray from God's commands. In the context of the Hebrew-Yiddish opposition, the role of the snake is particularly intriguing. The stereotypical characterization of both languages undergoes startling reversals for the purposes of the metaphor. Yiddish, traditionally emblematizing weakness, is here portrayed as the archetypal aggressive masculine entity—the snake—whereas Hebrew, metonymizing the "brave new Jew" that Zionism sought to create, takes on opposite, "feminine" implications of weakness and gullibility. Yiddish, sneaking up to entrap an unsuspecting Hebrew, was thus a resurgent threat to the community's faith in Zionism. This virulent review signaled the Hebrew culture's continued sense of insecurity, which gave rise to fears that persisted for years.

In *Dray* (September 1931), D. L. (Daniel Leybl) noted that the entire "bourgeois press" [50] attacked *May* and *Yuni*, and he compared the commotion to that "in the Jewish shtetl when the moon rises" (1931, col. 34). Leybl placed these Yishuv newspapers squarely within the locus of diasporic unreason—precisely the context that Zionist ideology repudiated. In the same publication, A. B. (Avrom Blay) ridiculed an advertisement in the Hebrew press for *Vos Arbetorins Dertseyln* (What women workers tell, translated and edited by Rachel Katznelson), the 1931 Yiddish version of the 1930 Hebrew anthology *Divrey Po'alot* (The woman worker speaks, also edited by Katznelson). The advertisement suggested that the book was suitable as a

---

heyb includes a translation of his short fable "The Scholar" ("Der Gelernter"), which I have not been able to find in collections of Wilde's works.

50. In the lingo of the time, this phrase denotes groups that did not subscribe to socialist-Zionist ideology.

gift for friends abroad. Blay pointed out the paradox inherent in placing such an advertisement in the Yishuv's Hebrew press and doubted whether all those who supposedly bought the book in order to send it abroad actually did so: "Why should those, who recommend a book for others to read, not read it themselves?" (1931a, col. 35). He implied that Yiddish readers in the Yishuv secretly bought the book for themselves (evoking the diasporic stereotypical image of men who read Yiddish as being effeminate).[51]

Yiddish continued to be characterized as a dangerously tempting entity in 1934. Y. Mitbonen, writing in *Gilyonot* (the other major literary magazine, besides *Ketuvim,* of the Yishuv) presented the language issue as a symptom of the cultural and political conflict.[52] Mitbonen feared for the future of Hebrew in a land that was being settled by immigrants *(mehagrim)* rather than by "ascenders" *(olim).* The implication here is that immigrants of the Fifth Aliyah were not motivated by proper Zionist ideology and that their decision to retain the mother tongue was a betrayal of Zionism: "Foreign [i.e., non-Hebrew] speech floods every corner of our lives. . . . Hebrew speakers have almost become a kind of national minority in this nation of foreign-language speakers" (1934, 290). Although Mitbonen did not detail the foreign languages spoken in the Yishuv, except for a brief mention of German,[53] he devoted several malicious sentences to Yiddish, the old linguistic and cultural nemesis of Zionism, the mother tongue characterized as a foreign language. Mitbonen's language echoed the most virulent anti-Semitic rhetoric: "In the midst of all this foulness, our old acquaintances the Yiddishists have appeared. These crevice-dwellers smell prey. Now that all our bad, despicable lusts have begun to rampage here publicly and unchecked— shall Yiddishism be absent from this glorious choir? And look, it has blessed us with its new newspaper in Eretz-Israel!" (1934, 290).

In graphic terms designed to evoke revulsion, Mitbonen was reviving the old specter of Yiddishism. Its adherents were "crevice-dwellers"—that is, insect pests or predatory vermin; yet he also depicted the craving for Yiddish as

51. This image was internalized by Jews early on; thus, Moshe Chanokh states in his 1602 Yiddish book of ethics *Der Brantshpigl* that he is writing "in Yiddish for women and men who are like women" (quoted in Niger 1985, 44).

52. "Mitbonen" is obviously a pen name, possibly of the poet Yitzchak Lamdan, the editor of *Gilyonot.* The name can be translated as "the observer."

53. Immigrants from Nazi Germany were then forming a distinctive community within the Yishuv; for a perceptive discussion of this group, see Segev 1993.

a constant, suppressed negative desire—a "despicable lust"—within the community. The newspaper to which he referred with such heavy-handed irony was the Yiddish biweekly *Nayvelt,* which had begun publication the previous year. Mitbonen placed Yiddishism at the head of the perceived political and cultural threat posed to Labor's hegemony by the changing demographics. The ambivalence of the Yishuv's relationship with Yiddish surfaced urgently: against a background of suppression to the point of denial, the danger of Yiddish was inflated in grotesquely sexual and bestial terms, and the mother tongue was made "other."

The Yiddish writers in the magazines used the elitism of Yishuv Hebrew culture as a cultural weapon. Echoing his socialist ideology, L. Litvak (a pseudonym of L. Cheyn) wrote in an article titled "Undzerer Kultur-problemen" (Our cultural problems): "The Hebraists consist of a specific section of Jewish society, namely, the average bourgeoisie. . . . Hebraism is a political class weapon in the hands of the wealthy Jewish classes. . . . [It] has created a spiritual desert for the simple worker" (1928, 26–27). Litvak expanded on the political aspects of Hebraism when he noted the incontrovertible fact that Yishuv culture was polyglot, or at least bilingual, and had been so since the beginning of Zionist immigration. Depicting daily life in the community, Litvak sarcastically equated the jabber of bad Polish and bad Russian of the diasporic homelands with the jabbering, halting Hebrew spoken by most immigrants. By doing so, he exposed the hypocrisy of the dominant Zionist circles that used the language issue as a political and cultural tool: "There [in the Diaspora] one jabbered a *kugl*-Polish [a *kugl* is a casserole consisting of leftovers] or a *kugl*-Russian; here one jabbers a broken Hebrew, which makes one a 'person of culture' as it were" (27). The imperfect Hebrew spoken in the Yishuv was no purer than the languages adopted in the Diaspora, yet those who spoke it were, by mainstream definition, "cultured."

Within the Hebrew culture, mainstream literary critic Yosef Seh-Lavan offered a more typical flattering reference to this elitism: "At the center of the Third Aliyah's literature towers [*mitnaseh*] the figure of the pioneering person [*ha-adam ha-chalutzi*] who considers himself responsible for the fate of the individual and of society, who is totally immersed in creating and building, who lives a life of integrity and truth" (1964, 858). Seh-Lavan's choice of the verb *mitnaseh* (hold oneself high), which conveys a sense of superiority, indicates his own awareness of the idealized, elitist self-image of the pioneers. Ironically, the Yiddish writers of the Fourth Aliyah, who dealt with the concerns and met the needs of a large proportion of the Yishuv, also fell squarely within Seh-Lavan's definition of "the pioneering person": they, too, were immigrants, imbued with a sense of personal and social mission and active participants in the Zionist project. These writers were marginalized by the dominant culture, yet it was precisely this marginalization that enabled them to critique the mainstream insightfully. Examination of the fiction in the Yiddish magazines indicates that much of the animosity toward the magazines, although ostensibly owing to the language choice, Yiddish, actually stemmed from the unorthodox thematics of the Yiddish writers. Many of their protagonists and characters are as consumed with issues of personal loss as with "creating and building," and some characters situated outside Zionism altogether are nonetheless profoundly affected by its impact. These thematics are often manifested in the choice of dialect and language framed and represented within Yiddish.

The Hebraists' vehement reaction to the Yiddish publications seems to have been only in part driven by political differences. It may have masked a fear that the mother tongue and its culture, repressed at such psychological cost, would reemerge. The creation of Yiddish literature in the Yishuv expressed the community's continuing ambivalence concerning the need to choose sides in the language dilemma, an ambivalence that most contemporaneous Hebrew literature did not address. With keen sensibility, Rachel Katznelson, in the conclusion of her foreword to the Yiddish *What Women Workers Tell*, expressed this ambivalence and suggested an alternative path of cultural development:

> It was also our purpose [in the anthology] to present emphatically the organic link between that which has been created in Palestine and the previous lives of the same people, to . . . try to reveal the blessed sources in Jewish and European culture from which the new Palestinian culture benefits. And the very fact of translation into Yiddish is, in a certain sense, a symbol of continuity, of cultural interconnectedness: as though this were repayment of a debt to someone to whom one owes a great deal. (1931, iii)

Referring to an organic link between the cultures, Katznelson blurred the powerful dichotomy created by Zionism. She not only admitted the essential and intricate causal relationship between the European past and the Palestinian present in Yishuv culture, but welcomed it as a vital resource for the development of the nascent community. However, no such formulation appeared in the Hebrew *The Woman Worker Speaks;* her inclusive cultural vision could not be part of a Hebrew publication in the Yishuv.

Thus, the political and personal problematics at play in Palestine beginning in the first decade of the twentieth century lingered well into the fourth decade. The persisting ambivalence on the language issue was usually concealed from the public gaze, yet, as we see, it is evident upon close examination of the speeches and writings of this period. The only part of the Yishuv that was not ambivalent were the Yiddish writers and readers who enabled the existence of these Yiddish magazines.

CHAPTER FOUR

Outcasts Within

The Yishuv Experience in the Fiction of Avrom Rivess

Each tent is a small world unto itself.

—Avrom Rivess, "Transplant," 1929

The fiction writers in the Yiddish magazines of the Yishuv were a typical cross-section of the young Jewish pioneers who immigrated to Palestine from eastern Europe in the 1920s, seeking to realize their Zionist-socialist ideals. Yet they were, of course, unique in their use of Yiddish. The fiction of Avrom Rivess represents the possibilities enabled by the use, against the cultural and political tide, of a proscribed language that was much more flexible than the officially sanctioned Hebrew and clearly much more accessible, in all its layers and nuances, to the Yishuv's reading culture. It was Yiddish, the "fusion" language whose components are clearly discernible through the thin film of its orthography, that facilitated the multifaceted expression of a nascent culture. The poetic antecedents of Zalmen Brokhes lie in late-nineteenth-century exoticizing romanticism, and his characters are unaffiliated individuals who display little if any social or national engagement. Rivess's sensibility, in contrast, was nurtured in both socialism and European Yiddish modernism, in particular its expressionistic strain. His Yishuv fiction, published locally between the late 1920s and the mid-1940s, expresses these affiliations while often sounding a piercing critique of the Zionist project.

Appropriating Modernism

Avrom Rivess (the pseudonym of Avrom Naimovitch, 1900–1963),[1] was born in the industrial town of Lomzhe (Lomza), Poland, where he was trained in a vocational school and worked as a railway laborer. As a young man, he was an active participant in the vibrant Yiddish cultural and political scene of his hometown and published stories in the local magazines *Der Oyfkum* (The uprising, 1919) and *Yidishe Lomzshe* (Jewish Lomzhe) (Kohen, Naks, and Shulman 1981, 8: col. 445). Underscoring his affiliation with modernist Yiddish culture, he joined several friends—among them the poet and translator Aaron Mark—in initiating the publication of *Tayfun* (Typhoon, 1923) in Lomzhe. *Tayfun*, a thirty-two-page "art-literature collection," included poetry, prose, and artwork (linoleum cuts) that consciously emulated the work appearing in such significant expressionist Yiddish magazines as the Warsaw *Khalyastre* (1922) and Uri Tsvi Grinberg's *Albatros* (1922–23). Rivess proudly noted in a memoir entitled "Chugenu ha-Sifruti" (Our literary circle) that Melekh Ravitsh wrote a favorable review of *Tayfun* in the important Warsaw journal *Bikher Velt* (Rivess 1952, 166). Like the title of *Der Oyfkum*, *Tayfun* expressed a sense of revolutionary change as well as a yearning for the radical and the extreme, with exotic overtones of the Far East—as distant as possible from the reality of Lomzhe. Its contents indicated a modernist disenchantment with tradition—Jewish or otherwise—and strongly voiced the disaffected individual who was seeking a dramatic break with the past and a new beginning; the expressionist writer was "a prophetic visionary called to explode conventional reality" (Sheppard 1991a, 277), a description that suits the *Tayfun* group as it does other contemporaneous avant-garde Jewish groups.

Characteristic features of expressionism are "a tendency toward the inflated and the grotesque; a mystical, even religious element with frequent apocalyptic overtones" (Furness 1973, 21). Modernist Jewish writers often combined Jewish and non-Jewish, biblical and postbiblical religious traditions in order to achieve maximum dissonance and thus shock the reader into a radically different awareness. Perets Markish's "Oyf Markn un

---

1. A pseudonym that may incorporate his mother's name—literally, "Riva's Abraham" ("Riva" is a diminutive form of "Rivka"). Owing to the sparseness of biographical material, I have not been able to ascertain the name of Rivess's mother, but such a device would have been strongly within the Yiddish literary tradition. It was adopted by writers such as Isaac Bashevis ("Bathsheba's") Singer and Semyon An-ski, born Rappoport, who may have derived his pseudonym from his mother's name (Kantsedikas 1994, 18). Use of the mother's name for identification further underscores the emotional power and feminine resonance of the language known to its speakers as *mame-loshn* (mother tongue).

Yaridn" (At markets and fairs), in *Di Kupe* (The pile [Markish 1921, 14]), has a pig urinating on the parchment that bears the Ten Commandments. This is a startling image of desecration incarnate, defiling the most hallowed of Jewish texts in a poem that is part of a cycle memorializing the victims of the Horodishtsh pogrom.

A measure of *Tayfun*'s radical poetics is the work of Mark Shturem (very likely Aaron Mark, using a pseudonym, "storm," that echoes the name of the magazine and conveys a timely cultural and political message). In his poem "Oyf Sheyd-veg" (At the crossroads), he explosively juxtaposes the most sacred with the most profane. He speaks of "the seven suns / with thousands of eyes / that illuminate the Holies of Holies [*kodshey-kodoshims*] / of human temples / and bang, smiling pleasantly, on / all the Gates of Impurity [*sha'arey-tum'ah*]" (1923, 25). In Jewish tradition, the one and only Holy of Holies was the locus of God's presence inside the biblical Temple of Jerusalem. When Shturem multiplies the single site and situates it in more than one human temple, he is desecrating the uniqueness of God's chosen abode. Because the biblical Holy of Holies was completely sealed off from the outside, the light of the formulaic, folkloric "seven suns" is a bizarre intrusion into this ultimate sanctum. Next, Shturem has the light of the seven suns banging away at the Gates of Impurity—a name derived from Kabbalah mysticism, where the figurative "forty-nine gates of impurity" *(mem-tet sha'arey tum'ah,* a number that squares the magical "seven") indicates the depths of wickedness and perversion. Later in the poem he describes "thousands of runged ladders / of black Golgothas [*golgotes*] / swinging in the storm, my brother" (27), evoking the shocking imagery used a year earlier by Grinberg in his "Uri Tsvi farn Tseylem" (Uri Tsvi in front of the cross [1922b, 3–4]).[2] Rivess's participation in this local collection of avant-garde writing indicates his affinity with contemporary radical Yiddish poetics.

Rivess's contribution to *Tayfun* in 1923, the short story "Bloye Roybfoygl" (Blue birds of prey), powerfully illustrates his Jewish and modernist concerns. The story begins with a deceptively traditional setting for a Yiddish narrative: the first-person narrator is traveling on a train. This setting is ostensibly in line with a stock theme of nineteenth-century Jewish literature: the railroad. As railroads became increasingly widespread throughout Europe in the nineteenth century, Haskalah thinkers perceived this innovation

---

2. In this striking poem, with its cruciform typography, Grinberg construes Jesus on the cross as his brother: "screaming, screaming, a scream of Jewish misery."

as a powerful instrument of progress that would disseminate modernizing values among Jews and improve individual and communal situations. Yet it soon became clear that, on the contrary, the trains had become a surrogate shtetl for traveling Jews. The railroad soon served as a grand metaphor for the inactivity of Jews as a community. David Roskies notes that as late as the first decade of the twentieth century, "trains and technology had benefitted Russian Jews very little" (1995, 177). Jews riding in railroad cars clung to their own distinctive culture in the very moment that the dominant non-Jewish society was contributing to their dislocation. An oft-quoted passage from S. Y. Abramovitch's Hebrew version of his 1890 story "Shem ve-Yefet ba'agalah" (Shem and Japheth on the train) spells out the metaphor: "the railway train is like a whole traveling city, with its multitude and uproar, with its inhabitants divided into groups and classes, with their hates and envy and competition and negotiation and quarreling" (1947, 399). Discussing Sholem Aleichem's 1911 "Railroad Stories," Hillel Halkin remarks that because Russian peasants rarely traveled and the aristocracy did not use third-class cars, most of the travelers in third class would in fact have been "Jews who tell each other stories" (1987, xxxiii). In Sholem Aleichem's stories, Jews, lively and talkative, are the majority of riders on the trains, yet they seem to be going nowhere. The train is a shtetl in limbo, with all its tedium and pettiness (Miron 1996, 136). By the turn of the century, the train, initially a symbol of modernization, had become "a negative trope of the breakdown of communal Jewish life: pogroms, exile, loss of meaning, alienation" (Garrett 2003, 94).

Rivess's "Blue Birds of Prey" reflects this shift and carries it further. The train is not a mechanism that links Jewish shtetls and functions as a cultural vehicle. Rather, it is a freight train carrying new army recruits who initially seem to have no ethnic markers or, apparently, any self-awareness. The riders are barely sentient, a type of freight. Whereas the train and the changing landscape through which it moves are described in active, personified terms, the human cargo is passive and inanimate. It is the train and rails that are endowed with life: struggling to climb a grade, the "iron creature wrapped in black drags itself uphill with its last bit of strength . . . the rails underneath groan heavily; the wheels press on them pitilessly. Heartrending screams rise from below" (Rivess 1923, 28). Both train and rails seem to be in pain, as the "iron creature" thrusts its spurs into the underlying rails that wail in protest. In a remarkably radical recontextualization of modernist motifs, the narrator first personifies and then Judaizes the factory chimneys of the approaching city: "The tall factory chimneys immerse themselves [*toyvlen zikh*] in the damp mist, stretch and yawn out of their long night's sleep" (28). The Hebrew-derived reflexive *toyvlen zikh* invariably refers to the ritual immersion in the purification bath *(mikve)* practiced by observant male and female Jews. By situating industrial chimneys in this context and by applying the Yiddish term derived from the sacred domain to the imagined polluting action of the smokestacks, Rivess outrageously reconfigures cultural elements through the language hierarchies of both Yiddish and Hebrew. The Hebrew term, sacralized by language and by context, is profaned by its location in this grotesquely incongruous setting.

The narrator's sensibility shifts into surrealism when a group of Jews fleeing a pogrom enters the train station and encounters seasoned soldiers in blue uniform—the "birds of prey"—who have come in on a different train as the narrator looks on. Consider this horrendous description:

> Stormlike, a wave of Jews frightened to death races through. Heads stripped bare, their hands stretched out in front, as though they would push away the stifling stench. Coattails flutter and flap in the air. They seek to hide away from the wild multitude of blue birds of prey. Copper faces, the eyes send out sparks of snake-fire, with lead straps in their hands, they move like wild animals hunting prey. The air trembles with the blows and screams of glee, bloodied faces, split heads, Jews with disheveled, bloodied beards, run wildly, crazily. Inhuman screams of pain burst out of their hearts. With catlike ease, a blue devil springs through, on his head a horned hat. With wild pleasure he smears his hands with blood. A venomous smile grimaces on his copper brown face. A sacrifice has been offered on the altar. (29)

In this apocalyptic vision, disjointed body parts and articles of clothing function synecdochally and represent a complete dissolution of the most elementary human values. The point of ultimate depravity, human sacrifice, is reached. Both the Jewish victims and their non-Jewish tormentors have lost all vestiges of humanity in being disassembled into body parts, as well as all chance of redemption. This ghastly spectacle of dehumanization stands in stark contrast to the personified inanimate smokestacks of the previously cited passage, which "purify" themselves as they "stretch" into the morning mist.

Rivess performs another subversion, this time of a European modernist trope, when he distorts the expressionist connotations of the color blue. In the color lexicon of high expressionism just before the First World War, blue denotes innocence and love. Thus, Franz Marc's 1913 postcard painting *The Mare Mother of the Blue Horses* depicts a blue mare and blue foals in a rolling forest landscape with green meadows and blue hills (Schuster 1987, pl. 11). The German expressionist poet and artist Else Lasker-Schüler, whose favorite color was blue, wrote to Marc, "Blue is the suitable color for Jesus of Nazareth" (quoted in Schuster 1987, 119). In his story, Rivess carries out the reversal of significance in a subtle progression, signaled by the opposition in the title "Blue Birds of Prey." He initially depicts the early morning sky, in which the chimneys perform their "ritual purification," as blue (Rivess 1923, 28). The very next paragraph signifies a change, when the blue becomes the color of a void *(tehomikeyt,* in which the Hebrew element *tehom* evokes the mythical chaos that predates Creation in Genesis 1:1).[3] From this locus of chaos, the menacing black troop train emerges "with a devilish rush." In a rapid transformation, the soldiers' flapping blue uniforms turn them into a host of "blue birds of prey" as they rampage through the station (29). Finally, in a total reversal of the expressionist trope, the soldiers become "blue devils."

In this early story, Rivess plays on the multiple cultural connotations inherent in the sacred context of Hebrew terms by transposing them into the different though subtly related secular context of Yiddish and expressionist color symbolism. This interplay between cultural contexts is an intimation of the remarkable possibilities available to a modernist Yiddish writer thanks to the receptiveness of the fusion language. Like Markish in "At Markets and Fairs," Rivess defamiliarizes Hebrew terms associated with the sacred domain by radically recontextualizing them. Thus, at the outset of his career, he was located squarely within the contemporaneous Yiddish avant-garde. In his later Palestinian work, he expanded his range of inter- and intracultural expression. Yiddish became the vehicle for delineation of cultural and personal dilemmas in a culture whose ideology rejected it.

Refiguring Stereotypes

After Rivess immigrated to Palestine in 1924, he worked at road building, swamp draining, and other paradigmatic pioneer occupations. He was one

---

3. See my discussion in chapter 1 regarding the significance of *tehom* in the Jewish imaginary.

of the founding members of the Yiddish Writers' and Journalists' Club in Palestine in 1928, while continuing to publish in the major Yiddish centers of Warsaw and New York. His stories appeared in the Palestine Yiddish magazines almost from their inception: in *Eyns, Tsvey, Tsvishn Tsvey un Dray* (all in 1929), *Dray* (1931), *Fir* (1932), and *Shtamen* (1936). His work also appeared in the collections *Bleter tsum Ondenk fun L. Malakh* (1936) and *Eretz-yisroel Shriftn* (1937), and in the two collections titled *Undzers* (1940, 1949); he was one of the editors of the latter volume. Just before the establishment of Israel, Rivess's first volume of stories appeared in Tel-Aviv, taking its title from a story whose theme is key in his work: *Iberflants* (Transplant [1947]). A novel, *Mit der Shif Chicherin* (On the ship Chicherin), appeared in 1959.

Rivess reevaluates the idealized paradigm of the Zionist pioneer. His stories from the late 1920s and 1930s, as well as some in the 1947 *Transplant,* are stylistically rooted in the European Jewish avant-garde, which was his first literary home. Yishuv life in these stories is quite different from the monotone socialist-Zionist construct that emerged as the literary norm for the Yishuv, in which the positive characters are workers who share a common goal and bond: realization of the socialist-Zionist ideology. A representative example of a contemporaneous mainstream genre Hebrew fiction writer is Yosef Arikha, who in a 1936 story describes the Palestinian landscape and places Arab and Zionist villages in the standard oppositional terms.[4] In the "Arab" landscape, "burial mounds and tombstones squat alongside the roads, as if sunk in eternal, frozen silence. The sun, sinking toward the west, throws shadows; the shadows of hills, rocks, trees, and houses, which combine in a single mask of darkness. The environment takes on an air of gloom" (1988, 139). Arikha characterizes the new Zionist settlements in a vein that is similarly monolithic but opposite in nature. The descriptions, scattered throughout the piece, mention white houses on "Hebrew" soil, where food is proffered to the visitor without asking and children receive "princely care . . . a handsome boulevard leads to the village. In the yard children shout

4. Shaked defines Arikha as typical of most Hebrew Palestinian fiction writers between the two world wars who attempted to present the ideal as though it actually existed and who depicted the Arab community in stereotypical terms (1983, 241, 319). For a different view of Arikha, identifying him as a picaresque writer rather than as a would-be realist, see Mahalo 1991, 102–34.

gleefully in the company of large dogs. . . . In the pen a flock of sheep herds together" (141).

In Arikha's depiction, the Arab scene is lifeless and depressing; the objects function as synecdoches for a culture that Zionism perceived as lacking in the desirable values of progress and optimism—they are "frozen," and the landscape itself has "an air of gloom." Even more powerful, characterization of the local Arab culture in terms of tombstones and burial mounds links it permanently with death. In Jewish tradition, objects and locations connected with death are rendered eternally impure and can never be transmuted into or replaced by anything of positive value. The very ground is forever tainted. In contrast, the attributes of the Zionist settlements carry a diametrically opposed valence:[5] instead of emblems of death in a sinister landscape, there are white ("pure") houses for living people (metonymized by food), who are oriented toward the future (reflected in the princely treatment of the children, who have shed the diasporic European stereotype that Jews fear dogs).[6]

Rivess delineates a much more complex and nuanced picture of Zionist and non-Zionist cultures and admits a different perspective on the Yishuv. Breaking stereotypes, he thus joins the Jewish Palestinian antigenre writers. His first Palestine story "Iberflants" (Transplant), subtitled "A Fragment," appeared in *Eyns* (Rivess 1929a).[7] The very title and subtitle of this early story connote a subversion of Zionism's linearity, which envisaged a steady trajectory of personal and national progress. By viewing the pioneers as "transplants" rather than as "returning sons," Rivess infuses the prospects of the Zionist project with ambivalence. The act of transplanting, though squarely within the metaphorical domain of Zionism with its ubiquitous organic imagery, is intrinsically fraught with danger: a plant uprooted from its original home will either reroot in its new location, or it will die. The subtitle underscores this connotation: the story is not a whole entity but rather a fragment.

5. Benvenisti cites such Hebrew literary representations of the local landscape, influenced by the Arab-Zionist divide, as prefiguring the actual process of geographical renaming implemented by the Israeli government after 1948 (2000, 55–70).

6. Rivess shatters this stereotype in his "In Straits," discussed later in this chapter.

7. In my discussion of this story, I use Rivess 1929a. This version was incorporated into the novella of the same name (also dated 1929), which provided the title for Rivess's 1947 volume of stories. Pilowsky notes that 1929, the date given for the 1947 "Iberflants" (Rivess 1947b), actually refers to the date its first version was published (1986, 342n. 46).

Rivess's deep-lying concerns about the future of Zionism surface in the opening passage of the story. "Transplant" begins with a description, conventional in Zionist literature, of a group of pioneers walking out to the fields in the morning under a pale dreamy sky over dewy grass, hoes over their shoulders, with flocks of sheep grazing in the distance. A Hebrew passage in this genre, similar in setting and form, by Avraham Reichenstein, runs as follows:

> A pale light trembles on the hilltops and a deep redness is soon infused into it. The redness grows lighter, becomes golden. Streams of light swell, run over the banks of hills, and flood the valley. . . . The plain where the plowers are working is full of wild, thorny trees and bushes. The plow often strikes against underlying rocks. The person holding the plow's handle breathes heavily, his mouth open, but his eyes, bathed in the morning's glimmer, shine with a magical light. (Reichenstein 1943, 2)

In this romantic description, the Zionist pioneers blend into the ancient landscape as they take on the age-old human role of tilling the land. The rising sun suffuses them with a sense of wonder and joy that provides compensation for the physical difficulties of plowing.

Rivess's passage begins in a deceptively similar fashion, but about halfway through an abrupt change in tone shocks the reader into a radically different awareness:

> So the sky was still dull. Blurred with dream, readying itself to burst forth with sunlight. The mountaintop lit up, a sunny stream poured over the dewy grass. Flocks of sheep gathered in clumps on the mountain's back, with gentle murmurs of bells. Tall staffs of shepherds, with curved handles, pointed into space. Whistling mountains here and there, plaintively, trilling and gurgling in tearful joy. Song sounded in sheeps' hearts. And when the gang arrived at the site, the sun was already gasping with heat, fierily licking exposed bodies. The steppe grasses were thick, not a bit of earth was visible. Wild spearlike stumps thrusting sideways threatened human movement with bloody stabs. Fear of snakes, coiled dreaming in malicious repose on green-lined earth. The head of a snake-circle quivered. Pointed upward with a bloody tremble in its flat eye, listening to the noise of human feet—disturbers of their fat, congealed sleep. (Rivess 1929a, 30)

The scene is pastoral and idyllic as long as humans are passive components of the bucolic landscape. However, once the "gang" arrives to start work, the entire landscape becomes their adversary: the sun is intent on roasting them alive, the thorny bushes on ambushing them and drawing blood, and venomous snakes on biting them. This is not a motherland welcoming its returning sons, but an alien environment doing its utmost to discourage the interlopers. The land becomes a grotesque apparition, described in expressionist syntax and shifting into the surreal. Isolated elements, abstract as well as concrete, are anthropomorphized and brought to the forefront synecdochally: the sun's hostile heat, the thorns that stab maliciously, the snakes seeking revenge for their disturbed sleep. This powerful description may be viewed as a complement, set in a Zionist context, to the scene in the 1923 "Blue Birds of Prey." Whereas the humans in the earlier story are dehumanized or rendered totally inanimate, the naturally inanimate and animal elements of the Palestinian landscape in "Transplant" are given a human motivation as they seek to harm the intruders. The resulting effects are mirror images of each other: each category is divested of its innate qualities in an insult to nature itself.

Rivess achieves an even stronger effect with similar expressionistic means at the outset of "In der Machne" (In the camp [Rivess 1929b]).[8] The virtual plotlessness of this piece echoes the lack of focus that seems to envelop the characters. The "camp" consists of a haphazard, motley assortment of Zionist pioneers who apparently have nothing in common, not even their goal. The story begins with the only moment of unity shared by the characters: as if in a trance, they come together in an ecstatic dance but in the process are deprived of their physical integrity:

A circle [of dancers] turns, arms twisted over shoulders. Knees bend into each other. Slowly at first, barely touching the earth with the sole. The more they dance, the faster and more urgently they go, with choked song. Truncated, brief. A twisted garland of drunken youths twirls, heads thrown back, manes shaking. It draws in an excited girl. A second jumps in. And the earth itself twirls with them. The song rasps, as if dying, in hot mouths. And

8. Somewhat confusingly, several characters and scenes of the 1929 "Transplant" (Rivess 1929a) also appear in the 1929 "In the Camp" (Rivess 1929b), as well as in the expanded "Transplant" of the 1947 volume (Rivess 1947b).

feet do not stop, landing with a heavy thump on the hard earth. A wild
carousel whirls in dumb madness, breasts heaving with glowing breaths.
(col. 3)

This is a fevered vision, in which human entities are fragmented into disjointed body parts that function autonomously. The spectacle of disintegration is heightened by the short, jerking sentences, some of which are
syntactically deficient. The festive "garland," with its positive connotations
of joyous celebration, first becomes a metaphor for drunkards and then is
transformed into a "wild carousel" *(vilde karuzelye)*, evoking the semantic
domain of carnival, where innocent pleasure and extreme debauchery can le-
gitimately coexist or even combine. Following Mikhail Bakhtin's characterization of carnival as a locus where convention can be overthrown, the
inconceivable can be done, and the unspeakable can be said, the startling
carousel image invokes a threatening loss of values.[9] Because this circle
dance is actually a combination of disparate elements, it cannot hold. The
initial image of unity, conveyed by the wheel figure, is gradually undermined,
until the description of the dance's conclusion seals its fate: "Finally, there
had to be an end to it. The garland fell apart, like a burned hayrick" (col. 3).
The dancers do not communicate within the circle, nor can they do so after-
ward because they are metaphorically reduced to flakes of ash. Once the moment of collective hysteria dissipates, they revert to their separate, isolated
lives. "Each tent is a world unto itself," remarks the narrator in the expanded version of the story (Rivess 1947b, 145). Rivess's utilization of the
carnival trope in this manner reflects a poetic relationship with European
modernist contexts, in particular expressionism, which is rare in the contemporaneous Hebrew culture of the Yishuv.[10]

In the remarkable opening scene, Rivess also subverts a major trope of pioneering literature—the "hora" circle dance (inspired by Romanian folk

9. Bakhtin characterizes what he terms "the life of the carnival square" as being "full of
ambivalent laughter, blasphemy, the profanation of all that was holy, disparagement and ob-
scenity" and even defines a specific "carnival anatomy" in which the parts of a dismembered
body are enumerated (1973, 107, 135).

10. A salient example of comparable expressionistic poetics in Hebrew is the antigenristic
work of Nathan Bistritsky, who describes a communal dance scene in similar terms of fragmentation and alienation: "Burning fingers joined fingers and a tiny fire sparked . . . until a flame-
circle burst out . . . hands felt as strong as branches . . . and bodies hung from hands as if wrung
out . . . mouths gaped wide open . . . and feet soared in the air" (1978, 284–85).

dance) that was an integral and much-valorized part of pioneering life. Virtually every mainstream contemporaneous description of the pioneer experience speaks of "ecstatic dancing" *(rikudim be-hitlahavut),* a group act perceived as a sacramental compensation for the hardships of daily life. It is no coincidence that the secular Zionist dance experience is presented in terms taken from the Jewish culture of Hasidism, which extolled faith above study and rationalist argumentation and in which dance is perceived as one of the means to achieve freedom from the material world while drawing closer to God. Memoirists of the Second and Third Aliyahs uniformly consider the hora as the climax of their daily experience. Moshe Shoshani describes the founders of Kibbutz Ganigar dancing: "The echo of our hobnailed boots . . . was heard strongly while we danced the long, tempestuous hora dances at night," a depiction that implies group unity and strength (1964, 474). Yehuda Chorin, writing about the early days of Kibbutz Gan-Shmuel, says, "After a hard day's work, the evenings were devoted to conversation, song, and ecstatic dancing," expressing the sense of the reward offered by the dance (1964, 465). In language that verges on the metaphysical, Tzvi Amrami remembers the rapture of hora dancing in the collective settlement of Deganyah Bet during the 1924 visit of the Hebrew-Yiddish poet Yitzchak Katznelson: "Our spirits ignited into dance, with the poet in the center, stirring us up. Old and young gambol and dance to the point where material existence is transcended [*hitpashtut ha-chomer*]" (1964, 469).

Rivess subverts the significance of the group dance as a vehicle of ecstatic communal experience when at the end of "In the Camp" he reformulates it as a metaphor for the essential isolation of the pioneers. He challenges another convention by situating the bizarre dance scene at the beginning of the story. The stereotypical Zionist memoir usually begins with a description of the group's departure for work in the morning and ends with the climax of the evening hora. Here, Rivess elaborates on his approach in the "Transplant" fragment, where he begins conventionally with idyllic "morning" imagery and proceeds to shock the reader by transmuting the landscape into a malevolent entity. In "In the Camp," he reverses "normal" order altogether (exemplified in the Reichenstein passage quoted earlier, where the dawn provides the setting for a pioneer plowing scene on the second page of the novel) and jars the reader by beginning the story at the end of the workday.

The sense of estrangement within the community is reinforced as Rivess fleshes out the characters of "In the Camp." Perhaps the most obvious misfit in the group is Keller, the *yeke* who sits scratching himself as he writes to his girlfriend in Germany about the "primitive, archetypal customs of the Arab creatures" in the stereotypical, orientalizing fashion of nineteenth-century travelers (Rivess 1929b, col. 5).[11] He is not inspired to write about his uplifting experiences as a pioneer, as required by the Zionist norm. Intensely dislocated, Keller is bedeviled and deeply threatened by his own racist stereotype, "the lurking vision of a dark monkey ready to spring onto his neck from the slanted canvas surface [of the tent]" (col. 5). Feelings of despair and loneliness are especially poignant in the depictions of the women in the camp. As noted, women in Palestinian Hebrew pioneer fiction are usually presented as objects of unfocused erotic desire or as personifications of others' homesickness, in which they function as mother or sister surrogates within the men's sensibility; rarely are they allowed to speak for themselves. By contrast, in "In the Camp" Rivess makes a significant attempt to present pioneer women's dissatisfactions and frustrations. Miriam and Tsila are tent mates, but Miriam cannot subscribe to the required sense of community. When the two women return to their tent after the dance, Tsila tries to comfort Miriam but is unsuccessful: "[Miriam] herself did not know why hatred toward the entire world swarmed inside her. She slid her hand out from under her friend's arm, letting it hang loosely in a kind of painful emptiness, remaining disconnected from the body. Like a cast-out fish on the shore" (col. 5). The image of the detached arm, emphasized through modernist syntax, particularizes the group's fragmentation during the dance as it zooms in on an individual whose body parts are detached from each other and from her own subjectivity. What little conversation there is between the two women revolves around unsatisfactory relationships within the group. In a later passage, Tsila sits patching her shirt impatiently while Miriam combs her hair, "silently, bitterly, her black eyes staring into a vast space." In a malignant and intensified reprise of Keller's monkey nightmare, "the silence crept down from the canvas walls and pinched itself around her. Very soon nothing would remain of her" (col. 6).

Before the characters of "Transplant" are differentiated, they are referred to collectively as a "camp of young people [*machne yungen*]" (Rivess 1929a, 31). In the very title of the story, Rivess is using the multivalency of the Yiddish *machne,* which can mean both "multitude" and "camp." The residents of the "camp" are soon revealed as a disparate collection of people

11. It is intriguing that later Jewish immigrants from Germany who came in the 1930s continued to be tagged disparagingly as *yekes* for decades.

differing in abilities, age, and ideological nuancing—a heterogeneity that Rivess exposes by exploiting the "openness" of his Yiddish medium, using a particular Yiddish dialect or even introducing inserts in another language. He initially deploys traditional techniques of characterization. The collective image that has been established is immediately subverted, first by the description of individual physical features. The first member of this "camp of young people," Shpigl, is an older man "of a certain age" *(in di shonim,* literally "in the years"), whose "bundle of years has made him stiff" (31–32). The next character, Rekhtman, is marked at first by external attributes—his clothing. His European dandyism *("frantishkeyt fun der alter heym"* [dandyism from the old home]) persists in the new homeland, where he avoids the hard work of tilling the soil for fear of wrinkling his trousers. Rekhtman is a cynic who does not admire physical labor and thus runs against the grain of the ideology that valorized labor and disdained the propriety of bourgeois appearances. His cynicism extends to the Zionist vision, according to which the benefits of labor would accrue to the entire collective: "We will forever be plowing our noses into the ground. Our petty bureaucrats [*pekidimlekh*] will stroll in the forest, not we" (32), says Rekhtman in "Transplant," combining the Hebrew *pekidim* (clerks) with the Yiddish diminutive suffix *-lekh.*

The heterogeneity of the group now begins to emerge in greater detail as Rivess employs a range of dialect and language variations in a form of Bakhtinian heteroglossia ("a multiplicity of social voices and a wide variety of their links and interrelationships, always more or less dialogized" [Bakhtin 1981, 263]) as well as actual polyglossia. In "In the Camp," Keller, the Jew from Germany is, in fact, speaking German transcribed as Yiddish. This was an established device as far back as Haskalah Yiddish literature, in which *daytshmerish* (pretentiously cultured, pseudo-German Yiddish) was used to ridicule Jews who adopted the outward trappings of culture, symbolized by German. Thematizing both the alien surroundings and the plurality of languages, Keller asks his tent mate, Rekhtman, for the name of the common Arab headdress, interpolating the Arabic plural *falacheen* (peasants) in his mispronounced and syntactically Germanicized Yiddish *("di shnire vas di fellachen oyf den kepfen tragen").* Rekhtman brushes him off impatiently in a very idiomatic Yiddish: "What is he bothering me about [*vos hakt er mir a tshaynik*], the *yeklman?*"—adding ridicule to the pejorative *yeke* by diminishing it to *yekl,* a Yiddish synonym for "fool." Keller's alienation is intensified by the fact that he has trouble articulating his thoughts even in his native language: he expostulates "to the devil!" (5) as he seeks the term that seems to hover at the edge of his consciousness.

For a better appreciation of Rivess's use of dialect, a few words are in order about Yiddish dialects and their social significance. Eastern Yiddish (as distinct from western Yiddish, the language of Jews in Germany and its surrounding countries) can be grouped in three major categories, popularly known by their geographic location: "Polish" (central), "Lithuanian" (northeastern), and "Ukrainian" (southeastern) Yiddish. The dialects developed centuries ago; Vilna became the geographical center of the "Lithuanian" dialect and Warsaw the center of the "Polish" dialect. The opposition between the dialects was heightened in the wake of discord between Hasidism (whose adherents were identified as speaking "Polish" Yiddish), based primarily in central and southeastern Europe, and the Lithuanian-centered movement (its members identified as speaking "Lithuanian" Yiddish). For unknown reasons, the "Lithuanian" dialect came to be construed as the more desirable of the two. Over time, a consensus emerged among secular young people who considered "Lithuanian" Yiddish more literary (M. Weinreich 1980, 18–20). The different dialects also denoted "strongly opposed stereotypes of mentality and behavior" (Harshav 1990, 79). Thus, in I. L. Perets's well-known story "Oyb nit nokh hekher" (If not higher [1990, originally published in 1900]), the "Litvak" (Lithuanian) who sets out to debunk a revered Hasidic rebbe is depicted as highly skeptical and somewhat arrogant. These stereotypes are still so ingrained that a modern dictionary defines *Litvak,* in addition to *Lithuanian Jew,* as "(proverbially) an incredulous, rationalistic, learned, strictly observant person" (U. Weinreich 1968, 224).

In "In the Camp," Rivess fleshes out Rekhtman's character by a conventional linguistic marker: Rekhtman speaks an idiomatic Yiddish that indicates his origin. When he says, *"di por hoyzn el yakh nokh trogn"* (I will still wear this pair of pants [Rivess 1929b, col. 5]), the use of the regional *el yakh* rather than the normative *vel ikh* is a representation of the Warsaw Yiddish dialect. A character who appears in the earlier "Transplant," bearing the lowly name Fussbeynkel (Footstool), is similarly marked: tired of working, he declares, *"Belgishe ferd zoln arbetn, nisht ekh"* (let Belgian horses work, not me [Rivess 1929a, 33]), using the nonnormative "Polish" Yiddish *ekh* for *ikh.* Also in "Transplant," Yeruchamzon the "Litvak" is immediately identified by his dialect, which often transposes *s* for *sh:* "*svayg soyn, stik neveyle*" (shut up, you scumbag) instead of the normative "*shvayg shoyn, shtik,"* and so on (32). He is indelibly stereotyped by his comrades, who term him *"Litvak-ganev"* (Lithuanian thief [32])—in the popular imagination, Lithuanian Jews use their proverbial quick-wittedness for devious purposes. Yeruchamzon carries on a running feud with the slow-witted Fussbeynkel in a type of comic relief. The two characters speak a Yiddish that is replete with idioms: *"er hot shoyn flign in noz"* (already he has flies in his nose), says Yeruchamzon about Fussbeynkel's restlessness in the later version of "Transplant" (Rivess 1947b, 146). Keller is stereotyped from the outset as a *yeke.*

In the earlier version of "Transplant," the Ukrainian Siomka Perlov, who survived a pogrom thanks to his non-Jewish appearance, hurls a Slavic anti-Jewish curse at his comrades: *"ekh ty zhidovskaya morda!"* (oh, you kike face! [1929a, 33]). Now that Siomka is in Palestine, says the narrator, he "bent his tongue and speaks in a newfound language—Hebrew" (33). In the expanded version of "Transplant," it is Siomka who voices a central tenet of the new Yishuv culture: "Here one is not asked where one comes from—one sprouts anew here" (1947b, 133). Applying conventional Zionist metaphorics, Siomka echoes the idea of creating new persons who will constitute the new nation in the ancestral homeland. It is the potential "slipperiness" of ethnic, regional, and linguistic categories that enables the "transplantation" of diasporic Jews. Yet, paradoxically, the characters in these early stories are immediately stigmatized as stereotypically representative of their diasporic locations. It is very clear from the conversation that no one in the pioneer group is speaking Hebrew; the old-new language does not fulfil its unifying function.

Mirror Images: Strangers and Us

"Zhukess" (Bugs [Rivess 1929c]) marks a different type of departure from the stereotypical Zionist narrative, with Yiddish serving once again as the vehicle for an unconventional view of the Yishuv. The protagonist of this story is an almost total anomaly in his society. He is immediately—and doubly—marked as an outsider when he is introduced in the first words of the story as *"der alter Rechavya"* (the old guy Rechavya [2]), a phrasing that instantly locates him in a complex cultural limbo. First, his rare biblical name is not traditional for Ashkenazis, the majority of Palestinian Jews at the time.[12] We soon discover that Rechavya is an Iraqi Jew and as such a member of the Sephardic minority in the Yishuv. His move to Palestine thirty years earlier

---

12. The name appears in I Chronicles 23, 24, and 26 in lists of Moses' descendants.

was sparked not by modern Zionism with its European roots, but by a traditional religious connection; he came "back to the land of the forefathers" (5). Second, his identification as "the old guy" makes him incongruous in a culture that idolizes youth and innovativeness. As he prepares to take a group of boisterous local Jewish teenagers to clear the almond orchard of insect pests, "he met the newcomers, young boys and girls, newly sprouted, very young, with pent-up anger in his eyes, so much that he felt a burning in his stomach" (2–3). The very youthfulness of his charges is an irritation rather than a delightful promise. His class situation also proves to be liminal: as a foreman for the Jewish property owners in a well-established colony, he is neither a penniless, socialist pioneer nor a relatively rich farmer who owns his own land. In a political limbo, he takes no stance in the ideological conflicts between the socialist pioneers and the nonsocialist old-timers. The fact that he is represented in Yiddish, a language that, although Jewish, is not his native one, underscores his displacement. Rechavya is doubly dispossessed from his own Iraqi Jewish culture in this society that flaunts the banner of a home for all Jews, by living in physical circumstances in which he is an isolated Sephardic Jew in a Europe-oriented context and by being forced into a European Jewish culture by agency of the language in which his consciousness is represented.

Hankering after the romanticism of the early days, he does not subscribe to the communal passion for settlement and construction on the land (in Zionist terminology, "making the desert bloom"). On the contrary, "inside the town borders he feels more and more imprisoned every day" (3), an ironic contrast to the meaning of his name, which implies spaciousness. Rechavya is deeply nostalgic for the days when "the land was free as far as the eye could see. . . . [E]verything here was empty. Naked fields. Jackals roamed here freely, their greedy snouts restlessly waiting for warm-blooded prey" (3–5). By giving the jackal a positive valence within Rechavya's sensibility, Rivess reverses the stereotypical role of this animal in Zionist culture and further underscores his protagonist's irregular cultural situation. The jackal—a ubiquitous, foxlike, nocturnal scavenger with a distinctive, penetrating wail—was usually construed as the epitome of everything negative and threatening that the Zionists sought to eliminate from the country, in particular Arab hostility toward the Zionist project.[13] For Rechavya, how-

---

13. Rivess again employs the jackal motif effectively in his 1944 story "In Klem" (In Straits [1947c], discussed later). In Hebrew literature, the theme of the jackal as an emblem of local

ever, the jackals embody the lost freedom of the open spaces that are now fenced in, and thus, by extension, they represent a loss of individualism. When he imagines the jackals positively, he is attributing a positive value to the "wasteland," which Zionism negated.[14]

Moreover, it is the newcomers and their alien, European values who are the major cause of Rechavya's frustration: "They who come from other countries, they totally spoil the world. They have corrupted Ovadya's son, Ovadya, who now dresses like the Ashkenazis" (4). Although Rechavya himself is an immigrant, he considers himself a native and feels profoundly threatened by the encroaching European modernity. Rivess persuasively represents Rechavya's inner consciousness by deploying the early modernist European technique of narrated monologue at key moments in the text. Dorrit Cohn defines this novelistic technique (also termed *style indirect libre*) as the presentation of a character's mental discourse in the guise of the narrator's discourse, maintaining the third-person reference (1978, 13–14). In Rivess's representation of Rechavya's nostalgia for the old days, Rechavya's consciousness is voiced halfway through the narrator's description: "[Then] he was the only shepherd, wandering with the flock of sheep anywhere he wanted, everything belonged to him . . . Why, today one can't even give a yell out loud . . . Hemmed in on all sides . . . Brick walls and enclosing fences . . ." (Rivess 1929c, 3, ellipses in the original). The shift into the character's perspective is marked by the move into the present tense, in an idiom different from that of the narrator. Rivess uses narrated monologue in other stories as well to provide insight into his characters' sensibilities.

The representation of Rechavya's inner consciousness is all the more effective because it is a translation of one idiom into another. Rechavya would probably be thinking in his mother tongue, Arabic, or in the Jewish Baghdadi dialect—both Semitic languages—yet his thoughts are transmitted in Yiddish, primarily a Germanic language. The effect upon readers occurs in two phases: our first reaction as Yiddish readers is empathy with Rechavya's unhappiness because his plight is made immediately accessible. Only when we

---

hostility is developed perhaps most notably in the work of Amos Oz several decades later, titled *Artzot ha-Tan* (The lands of the jackal [1965]).

14. This positive view echoes the romantic, idealizing depiction of the "untamed" land, expressed in the popular song "Yafim ha-Leilot bi-Khna'an" (Lovely are the nights in Canaan), in which the refrain glorifies the melancholy wail of the jackal; see my discussion of a different echo of this song in chapter 2.

become aware of the discrepancy between Rechavya's inner language and the language of his represented thought do we grasp the extent of his dislocation. The resulting portrayal of cultural conflict is rare in Yishuv literature. Rechavya's represented language reflects his cultural difference: he was educated not in a modern European Jewish school with teachers who sought to instill European languages and values, but in a Baghdad synagogue.

Unlike the representations of the speech of European immigrants in Rivess's earlier stories, Rechavya's speech is laced with Arabic idioms rather than with European or Yiddish ones. He uses Arabic exclamations such as *"yallah"* (get a move on) for the Jewish youngsters (3) and addresses the Arab worker Mustafa familiarly with the Arabic greeting *"kif chalak"* (how are you [6]). Rechavya's exchanges with the local youngsters are represented as standard Yiddish liberally interspersed with transliterated Arabic phrases that convey his cultural milieu (his knowledge of Arabic most likely stems equally from his past in Baghdad and from the decades he has spent with Arab laborers in Palestine). This familiarity with Arab culture again marks Rechavya as an exception to the Zionist norm of the 1920s and as a throwback to the cultural ambiguity of the Second Aliyah period with its idealization of that culture. He is at home in the Middle East but alienated in the Jewish Yishuv, where his home ought to be; he seems to have no friends in the settlement and is most comfortable in the company of the native Arabs. The Jewish teenagers who by their very existence assure the future of the Zionist project are a source of irritation to him. At the close of the story, Rechavya is disappointed in the younger generation. In fact, we begin to suspect that the rowdy teenagers are the real "bugs" of the title. When one of the boys releases the captured insects, Rechavya says: *"N-n-eh,* children, what a savage that is. He will never become a respectable person [*layt*]. To the devil . . ."* (11, ellipsis in the original). For Rechavya, the true goal is the vision of becoming a "respectable person" in traditional terms taken from the social lexicon of European Jews, rather than the Zionist dream of creating the "new Hebrew."

Although the entire Yiddish project in the Yishuv constituted a violation of Zionist ideology, the deviation from these ideological standards is perhaps most striking when Rivess uses Yiddish, the Jewish language that was construed as non-Zionist, to portray the sensibility of alienated non-Jewish protagonists. Yishuv culture was engrossed with the challenges and problems of the Zionist project almost exclusively from its own point of view. In the works coinciding with this project, the local Arab natives, the most commonly depicted non-Jews, were usually limned in stereotypical orientalizing terms as part of an exotic, static "native" backdrop. Moshe Stavi's 1930 collection of stories *ha-Boker Or* (At morning light) includes Arab "folktales" and vignettes in the prevalent rather patronizing anthropological vein, emphasizing the conventional view that Arabs lacked initiative and energy in the European sense.[15] His story "Ba-negev" (In the Negev [Stavi 1930, 14–32]), for instance, depicts a small farming community of Arabs beset by drought and stolidly awaiting the visit of tax assessors, and characterizes them monolithically as follows: "The village waited for the assessors, waited longingly, with strange submissive patience and stupid humility" (15). Throughout this story and others, Stavi does not individualize the Arab villagers.

Rivess therefore charts new thematic territory in "Tayve" (Lust [Rivess 1936, 40–45]), a coming-of-age story written from a highly marginal perspective. The protagonist, Salach, is a local sixteen-year-old male Arab whose world is beginning to oscillate between Muslim tradition and the new European Zionist values that are gradually affecting the ancient Mediterranean port city of Jaffa, where he lives. He has been the only male in his family since the death of his father in a coffeehouse brawl three years earlier. Salach's existence is liminal: neither boy nor man, lacking a father but not yet one himself, he prefers to spend his time on the beach—the borderline region where outside influences collide with local ones. Salach does not join the undifferentiated, barely human "piles of Arabs sitting with their legs folded under, who sit side by side, more silent than speaking" (40) and who are absorbed in the rhythmic fingering of their worry beads—a stock Western metonymy for the "passivity" of the East. Neither is he a participant in the "rows of naked slaves," the stevedores and porters who carry loads from ship to shore. He sits solitary on the sea wall that demarcates and protects the familiar from the alien, "gazing out to sea with eyes wide open" (40). It quickly becomes clear that Salach is in the process of choosing between a modern world and his own traditional one.

Salach is enthralled by the developing Jewish city of Tel-Aviv, adjoining Jaffa "on the flat beach, where thousands of white houses and long tidy streets are being built" (42). In an expressionist reversal of conventional European tropes, the bright new homes and straight, clean streets spell out temptation, as opposed to the "dark, narrow alleys of Jaffa with the extin-

---

15. As mentioned, Stavi was one of the Yiddish writers of the Second Aliyah who began his career in Yiddish (using his original name, Stavski) and later switched to Hebrew.

guished, boarded-up houses" (43). When seen through Salach's sensibilities, it is the new settlers who are the exotics, with a culture that is unsettlingly attractive. The political and erotic stereotypes of the dangerously seductive Arabs are overturned: it is the Jews who threaten to corrupt him. Wandering through Tel-Aviv, Salach "is totally intoxicated as if by wine" (43). This comparison indicates the first breach in his traditional system of values because devout Muslims are forbidden to drink alcohol.

Salach struggles with his own developing sexuality, terrified of the freedom that the Jewish women seem to promise. He compares the Jewish women with his own sisters: "They [the Jewish newcomers] are rich, their wives are beautiful and go about free and clear with bared bodies. He was seized by an aversion to his home with its barred windows. Muslim women, shrouded in black from head to toe, come to chat with his mother—and when they see him, the big youth, they quickly conceal their faces with their black veils. When his four sisters are grown, they will also cover their faces" (42). At this significant juncture, when modernity is identified with open sexuality, Salach's confusion is revealed through narrated monologue marked by a shift into the present tense and the protagonist's idiom as he sees himself through the women's sensibilities ("when they see him, the big youth, they quickly conceal their faces with their black veils"). He appears to attach no sexual significance to the Muslim women he usually encounters; they are identified either with his mother's friends or with his prepubescent sisters. The Jewish women of Tel-Aviv, in contrast, dressed in European fashion, are probably the first ones he has ever seen uncovered. This vision conjoins with his own sexual awakening, and the Jewish women become emblems as well as objects of an erotic desire he has not experienced previously.

In this world of upset certainties, the distinctions between animate and inanimate blur in Salach's heightened awareness as he roams the streets of Tel-Aviv:

> The electric signs in enormous show windows dazzled and confused him. So many elegant mannequins beckoned and smiled at him from the display windows, with naked shoulders and hands so artfully placed at their waists. Suddenly he was attracted by a movie advertisement: a greenish light flowed up and down a gigantic wall. Two crude heads, a man and a woman, cut out of colorful cardboard, kissed each other on the lips. (43)

The store mannequins and the cut-out figures in the movie advertisement seem alive, beckoning him and kissing each other. The cardboard figures take on added significance in Salach's lexicon of tropes because of their illumination in green: in Muslim tradition, green is the color of paradise, where easy access to women is a key component of masculine pleasure. Thus, the liquid green radiance turns the cardboard kiss into a glimpse of heaven. When he enters the cinema, the boundaries between the swiftly moving shadows on the screen and a flesh-and-blood, bare-shouldered woman in a seat across the aisle are totally obscured:

> Salach blinked his eyes, unable to grasp the speed with which the images changed—and now he was tempted by a fat woman in a seat across from him, the deep exposure of her fleshy shoulder drove him crazy, his chest became hot—and here on the screen he again saw half-naked dancers lifting their shapely legs. His eyes burned, boring into the bare shoulder across the way. His seat could no longer hold him. The light came on in the hall. On leaden feet, he went outside to refresh himself in the open air. (43)

At the close of the story, the ambiguity of his cultural situation, which has been compromised by his glimpse into alien values, forces him into the sea, where he spent many hours as a child diving for coins thrown by tourists—now not a workplace but the site of erotic play. On impulse, he plunges into the waves to "rescue" a Jewish woman who is playfully tussling with her boyfriend. As she whines childishly that she is afraid, "Salach feels that he would like to carry the pretty girl far, far away in the sea. But he cannot speak, he is as mute as a fish. He repeatedly utters a wild cry from his breast and somersaults into the noisy water" (44–45). Salach, who has lost the ability to communicate with his own culture, chooses water—the element in which human voices are inaudible and human identity is obscured. In an expressionist moment of alienation, disembodied shouts from the beach make a fragmented attempt to label the threatening Other: "Wet bodies with open mouths were astonished. 'A fish! A whale has lost its way! . . . There he is! A little Oriental Jew [*frenkl*]! An Arab!' " (45). Indeed, Salach is like a whale in danger of beaching on an alien shore. He swims away powerfully toward Jaffa, becoming part of the seascape, in which "sky and water flowed together into one blueness" (45). He has found refuge in the blue sea, with its expressionist connotations of love and innocence—the same sea on whose shore we first glimpsed him as a child longing for his dead father. For the moment, the sea-land opposition has been settled in favor of the former.

An early key image of the story prefigures its end through the use of a biblical simile. As Salach sits on the seawall, he ruminates about the great numbers of Jews that he has seen arriving in the country and "are already as numerous as sand on the seashore" (42). As noted previously, his incongruous position is initially indicated when his non-Jewish sensibility is articulated in Yiddish. Now Rivess ironizes Salach's situation by having him, the Arab, use a traditional biblical phrase that is an integral part of Jewish discourse. Salach quotes almost verbatim from the Bible, where the phrase "as numerous as the sand on the seashore" is a common simile for a populous, powerful folk. Though the phrase is sometimes used in the Bible to denote a conqueror who will overwhelm Israel (Jud. 7:12; I Sam. 13:5), it is most significantly linked with Genesis, when, after the Binding of Isaac, God promises Abraham, "I will multiply your descendants as the stars of heaven and as the sand which is on the seashore" (Gen. 22:17). Ever since, Jews have adopted the phrase to denote Jewish prosperity and power.[16] Thus, Salach's instinctive perception that his native culture is doomed by Zionism is imparted through the most conventional biblical expression for the success of the Jewish people—comically secularized by reference to the newcomers' habit of playing on the beach. Rivess could have presented the biblical quote in the original Hebrew—accessible to Yiddish readers—but he instead gives it in Yiddish, the language that Zionism considered subversive. Using Yiddish as a vehicle to convey Salach's ambiguous, confused state further complicates his quandary because it exposes the inherent colonialist dilemma of the situation: the native Palestinian non-Jew is displaced by using the dominant Jewish lexicon of images and the de facto language of Jews in Palestine. Though Salach flees back to his dark home as the story ends, he has in fact been deprived of his heritage and belongs to neither world.

In "Lust," schematic and simplistic as its protagonist is, Rivess provides a rare critique of the effect of European modernity in general and of Jewish settlement in particular on time-honored local Arab culture. Salach, disaffected with his own tradition and ill at ease with the new ways that confront

16. The description of King Solomon's reign, the idealized Golden Age of biblical Israel, has "Judah and Israel . . . as many as the sand by the sea; they ate and drank and were happy" (1 Kgs. 4:20). The simile reappears in Isaiah (48:19), obviously echoing earlier occurrences, to signify the reward awaiting the Israelites if they follow God's commandments.

him, may perhaps be construed as a prototypical Arab *talush,* alienated and
set adrift through the intrusion of modernity represented by the agency of the
Zionist pioneers. His ethnic identity is obscured, as the Jewish bathers on the
beach try to identify his affiliation, appending a diminutive to the Yiddish
derogatory term *frenk* for eastern Jew: "A *frenkl*! An Arab!" (45). Gila Ramras-Rauch charts the development of the Arab figure in Hebrew Yishuv and
Israeli literature from the beginning of the century; she cites Brenner as the
writer who, in *Shekhol ve-Khishalon,* "depicts for the first time the entrance
of the Arab into the Jewish psyche" (1989, 44). If we reverse this definition,
Rivess may be considered one of the few (if not the only) Jewish Palestinian
writers of the period who portray the Jew entering the psyche of the Arab
and the consequences of this intrusion.[17]

Rivess expands the definition of alienation in his 1944 "In Klem" (In
straits [Rivess 1947c, 36–48]). The protagonist, Popiel, is perhaps the ultimate outsider in a Zionist environment: an anti-Semitic non-Jew who finds
himself in Palestine unwillingly as part of the "Anders army."[18] As in Rivess's
earlier stories, representation of the protagonist in Yiddish produces a powerful irony: this anti-Semite is made to formulate his consciousness in the language that emblematizes the people he despises. Popiel is bitterly unhappy in
Tel-Aviv. His sense of estrangement in an alien world is concretized in the
opening sentences of the story: "The next morning, after a night of jackal
wails from the sandy deserts, Frantishek Popiel moved himself out of his tent
into the dawning outdoors. During the few days that he has been here in the
Polish camp, since they were evacuated from Persia, he has been seeing himself solely as if imprisoned among the canvas tents, drawn taut by rope" (36).

---

17. The thematic of "the Jew in the psyche of the Arab" was not picked up again in a major
way until A. B. Yehoshua's *ha-Me'ahev* (The lover [1977]), in which one of the main characters
is an Arab teenager who is at home neither in his native culture and society nor in Jewish Israeli
culture and society. For a survey of changing attitudes toward the native Arabs in Hebrew literature, see Ben-Ezer 1992.

18. After being attacked by Germany in 1941, the USSR released Poles who had been held
since 1939 because they had refused to join the Soviet army. Headed by General Wladislaw Anders, seventy-seven thousand men and as many as one hundred thousand women and children
dependents reached Palestine by way of Persia in 1942. The men underwent extensive training
by the British army and eventually fought alongside British units in Italy from 1943 to 1945. Approximately four thousand European Jews managed to join Anders, seeing this as their chance
to circumvent the British Mandate's strict limits on Jewish immigration to Palestine; three-
quarters of these Jews deserted and remained in the Yishuv (Dear 1995, 36–37).

The deceptively straightforward first sentence is fraught with complex cultural and ideological implications. Images of morning and dawn were highly significant and ubiquitous in modern ideologies in general and in Zionism in particular: the emergence of a new society was often likened to a "new dawn." Popiel, however, coming out of the tent after a sleepless night, is exchanging one uncomfortable situation for another.

Rivess applies a literary convention of the Yishuv when he uses the jackal as an emblem of all that is inimical to Europeans in Palestine, but Popiel's attitude toward jackals is different from that of conventional Zionists or even that of Rechavya in "Bugs." This stranger, unlike the Zionists, has no motivation to overcome the innate hostility of the country symbolized by the animals, nor does he regard the jackals with nostalgia, as Rechavya does. For him, the jackals and the sandy deserts are a permanent menace, resistant to metaphorical sublimation. Rivess's use of the reflexive verb compound *"zikh aroysgeklibn"* (moved himself out of), which usually implies "to move out of one's lodgings," to describe Popiel's exit from his tent emphasizes Popiel's sense of being adrift; the tent is a shelter, not a home. The second sentence of the story is couched in the present tense, emphasizing Popiel's sense of ongoing punishment. In what may be an eerie gesture toward the concentration camps of Europe, whose existence and role were becoming known in the Yishuv by 1944, Popiel considers himself imprisoned in Palestine.

Popiel, in civilian life a tax collector, curses when he identifies "Jewish faces" among his fellow trainees. In the cultural climate of the Yishuv, this non-Jewish character is doubly displaced by Rivess's deployment of polyglossia. Popiel's situation is further complicated in a virtuoso passage in which he watches Zionist pioneers crushing rock for a new road. The cultural problematics of the Yishuv are conveyed through the prism of his sensibility, as he and the reader are exposed to three transliterated languages within the frame of a fourth. First, Popiel is addressed in an idiosyncratic transliteration of Arabic: *"Markheba, ya efendi!"* (Good morning, master! [37]). Then,

a sunburned youth, like a lump of copper, yelled from atop a pile of stones: *"Ya selami, 'panye plutonovi!'"* [Peace be with you, "Mr. Platoon Commander"]. Hammers struck the rock rhythmically and words flew: *"Finfte Aliye!"* [Fifth Aliyah!] *"Yetsies Poyln!"* [Exodus from Poland!] *"Fule zhmenyes sertifikaten!"* [Fistfuls of certificates!] *"Okh un vey tsu mayn tatn!"* [Misery and woe to my father!]. A youth interwove into the stone clacking: *"Zbuduyen doley, zbuduyen vyentsey—zbuduyen pyentro do sto tishentsey!"* [We will build further, we will build more, we will build ten thousand floors!]. (37)

This extraordinary linguistic melange, the words flying in the air like stone chips, incorporates Yiddish (the frame language), Arabic *(marcheba, ya efendi; ya selami)*, Hebrew *(aliyah; yetsies*—the Yiddishized form of *yetsi'at,* the word used in construct form to describe the biblical Exodus from Egypt), the international lexicon *(sertifikaten* with a Germanic ending, used in the context of British government terminology), and Polish *(panye plutonovyi* as well as the chant that seems to taunt the Polish bystander). The result is a vivid illustration of the multifaceted cultural swirl into which Popiel has been thrust.

The social intricacies that this polyglossia indicates are complex. In a society where the Jewish pioneers are dominant, Popiel is first hailed by the Jewish workers as an Arab landowner *(efendi)*. Next, both his ethnicity and his military affiliation are mocked in the very act of acknowledgment when he is addressed derisively in Polish, after an Arabic salutation *(Ya selami),* as *"panye plutonovi"* (Mr. Platoon Commander). He serves as a conduit for some of the dissonances in Yishuv society as he hears the exchange "Fifth Aliyah /Exodus from Poland / Fistfuls of certificates" (during the Fifth Aliyah, the British Mandate authorities granted immigration permits, "certificates," to those who could prove that they possessed a specified amount of money).[19] *"Yetsies Poyln"* incorporates *yetsies mitsrayim,* the hallowed term for the original Exodus from Egypt, but is also an idiom for a long, hard ordeal; here it satirizes the Fourth ("Grabski") Aliyah. "Misery and woe to my father," a stereotypical Yiddish phrase denoting misfortune, seems to sum up these "disasters." Finally, the Jewish pioneers from Poland voice, in Polish, what seems to be a mocking variation on a popular Hebrew song that extols

19. This proof of funds was often a fiction. In the 1930s, for example, individual members of the Ha-shomer Ha-tza'ir youth movement in New York shifted the same lump sum between their personal bank accounts and fooled the British authorities into believing that each of them was wealthy. (Segal 1990).

the act of building the Jewish homeland.[20] Popiel, who cannot join in this bantering exchange that he perceives to be directed at himself (at least the part that is in his language), feels "the earth burning under his feet" (37) when the Zionists voice this future-oriented song. He quits the scene in a futile rage as the transliterated languages create a bewildering cultural kaleidoscope that prefigures his own confused sense of identity.

After Popiel is exempted from active service because of his health and is relocated in Tel-Aviv, he is cut off from the society of his fellow soldiers and totally isolated. He cannot communicate even with his roommate, a deaf Polish sailor. Utterly displaced, he finds some solace and company in a Polish bar that has been incongruously transplanted to Tel-Aviv. Popiel blames the Jews for his plight and cannot accept the fact that in his new topsy-turvy existence the Jews are in a superior position. Underscoring this reversal of status, his Jewish landlord, Rindfleysh (Beef), is always accompanied by a dog. The image of the Jew with the dog compounds Popiel's disorientation because, according to European stereotype, dogs, owned by non-Jews, metonymize anti-Semitism. This barking "Jewish" dog, expressing Jewish dominance and seeming to seek a Jewish revenge, is the marker for Popiel's anti-Semitism, articulated in Yiddish through his confused consciousness. The text thus becomes a type of "Jewish revenge" at the same time that it forces the Jewish reader to humanize even the racist. This revenge is all the more striking given the date of the story—1944, when the full extent of the catastrophe striking the Jews in Europe was beginning to be known (Kronfeld 1999).

Popiel's existential crisis deepens dramatically when he comes to doubt his very identity during a religious pilgrimage to Jerusalem, Bethlehem, and Nazareth. The train trope, which Rivess first manipulated in his 1923 "Blue Birds of Prey," is reworked, as Popiel is situated on the train to Jerusalem, along with other Polish pilgrims en route to Catholic holy sites. In this displacement of the diasporic Jewish train culture into Yishuv society, it is the Poles who are members of a minority group and take on a "Jewish" identity as they create a traveling community. As the train winds toward Jerusalem, Popiel feels increasingly menaced by the very landscape in an inversion of the

20. The first line of this song runs *"Anu banu artza livnot u-le-hibanot ba"* (We have come to the land to build and be built [to be rejuvenated] in it). The phrase *livnot u-le-hibanot* (to build and be built) became a code phrase for the Zionist ideal in which settlement in Palestine would provide the remedy for the ills of the Jewish people.

landscape-train relationship in "Blue Birds of Prey," but conveyed by similar expressionist techniques: "The train winds, snakelike, along the mountain slopes. . . . Here come mountain cliffs, hanging upside-down, touching the train's windows and bringing darkness to Popiel's eyes. Soon the train rushes into an abyss again, while on the other side shrouded mountains appear, tall, gigantic, endless" (44). Whereas in "Blue Birds of Prey" the serene landscape poses an extreme contrast to the violence represented by the train, here the hills and valleys—in actuality quite moderate—are exaggerated and take on hostile qualities. In an expressionistic move, the rocks become cliffs that seem to attack the train's windows, the hills loom sky high, and the valley is transformed into an abyss. The train, a traveling enclave of "our own kind, Catholics [*eygene mentshen, katoliken*]" (43), is an island of security in a topsy-turvy world that Popiel perceives as threatening.

Expanding the mirror image, Rivess presents the Holy Land through a sensibility that excludes everything inconsistent with the protagonist's own religious culture. Popiel cannot acknowledge, much less appreciate, anything related to modern Palestine or to the Zionist Yishuv (in much the same way that Zionists excluded full awareness and perception of the country and its native population, Jews as well as Arabs). He sees in Jerusalem only that which is connected with various Christian churches; he is bewildered by the sheer variety of Christian denominations, identified by their clothing. These brands of Christianity are more alien to him than the Jerusalem Old Yishuv Jews, who resemble the Jews he knows from Poland: "Monks in long beards and conical hats . . . Capuchin monks in yarmulkes, long belted brown robes, barefoot in sandals . . . priests in broad-brimmed hats and black fluttering coats [*kapotes*] . . . strange-looking monks with black hoods over their eyes" (44). The parade of Eastern and Western church functionaries—Armenians, Franciscans, Greek Orthodox—is characterized by descriptive terms for traditional Jewish garb (yarmulke, *kapote*) with which Popiel is familiar, despite his hostility. This confusion between Christians and Jews seems to foreshadow the ultimate disintegration of his personality. As the nomadic community of Christians travels to the holy sites of Bethlehem and Nazareth, Popiel is impatient to see "where the cradle of Lord Jesus stood, to see the fields where he tended the sheep, the holy mountain on which he stood and where he ascended to heaven" (45). By filtering a view of the Land of Israel through the selective vision of a non-Jew, radically defamiliarizing the Zionist experience, Rivess tacitly admits the legitimacy of a different perception while exposing the limitations of a hegemonic view. Though Salach in

"Lust" is alien to the Yishuv, he is nonetheless a native son of the land. Popiel, however, is a complete stranger who cannot adjust his perceptions and thus offers unique insight into his own condition and that of his surroundings.

In the climactic scene of the pilgrimage, the Christian Popiel undergoes a shift that completes his self-alienation: he develops the theory that the Jews are half-Christians. He is even more shocked when he grasps that, by the same token, "we Christians are half-Jews. . . . It seemed to Popiel that he was drawn back to the Jewish Tel-Aviv, to his half-brothers. . . . The idea that he was half-Jewish continued to torment him. . . . Now on the streets he was more assertive, striding with a sure step, just as if he had a share in the trade of the crowded stores" (45). His world and identity blur as he descends into uncertainty. As he muses alcoholically, his very name is incorporated by alliteration into the cultural no-man's-land where he is now located: the name "Popiel" resonates as he mutters "Poyln-Palestina, Palestina-Poyln" (46). The two homelands, Jewish and Christian, are now conflated. As the story draws to a close, even Tel-Aviv's blue sea (the native Salach's way home), which had comforted Popiel when he envisioned it as his lifeline to his home in Poland, fails him when the beach is overrun by Jews. It is Rosh Hashanah, the Jewish New Year, when Orthodox Jews observe the custom of figuratively casting out the previous year's sins by standing at the shore of a river or a sea and praying. "The sea caused him to forget the city, the people. . . . He longed to swim away into the sea's distance; would he get to Poland? He stood for a long time on the cement pier, lulled by the music of the sea, and did not notice that behind him, out of all the streets, crowds of Jews poured out to the sea" (46). As the Jews, men and women, pray beside him, he is gripped by rage: "They have seized even the sea, devil take them!" (47). In the end, Popiel cannot locate his own space, nor can he identify his own person: "He could not grasp where he was: In Poland? In Palestine?" (48). The eternal outsider, the Jew, is here transmuted into the Pole, who is an outsider in this Jewish context. Popiel's sense of dislocation and loss of self in a situation not of his choosing seems to express much of the ambivalence that the Zionist pioneers felt toward their designated homeland. This shift in perspective brings into sharp relief problematic aspects of the Zionist project. Ultimately, the question of whether the Jews can ever be fully at home in Palestine is filtered through Popiel's sensibility. Can the Jew, as a half-Christian, ever be more at home in Palestine than is Popiel, the half-Jew? The answer seems to be highly doubtful. Even the Jews are doomed to be outsiders in this land where cultural heterogeneity—manifested in multilingualism—is the norm.

The Reluctant Penitent

The title of Rivess's 1932 story "Der Bal-tshuve" (The penitent [Rivess 1947a, 84–106]) illustrates some of the problematics involved in constructing a new Jewish identity in Palestine. The Hebraic term *ba'al-tshuva (bal-tshuve* in Yiddish pronunciation), literally "one who has returned (to the fold)," is reserved for nonobservant Jews who become religiously Orthodox. In keeping with his modernist poetics, Rivess again recontextualizes terms from the domain of ritual. Here he applies *bal-tshuve* to the defiantly secular and humanistic—but, in his perception, no less rigorous—belief system of socialism, a decisive ideological element of Yishuv culture.[21] Zeligman, a sixty-eight-year-old Polish Jew, was a rich businessman and property owner until his business declined and he was forced to immigrate to Palestine, where his son settled thirteen years earlier as an ardent socialist Zionist. However, by the time Zeligman and his wife arrive in Palestine, the son is no longer a socialist and has established a thriving contracting empire in Tel-Aviv. Zeligman, who was firmly opposed to the workers' movement in Poland, becomes disenchanted with his son's labor practices in Palestine and, to his own surprise, finds himself siding with the laborers. Thus, though *zeligman* is Yiddish for "happy person," Zeligman in Palestine is bitterly unhappy. In Tel-Aviv, where his son takes pride in his success, Zeligman suffers an apparent heart attack at the close of the story and collapses on the street in front of one of his son's construction sites.

In contrast to most Hebrew literature of the Yishuv, obsessed as it was

21. The recontextualization of religious terms in the secular Zionist domain was fairly common in contemporary Hebrew literature as well. A famous case in point is Avraham Shlonsky's treatment of the tallith (prayer shawl) and tefillin (phylacteries bound with thongs on the left arm and head), key Jewish ritual objects, in his 1927 poem "Amal" (Toil): "My country is wrapped in light like a tallith. / Houses stand like tefillin /and like tefillin thongs roads stretch down, paved by hands" (1927b, 98). Shlonsky's refiguration of the land as a male Jewish body, wearing the obligatory emblems of observance, was a shocking departure from the traditional lexicon of Jewish literary devices. As I show in chapter 5, the Yiddish poet Rikuda Potash, in dialogue with Shlonsky, takes this refiguration further, beyond the realm of Judaism, in her poem "Bovlishe Geter" (Babylonian gods).

with a sweeping negation of the diasporic past in its zeal to create a new society, Rivess provides rare insight into a diasporic Jew's deep-lying reluctance to leave Poland and his profound disenchantment with the Zionist reality of Palestine. This insight is achieved by an ironic play on the conventional Zionist botanical imagery that depicted diasporic Jews as "rootless." In "The Penitent," the metaphor is reversed: Zeligman's roots are deep in Poland, and uprooting him proves to be a catastrophe. The descendant of generations of property owners, he possesses grain mills, forests, and fields, all richly productive until recently. When his wife begins to agitate to join their son and his young family in Palestine, Zeligman feels that "he was too strongly rooted here to be pulled out of the earth" (1947a, 90). He resists the pressure to emigrate, even though his businesses are losing money: "Like an old tree, rooted in Polish soil, Zeligman did not let himself be bowed or broken by the sudden storm that laid waste Jewish life" (91). Once he is on board the ship to Palestine, he "so painfully felt a void in his heart. For sixty-eight years he had been rooted in Polish soil, and now like a naked tree, with no soil around its roots, he came ever nearer to the shores of his son's land. The closer he felt to the new land, the more strongly he felt the loss of the torn-away soil" (95–96). Like Hirshenzon, Rindfleysh's partner in "In Straits," who came to Palestine only after Popiel as tax collector had impoverished him (Rivess 1947c, 41), Zeligman feels no emotional attachment to the Promised Land—neither through Jewish tradition nor through Zionist ideology.

He who was rooted in Poland cannot put down roots in Tel-Aviv, literally because he perceives no earth there. For him, the new Jewish city consists solely of cement and mortar, ironizing a popular Yishuv song of the 1930s that praised a vision of "dressing" the land "in a garment of cement and mortar."[22] As Zeligman stands atop one of his son's structures and surveys Tel-Aviv, the emblem of Zionist aspirations to create an "organic" Jewish culture, he cannot see any soil or sign of life. Rivess describes the scene in geometric terms, using disjointed expressionistic syntax: "Far and wide around spread squares, plazas, houses piled on top of houses. . . . The streets intersected, divided into quarters—ever farther and more compactly, it sank toward the blue, immense, distant sea" (1947a, 101). The ordered planning

---

22. From a popular song with words by Natan Alterman and music by Daniel Sambursky. The song is known by its first line, *"be-harim kevar ha-shemesh melahetet"* (in the hills the sun is already blazing).

of Tel-Aviv, which for Salach in "Lust" emblematizes the alluring aspects of modernity, is for Zeligman contrived and unnatural.

As Zeligman walks through Tel-Aviv, the only way he can see himself attached to the ground is in death. When he sees a tombstone carver's samples displayed on the sidewalk, he defines himself oxymoronically as "a living tombstone in the midst of all the tumult" (99). Zeligman admits to himself that he is "disgusted with his new home—he would like to flee from this home to where the pepper tree grows" (100). "Where the pepper tree grows," an idiom meaning "the ends of the earth," resonates ironically with the baggage of early Zionist popular songs, one of which (adapted from a German patriotic song)[23] romantically depicted an idealized Palestine as "the place where cedars grow." In 1929, the major Yiddish poet and Yiddishist Yankev Glatshteyn published his poem "Dort un di Tseder" (There where the cedars) in dialogue with the same Hebrew song, thus depicting the plight of those in Palestine who are silenced by Hebraist zealotry.[24] In a complex intertextual and interlinguistic reference, Rivess utilizes the Yiddish idiom, the Zionist Hebrew song, and the non-Zionist Yiddish poem to emblematize Zeligman's situation. The lowly, common pepper tree of Tel-Aviv, rather than the lofty cedar with its biblical overtones (which does not grow in Tel-Aviv), becomes the negative icon of Zeligman's subverted paradise. With these images, Rivess overturns the basic premise of Zionism that diasporic life is "unnatural" and that Jews can be redeemed only through their return to a "natural" way of life in the traditional homeland. Zeligman's life has followed the opposite track. He, who was supremely confident of his social position in Poland and opposed socialism, has undergone an epiphany, the "repentance" intimated in the title. His disillusionment is complete when he realizes that although he has "come as a penitent" to the new land, "to begin life anew . . . [i]n the end he sees the same as in the shtetl. This son of his is a continuation of himself. It should have been different!" (98). The socialist-Zionist ideal has collapsed in the reality of Palestine. The firebrands who as-

23. The German "Die Wacht am Rhein" was written by Carl Wilhelm and Max Schneckenburger in 1840; the words were first reworked by Zionists in German and then rephrased in Hebrew. The Hebrew lyrics to "Sham Bimekom Arazim" (There where the cedars), like the music, are unattributed in Luncz 1918, a 1903 collection of "national and popular songs sung today in the towns and settlements of the Holy Land" that by 1918 had been reprinted at least five times.

24. Glatshteyn 1929, 72. See Seidman's perceptive reading of this poem (1997, 122–23).

pired to create a new society have become capitalists, contractors who exploit the labor of others and perpetuate the diasporic models. This is a critique of a socialist Zionism that is unable to live up to its ideology.

Rivess uses the concepts and tropes of Orthodox Judaism to expose the hypocrisy and contradictions inherent in the practical application of ideology. The irony of Zeligman's "conversion" to socialism is heightened by his own earlier interpretation of the image of (the Jewish) Karl Marx in a red-bordered socialist picture in Poland: "Marx, with curly disheveled hair and a rabbinical beard" (93). This description ridicules the religious fervor of many Jewish Marxists who revered Marx much as Hasidim revere their spiritual leader, the rebbe. Yet as Zeligman begins to embrace Zionism, he himself hangs a Zionist calendar on the wall with the image of the movement's founder, "black-bearded Dr. Herzl" (94). Theodor Herzl's square black beard, often characterized as "prophetic," was a trademark of his appearance. Zeligman eventually replaces one "prophetic" figure with another, both marked by their "Jewish" beards.

Zeligman's eventual disenchantment with Zionism is foreshadowed, while he is still in Poland, by the comical name of the president of the local Zionist association, who is also the Hebrew teacher: "Lokshin" (93). The name, a variant on *lokshn* (noodles), sets up Rivess's rather heavy-handed irony toward the Zionist project; in Yiddish folk lingo, *farkoyfn a loksh*, or "selling a noodle," indicates a confidence game. Lokshin, who is the town's chief Zionist, is a glib pitchman for a hollow ideology because he has no intention of emigrating to Palestine. Rivess also uses a subtextual implication of *lokshn* to needle the ideologues who posited Hebrew as a central feature of Zionism. *Lokshn* is the first element of the idiom *lokshn-koydesh* (holy noodles), a mocking variation on *loshn-koydesh* (the holy tongue), the Hebrew-derived Yiddish term for Hebrew (Harkavy 1928, 271); it also evokes the ironic idiom *toyres-lokshn* (noodle Torah), which mocks something that pretends to be true but is not (Harkavy 1928, 521). The negative connotations of *lokshn* as a euphemism for deception resonate in a degradation of the language that is doubly sacred, both to traditional Judaism and to Zionism. Lokshin himself, who is characterized by his "Gentile [*goyishe*] mustache" (Rivess 1947a, 93) rather than by the "rabbinical" beard that marks both Marx and Herzl, is not depicted as a Hebraist. He does not converse in Hebrew, and even his Yiddish is "fake." It is represented as pretentious *daytshmerish*, fashionably adorned with French in the manner of Polish nobility: "*yo, yo, das yidishe folk hat da kayne tsukunft—adye*" (Yes, yes, the Jewish people has no future here—adieu [94]). Thus, the Hebrew teacher, who not only resembles a Gentile but also attempts to speak like one, is actually alienated from Jewish culture as well as from Zionism and is the harbinger of the alienation that overwhelms Zeligman in Palestine.

This alienation is heightened by the character of Zeligman's son's wife, Ora (a distinctly nondiasporic name). She is Sephardic, and the description of her is rich in the exotic overtones that this non-European origin implies: "She keeps smiling to the newly arrived parents with the strange charm of a faraway land" (96). This sense of estrangement now extends to the parents' perception of their son: "Papa and mama [*tate-mame*] soon sensed a foreignness in him. It was really possible that this strangeness was borrowed from his newly acquired Sephardic wife" (96). The familiar joint term for parents, *tate-mame*, in conjunction with Ora's identification as "other," evokes the cultural distance between the basics of European Jewish tradition and the complexity of the Yishuv. No communication is possible between them and their daughter-in-law because Ora knows no Yiddish.

Rivess's exposure of the class conflict in the forming Yishuv takes an unexpected form when he portrays the hypocrisy of idealists-turned-opportunists such as Zeligman's son. This is a powerful reversal of the convention that marks the older generation as reactionary and the younger generation as progressive—a general principle of modernity as well as of socialist Zionism. Paradoxically, the father, who scorned the socialists in his hometown and immigrated to Palestine out of economic necessity rather than out of ideology, now upholds the social vision of Zionism. The son is the one who exploits his workers and whose "good fortune came from swindling, not from good deeds" (102). Zeligman is shaken to the core when he is recognized by the son of one of his former employees, now a laborer at his own son's construction site, who says, "My father gave his life for you, and I mine—for your son" (104). Once he realizes that his son has abandoned the ideals of social justice, he has nothing by way of compensation for his own disappointments, and the tragedy is inevitable. Zeligman collapses on the sidewalk. His premonition of himself as a "living tombstone" is literalized as he "rolls with a dull thud off the sidewalk onto the hot, hard cement" (106). Cement, the substance that has become the means and the emblem of success for his son and for Zionism in general, is Zeligman's deathbed and gravestone. By identifying cement as a place of death, Rivess sardonically refigures another trope of Yishuv culture: the popular song's vision of "dressing" the land "in a garment of cement and mortar." Zeligman's death indicates the terrible cost exacted by the growing Yishuv from both the individual and the community.

Rivess began as a revolutionary high modernist in 1923, when he joined the avant-garde. His sympathetic portrayal of Zeligman as a representative of an older, yet paradoxically more liberal and self-critical ideological approach, signifies a major shift of perspective away from the ideological terminology of extremes. The diasporic sensibility of Zeligman is revealed, through his native language, as more humanistic and less hypocritical than that of radical Zionism, which often adopted slogans while ignoring the social situations it created.

Rivess's individualism as a writer who refused to adopt conventional positions is obvious in the 1948 review of *Transplant* by Y. Z. Shargel, one of the founders of the 1928 *Onheyb* and a frequent contributor to the Yiddish magazines of the 1930s. Shargel accused Rivess of being something of an outsider. Rivess, he wrote, "does not see the young people [of Israel]. . . . [H]e lacks a central idea to inspire him in his struggle for Yiddish fiction in Eretz-Israel" (1977a, 48–49). Rivess's language was too firmly "rooted in deepest *yiddishkeyt,* reminiscent of the best traditions of Yiddish creativity in Poland" (48). In the Israel of 1948, during the first flush of independence and national pride, *yiddishkeyt,* the cultural and emotional quality associated with being Jewish, was an undesirable attribute because of its associations with the Diaspora. By this time, even the bearers of Yiddish culture in Israel considered "the best traditions of Yiddish creativity in Poland" to carry a negative valence. Significantly, Shargel applauded the expanded version of the "Transplant" story, which ends on a hopeful note and considered it "suitable for today" (50). Yet he summed up Rivess as "still a 'stranger' and a 'greenhorn' in his work" (48). Shargel's verdict is hardly surprising because four out of the seven stories in *Transplant* were written between 1929 and 1936, when the vast majority of the Yishuv consisted of just such "strangers" and "greenhorns." Shargel seemed to be devaluing Rivess's socialist and Zionist concerns as well as his expressionist style when he decisively relegated Rivess's work to the ranks of diasporic creativity. However, Rivess's use of Yiddish is actually ultra-inclusive. He straddles both the Marxist concern with an urban proletariat relocated in Palestine and the issues of the new rural proletariat forming in the Yishuv. Employing the language that was construed as anti-Zionist, he delineates some of the paradoxes and problematics of Zionism. In the metaphor that is so pervasive in his work, he may be said to have transplanted a modern version of *yid-*

dishkeyt into the new soil, melding together different contemporary issues by means of the traditional language. He thus exemplifies certain possibilities in Yiddish prose that most of his contemporaries in the area did not explore.

Michael Gluzman, analyzing processes of marginalization by the Hebrew canon, states that "the exclusion of the transgressor becomes essential, thus enabling the center to maintain its identity and hegemony as well as to reify its power" (2002, 144). Obviously, even the "canonic" Yiddish culture of Palestine, itself a minority, needed to delegitimize and discredit alternative voices within it, considering them a danger to its own position. The particular combination of *yiddishkeyt* and modernism that was an integral component of Avrom Rivess's poetics was ostracized because it did not conform to the Zionist construct. The "transplant" of modern Yiddish culture itself was doomed to failure. Only six Yiddish magazines were published between 1940 and 1945 (compared with nineteen between 1928 and 1939), as the Yiddish-speaking Jewish centers of Europe were destroyed. Yiddish literary production in the Yishuv was reduced to a trickle. Yet it was at this point that an alternative Yiddish vision of Yishuv culture began to take shape in the poetry of Rikuda Potash.

CHAPTER FIVE

Writing as a Native

The "Canaanizing" Poetry of Rikuda Potash

"My god is an orphan
amid fire,
storm,
in no one's land"

—Rikuda Potash, "Babylonian Gods," 1967

This analysis of Rikuda Potash's nativist poetry rounds out an examination of the cultural problematics of Jewish reterritorialization in Palestine and poses an intriguing option. Potash (1906–1965) began to write in Poland, immigrated to Palestine in 1934, and continued to write in Yiddish until her death. Because her output reflects both the prestatehood and statehood experiences, this concluding section goes beyond 1948, the chronological endpoint of Zionist Palestine. Potash was not part of the turn-of-the-century poetic tradition like Zalmen Brokhes, nor was she involved in the prestatehood literary scene like Avrom Rivess. She embodies the quandary of the Yiddish writer, a resident of "Yiddishland," that imaginary land constituted by Yiddish language and literature. Once such a writer is resituated in the physical homeland, where the forming society opposes Yiddish, how can the resulting cultural dilemma be reconciled?

Potash's nativist work constitutes a possible solution. For her, the permutations of the immigrant position—from alienation to criticism—culminate in a hybrid construct. The "Canaanizing" poems I discuss in this chapter, representing a quantitatively small but poetically crucial portion of her output, combine her European-nurtured sensibility with a keen awareness of ancient Near Eastern traditions and thematics. Though she was not affiliated with the contemporaneous Hebrew "Canaanite" writers (or with any other Hebrew or Yiddish group), her poetry eclectically blends "Canaanite" thematics with modernist European poetics, through the vehicle of Yiddish—the fusion language that is admirably suited to this project. Potash's individualistic vision merges cultural and linguistic differences in a critique of monocultural and monolingual nationalism that is unusually rich in allusions and maintains a dialogue with the significant work of major Yiddish and Hebrew writers. Her output is simultaneously anchored in and displaced from the landscape and culture of the traditional homeland, echoing the traditional situation of the Jewish artist who is at home nowhere.

This complicated location led to her multiple marginalization. First, by writing Yiddish in Palestine, she was naturally rejected by the surrounding dominant Hebrew culture. Second, her individualism ran counter to the collective spirit of the Yiddish cultural establishment that had developed in Israel, which subscribed to mainstream Zionist values. Finally, the Yiddish literary establishment abroad considered her too naturalized in the Yishuv because her language contained an unusually large number of Hebrew words. I posit that Rikuda Potash's nativism and her syntactic and lexical practices form a unique strand of Yiddish modernism that drew on European and ancient Near Eastern sources but could develop only in Hebrew Palestine/Israel.

Poetic Roots

Rikuda Potash was born in Czestochowa, Poland, and began writing and publishing poetry in Polish as a teenager. Named Rebecca, she apparently adopted the name "Rikuda" (derived from the Hebrew root *r'k'd*, "dance") in early youth (Narkiss 1997). Following the traumatic Lemberg pogrom of 1918, in which seventy Jews were killed, she switched to Yiddish and began publishing poetry in 1922 in the *Lodzher Folksblat*. She moved to Lodz in 1924 and continued to publish in the Yiddish periodicals of Warsaw and Lodz. Her voice was recognized as significant when four of her poems were included in Ezra Korman's 1928 anthology *Yidishe Dikhterins Antologye* (Anthology of Yiddish women poets [255–59]). Her first volume, *Vint oyf Klavishn* (Wind on keyboard), appeared in 1934, the year she immigrated to Palestine with her young daughter to escape a traumatic marriage (Narkiss 1997). Potash settled in Jerusalem, where she was the librarian of the Bezalel Art School and Museum until her death; the books provided her own art with vital sustenance. Potash apparently published little in Palestinian Yiddish publications (perhaps no more than twelve poems, all in the biweekly *Nayvelt*),[1] including the magazines of the late 1930s. Her collection *Fun Kidron Tol* (From the Kidron Valley) appeared in London (Potash 1952); another volume of poetry, *Moyled iber Timna* (New moon over Timna), was published in Jerusalem (Potash 1960). Two volumes were published posthumously: *Lider* (Poems [Potash 1967]) and a collection of short stories and sketches, *In Geslekh fun Yerusholayim* (In the alleys of Jerusalem [Potash 1968]).[2]

Many of Potash's early poems reflect contemporaneous modernist trends. "Kuntsen-makhers" (Illusionists), which opens *Wind on Keyboard* (Potash 1934, 7), is totally devoid of Jewish content while thoroughly modernist in its poetics. Her choppy, synesthetic vision, simultaneously disintegrating and conflating sight, sound, and touch in a street scene unanchored in time or place—the "ever-recurrent and variously momentous instant" typical of symbolism (Scott 1991, 207)—foreshadows her later work.

Illusionists[3]

A quilt was spread in the middle of the yard
A great crowd rushed in.
Heads pushed through balconies and windows
and hot, burning, the sun sidled near.

1. Although Potash was not aligned politically with Left Po'alei Zion, the party that backed *Nayvelt,* the newspaper was the only regular venue for Yiddish in the country when it began publication in 1934.

2. The poems and stories are undated, yet the posthumous volumes seem to present the works in chronological order: the first group in *Lider* (Poems [1967]) contains most of the poems in her 1934 volume, whereas the later poems are replete with Palestinian thematics. I have not been able to establish the full publishing history of these books. *Fun Kidron Tol* (From the Kidron Valley [1952]) appeared in London. *Moyled iber Timna* (New moon over Timna [1960]) was published in Jerusalem by Tarshish Press and was printed at the facilities of the prestigious mainstream Hebrew newspaper *Ha'aretz*. The posthumous *Poems* appeared under the auspices of the Association of Yiddish Writers and Journalists in Israel; *In Geslekh fun Yerusholayim* (In the alleys of Jerusalem [1968]) was published by Yisro'el-Bukh Press in Tel-Aviv.

3. At the expense of elegance, my translations of Potash's poetry represent an effort to retain the Yiddish syntax as well as to reproduce her sometimes unconventional practices in order to convey the modernist effect of her writing style.

On the quilt a child collapsed on his knees
and a man with broad shoulders stuck a knife
into the tiny thin body lying on the ground,
a woman in a top hat he held with the edge of his lips;

held her by the toetips for a few minutes
and an old illusionist lay as if cut down.
Soon a street-organ intoned its "didl-didl"
and the old man, like a dog, barked in fear.

Then a small, thin childish body
went for a walk on its head as if on feet
hung a while like a cripple
crucified with its hands on a spear.

And when the organ stopped its "didl"-ing
a long sword still gleamed in the air
and a yellow cap, faded by the sun,
took a leap up in the air.

Someone refolded the quilt,
a red ribbon of blood hung over his forehead.
They gathered up a few pennies from the ground
and away they went to other yards and gates.

This street scene, depicting the stages of an ostensible tragedy in which a child is apparently tortured as part of the show and seems to be dead, is narrated dispassionately. The rhetorical distance itself, manifested in her symbolistic use of particle or adjective as adverb ("the old man . . . barked in fear"), underscores the crowd's simultaneous attraction and repulsion to violence as spectacle.

Richard Sheppard characterizes German expressionist poets before the First World War as standing "not within . . . but on the extreme edge, or some precarious vantage point from which the panorama is valid both as an objective picture and as an image of their subjective condition. In this way they seem both involved in and detached from their vision, fascinated and repelled by its horror" (1991b, 384). This is the stance of the observer-speaker in Potash's 1934 poem, perhaps one of the "heads pushed through windows," who seems in thrall to the gruesome scene. Accentuating the

קונצן-מאכערס

מען האָט געשפּרייט אַ קאָלדערע אויפֿן מיטן הויף
ס'איז געװען אַ גרויסער אָנגעלויף.
קעפּ פֿון פֿענצטער און באַלקאָנען האָבן זיך ארויסגעשפּאַרט
און אַ הייסע, אַ צעגליטע האָט די זון זיך צוגעשאַרט.

אויף דער קאָלדערע האָט אַ קינד די קניען אײַנגעבראָכן
און אַ מענטש מיט ברייטע פּלייצעס האָט אַ מעסער אײַנגעשטאָכן
אין דעם קליינעם דאָרן גופֿל, װאָס איז אויף דער ערד געלעגן
אַ פֿרוי אין אַ צילינדער האָט ער אין די ליפּן ברעגן

צוגעהאַלטן ביי די שפּיצן פֿיס עטלעכע מינוטן
און אַן אַלטער קונצן-מאַכער איז געלעגן װי צעשניטן.
באַלד האָט אַ קאַטערינקע דידל-דידל טענער צוגעשפּילט
און דער אַלטער האָט װאַ'אַ הונט דערשראָקן צוגעבילט.

דערנאָך האָט אַ קליין דאַר קינדיש גופֿל
מיט קאָפּ אַרומשפּאַצירט װי מיט פֿיס
אַ װײַיל געהאָנגען װי אַ קריפּל
געקרייציקט מיט די הענט אויף אַ שפּיז.

און די קאַטערינקע האָט דידלען אויפֿגעהערט
האָט נאָך אין דער לופֿט געבלאָנקט אַ לאַנגע שװוערד
און אַ קאַשקעט אַ געלער אָפּגעשאָסן פֿון דער זון
האָט אין דער לופֿטן אַ הויכן שפּרונג געטון.

האָט װער צוריק די קאָלדערע אײַנגעפּאַקט,
אַ רויטע סטעטנגע בלוט איז געהאָנגען אויף זײַן שטערן.
עטלעכע גראָשנס פֿון דער ערד צונויף געקליבן
און אַװעק זענען זיי צו אַנדערע הייף און טוירן.

9. "Kuntsenmakhers" (Illusionists), poem by Rikuda Potash.

grotesqueness of the theatrical deception, body parts are separated from their physical context and given a perverse autonomy, as lips function in place of hands and a head is made to do the work of feet. The characters are dehumanized and bestialized when the old contortionist is first cut up and then barks like a dog. Inanimate objects are endowed with life, either personified or acting as metonymies for the human agent they replace or figuratively dismember: the sun shuffles along, the street organ plays on its own, the sword continues to emit light, and the yellow cap leaps into the air with no obvious causative agent.

The scene reinscribes a reigning "carnival anatomy" that is characterized by parts of dismembered bodies (Bakhtin 1973, 135). Whereas Avrom Rivess drew on the carnivalesque to express the alienation within a group of Zionist pioneers in "In the Camp," Potash evokes a more sinister echo as she reaches further into modernist experimentation. In eastern European Jewish culture, fairs and carnivals were the location where pogroms were brewed and when society's conventions broke down. The Yiddish *yerid* (fair) has a secondary meaning of "tumult, uproar." In Potash's carnivalesque minisociety on the quilt, it is the weaker members—the woman, the old man, the child—who are forced into unnatural, life-threatening situations. Yet Potash subverts the horror in advance: after all, the characters are *kuntsen-makhers*, tricksters, illusionists. Although the word implies deception, it nonetheless incorporates a positive sense of the skills that are an essential element of art.[4] Everyone knows that magicians' acts rely on smoke and mirrors, yet the viewers are inevitably spellbound, to the point where they begin to doubt all reality.

This *ars*-poetic poem, the first one in Potash's first volume, functions as a type of credo, interrogating and broadening the bounds of her art. It places in question the artistic process itself: the narrator's refusal to judge simultaneously replicates and condemns the artist's aestheticization of pain. The metapoetic and meta-artistic dimension of the poem are exquisitely thematized through its Yiddish title, "Kuntsen-makhers." The poem is also in dialogue with a well-known story by the premodernist I. L. Perets, "Der Gilgl fun a Nign" (The reincarnation of a melody [Perets 1930, 116–35]), which thematizes art by following the changing functions of a Hasidic melody. In Perets's story, the tune reaches its lowest status when it is played by a street organ as part of a performance by "illusionists" with an abused child in a courtyard. In Potash's "Illusionists," we see the modernist, fragmented depiction of a similar street performance with music, also culminating in the image of a "crucified" child, challenging Perets's premodernist conception of art.

Potash's move to Palestine in 1934 was crucial artistically as well as personally. The relocation, motivated by personal issues rather than by Zionist ideology, did not necessarily imply a break with modern European culture,

---

4. The first component of the Yiddish word *kunts*—an act of trickery—is a metathesis of the German *Kunst,* which originally meant "skill" and in the nineteenth century came to mean "art" in the modern sense, in both German and Yiddish.

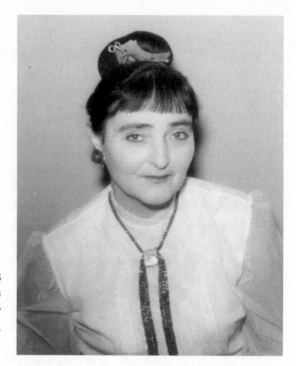

10. Rikuda Potash; photograph by Aviva Fuchs, 1960; courtesy of Aviva Fuchs.

but rather an expansion of vision to include local elements. Once in Palestine, she did not automatically subscribe to all components of the mainstream Zionist cultural ethos, with its negation of Yiddish and its collective imperative to settle the land. Potash made her home in a Jerusalem with a strong international flavor, as European Jewish intellectuals created a transplanted subculture. Major Jewish figures from Germany and Austria, such as the philosopher Martin Buber, the Bauhaus architect Erich Mendelssohn, and the modernist artist Anna Ticho, established what has been described as a "literary salon, reminiscent of Berlin and Vienna" (Zalmona 1981, 39). The home of Potash's brother, Mordecai Narkiss, a local artistic authority in his capacity as director of Jerusalem's only art museum and school, was a meeting place for leading local painters and writers. It was probably through Narkiss that she met the key German Jewish expressionist poet and visual artist Else Lasker-Schüler, something of a cult figure for Yiddish modernist writers, especially women,[5] who was forced to flee from Nazi Germany and

5. Early-twentieth-century Yiddish poet Anna Margolin wrote enviously, "Ah, would that I were worthy of being the great Else's pupil. But I am not" (quoted in Novershtern 1991, xlvi).

lived in Jerusalem from 1939 until her death in 1945. As a member of the German Austrian "cultural salon" of Jerusalem, Lasker-Schüler would bring her sketches for Mordecai Narkiss to evaluate (Narkiss 1997). Potash's profound connection with the "vast network of cultural codes" (Mitchell 1994, 13) that constituted the local landscape was undoubtedly strengthened by her close personal and artistic relationship with the major Palestinian Israeli painter Mordecai Ardon (1896–1992). The connection with Ardon, who was trained in the Berlin Bauhaus and deeply committed to the Palestinian landscape, was highly significant for both of them (Michael Ardon 2001). At least four of Ardon's paintings focus on "Rikuda" (Vishny 1974, 221–30); he also created a posthumous "Ex Libris" for her (ill. 11). Two paintings dedicated to her were created after her death: *Birthday of the Blue R.* on the first anniversary (1966) and *La Rosette pour Rikuda* (1986–87), which was used as the cover of the catalog for his last exhibition (1989). Other portraits of women also seem to be inspired by Potash (Schwarz 2003, 62).[6] Potash's work for the next thirty years seemed to oscillate between and be informed by two cultural poles: the local and the European, a key duality that reveals the sources of the cultural amalgam that emerges in her art.

Potash's particular voice can be better appreciated with a brief examination of the life and work of two mainstream Yiddish writers of the Yishuv. Pilowsky notes that "the function of Yiddish poetry [in the Yishuv] up to 1948 was to serve as an additional agent of propaganda for the socialist Yishuv" (1986, 317). The Israeli Yiddish poet Aryeh Shamri (1907–78) is perceived as a spokesman for the Yiddish mainstream in the Yishuv, which reflected the dominant ideology of socialist Zionism. Shamri's own course was typical: he immigrated to Palestine in 1929 as part of a Zionist youth group and was a member of the leftist Kibbutz Ein-Shemer from 1930 until his death. His poetry of the 1930s speaks for the collective in general and for left-wing Zionism in particular by extolling the virtues of communal life in a kibbutz.

Shamri's earliest Palestinian work, which established his reputation in

6. Studies of Ardon are numerous and extensive. Vishny 1974 is generally considered the authoritative monograph, and articles by Zalmona (1981) and Barasch (1981) cast greater light on Ardon's position in the art of both the Yishuv and Israel, the cultural milieu in which Potash found herself. In his wonderfully articulate Yiddish memoirs, which recount his artistic sources and development, Mordecai Ardon (1988, 1989) considers Potash one of the three most important women in his life, along with his mother and his wife. The vital poetic connection between these two artists is the topic of a separate study; see Schwarz 2003, 62–63.

מספרי ריקודה פוטאש תרס"ו–תשכ"ה

11. Mordecai Ardon, *Ex Libris Rikuda Potash*, n.d.; courtesy of
Michael Ardon and the Department of Manuscripts and Archives,
the Jewish National and University Library, Jerusalem.

1936, is "Leyzer Tsipress" (Shamri 1970), a *poema* named for its protagonist, a young male European Zionist who is part of a group building a new
kibbutz. The poem clearly conveys the message of socialist Zionism with its
call for national and personal self-redemption through communal action.
The protagonist's first name, "Leyzer," is derived from the Hebrew "Eliezer"
but is also a component of the Yiddish *derleyzer* (redeemer), an allusion to
his participation in the socialist-Zionist enterprise of national redemption

through communal action. Upon his arrival in the country, Leyzer is even referred to as *"eyner fun di derleyzers"* (one of the redeemers [17]). "Tsipress,"
the second component of his name, locates him in the Land of Israel: cy-
presses are not a northern European tree.[7] Even before Leyzer immigrates, he
is characterized as belonging to a mystical group that Jewish tradition considers an elite: he is one of the *"lamed-vav,"* the legendary circle of thirty-six
anonymous righteous men whose good deeds sustain the world and among
whom one will be revealed as the Messiah. Leyzer justifies his departure for
Palestine as a response to the call: "Enough of waiting on a threshold / with
tearful, unheeded entreaties" (13). The imperative to act carries over to
Palestine: he tills the fields and plants the commune's orchards. Throughout
the poem, Shamri locates his protagonist in the communal framework and
the communal enterprise. As a well is dug in the climactic final section of the
poem, Leyzer's sorrow is for the group's parched fields; and once the water
gushes forth, his joy is for the kibbutz children, the future of the collective.
His expressions of individual struggle, such as homesickness (30) and sexual
longing (31) are also within the framework of the problematics sanctioned
by major Hebrew writers of the time, such as Brenner and Bistritsky.

Another important mainstream Yiddish poet of the Yishuv, Yosef Papiernikov (1899–1976), explicitly distinguished between his intimate poetry
and the part of his oeuvre that was mobilized in the interests of socialist
Zionism (1938, 3). Papiernikov first came to Palestine in 1924 and published
more than twenty books of poetry there. Pilowsky notes that Papiernikov's
"mobilized" poetry tends to "a monodimensional declarativeness that 'flat-
tens' his work" (1986, 298). His intimate poetry, however, is lyrical and
presents the thematics of love, death, and landscape. According to Pilowsky,
these poems, which are "free of socialist-Zionist identification, constitute his
best work" (1986, 301).

It is against this background that Rikuda Potash's work should be read.
Unlike central figures such as Shamri and Papiernikov, she did not affiliate
herself with and never spoke for a collective—poetic, ideological, or na-

---

7. "Tsipress" may also be a matronymic form: "Tsipora" (Yiddish "Tsippe") is a feminine
name, and the suffix *-ess* denotes the possessive. The name could thus be construed as "Tsipora's
Leyzer," just as Avrom Rivess's pen name may incorporate the name Rivka or Riva (see chapter
4, fn. 1).

tional; she followed her own idiosyncratic vision.[8] Living in the Yishuv, she was located between worlds and created one of her own.

Homeless Wanderers, Foreign Gods

Paradoxically, Potash, although writing in Yiddish, seems close to the Hebrew extreme nativist "Canaanite" movement of the 1940s, or rather to cultural elements associated with that movement. As noted earlier, "Canaanism" had the national goals of "restoring" a cultural context that was assumed to have been part of the ancient Near East and of creating a Hebrew culture in the land of the Hebrews (Ratosh 1982, 39). "Canaanism" based itself on what James Diamond defines as "a vitalistic consciousness that was new and secular and qualitatively differed from the past, the religious tradition, and the Diaspora" (1986, 19). In this context, *Jewish* was understood as a religious definition, whereas *Hebrew* was seen to signify a generic prebiblical nation comprising various regional groups mentioned in the Bible (Amorites, Moabites, Phoenicians, and so on) that were united by common cultural ties. The national enterprise in Palestine was rooted in Hebrew, the original local language and the only possible vehicle for national creativity in the country. "Canaanism" politically envisioned a "secular entity that would seek to embrace and gradually assimilate all non-Arab minorities indigenous to the region . . . into a new Hebrew confederation" (Diamond 1986, 3).

Although the political ideology remained confined to the fringes of the Yishuv, "Canaanism" had a considerable cultural effect. This effect has been viewed as an offshoot of the tendency in European art, beginning in the mid-1930s, to return to ancient and archetypal myths, reinforced by Jungian psychoanalytic doctrines (Zalmona 1998, 66–67). However, similar chords had been struck in Hebrew literature as early as the 1890s by the major premodernist European Hebrew poet Shaul Tchernichovsky (1875–1943). Some of Tchernichovsky's poems that idealize a "pagan" Hebrew past can, in hindsight, be considered proto-"Canaanite." These poems—for which he was strongly criticized at the time—apostrophized ancient Near Eastern and Eu-

---

8. Chaim Leyb Fuks, to whom she was married, notes in his memoir of Lodz that she refused to identify herself with any of the local literary groupings (1972, 167). Potash's nephew Bezalel Narkiss remembers her as saying about other Yiddish writers in Palestine: "I have nothing to do with them" (Narkiss 1997).

ropean deities. In addition, Hebrew fiction that could be construed as nativist was being written in Palestine as early as the First Aliyah (Y. Shavit
1984, 156); and some of Zalmen Brokhes's Yiddish work in the second
decade of the twentieth century reflects a different strand of nativism. Such
vitalistic forces found political expression in "Canaanism."

"Canaanism," like mainstream Yishuv culture, drew much of its inspira-
tion from archaeological evidence. The archaeological discoveries at Ugarit
in the 1920s and 1930s, which indicated close links between the Hebrews of
the Bible and the surrounding cultures, were key elements of this orientation.
Archaeology, of course, is crucial to any modern discourse of national identity; it retrieves the factual, tangible evidence of the narrative that, grounded
in the past, facilitates a reconnection with original space and grants the present its meaning (Ezrahi 2000, 6). In the first decades of Israel's statehood, archaeology took on the dimensions of a national mania (Elon 1971, 291).
New discoveries substantiating the Jewish link with the land were top news
items, and thousands of Israelis practiced archaeology as a hobby; archaeology exhibitions, lectures, and clubs drew wide audiences and memberships.
Speaking from a perspective within Israel's academia, Charles Liebman and
Eliezer Don-Yehiya consider archaeology to be a key symbol of Israel's "civil
religion of statism" between 1948 and 1956, to the point that it "assumed
cultic aspects" (1983, 110).

By the 1950s and 1960s, however, such influential Hebrew poets as
Natan Zach (1930–) and Yehuda Amichai (1924–2000) were blazing the
way for a reevaluation of the role of archaeology, among other components
of mainstream Zionism. Amichai, for example, not only uses a non-Jewish
archaeological artifact as a simile in "be-Emtza ha-Me'ah ha-Zot" (In the
middle of this century), but relocates it from the domain of history to that of
intense personal rather than collective experience: "In the middle of this century we turned toward each other / half-faced and full-eyed / like an ancient
Egyptian painting" (1977, 187). Discussing Yonatan Ratosh's early poetry,
with its "pagan" thematics, Gertz notes that modernist poetics, which blur
the boundaries of time and space and tend toward abstraction at the expense
of realism, do not favor ideological messages (1985, 126). Potash is related
to this modernist trend in Yishuv letters, when she reconfigures biblical and
archaeological elements that were conventionally viewed as having a nationalist function and that could be labeled "Canaanite." Yet, paradoxically, she
couched this reconfiguration in the diasporic language despised by extreme
nativists such as the "Canaanites." The term *Canaanizing,* as used in this

chapter, is meant to distinguish Potash's work from that of those poets who were affiliated with the "Canaanite" movement.

The particular nature of her amalgam of ancient Near Eastern traditions is indicated by the title of the section "Di Shrift fun Kena'an" (Canaanite writings) in *Poems* (1967, 149–71), which evokes both the artifact (script) and the content of an ancient document. The section includes poems with Mesopotamian themes, recontextualized according to Potash's modernist sensibility. Thus, "Kena'aner Dikhtung" (Canaanite poem [156–57]) brings together the god Adad and the historical figures Sennacherib and Nebu-chadnezzar, who interact in a Mesopotamian palace scene. In "Mesopo-tamishe Harpe" (Mesopotamian harp [159]), the speaker plays on a musical instrument used by King Sargon II of Assyria; and in "Ashtoret" (Astarte [158]), the mythical goddess-queen, consort of the Mesopotamian chief god Baal, is transmuted into a Yemenite Jewish woman selling peaches in Jerusalem.

Although the locations of her book titles are geographically concrete and rooted in the Bible, they harbor ambiguous associations: neither Kidron nor Timna are associated with sacred sites of the Bible or with its Zionist re-covery. On the contrary, both locations are traditionally linked with pagan-ism. The biblical Kidron Valley, which provides the title of her 1952 volume, marks the border of settled, Israelite royal Jerusalem: King David, fleeing from his rebellious son Absalom, crosses the Kidron as "all the country wept aloud" at the threat to God-given authority (2 Sam. 15:23). It is also the site where pagan idols that threatened the state religion were destroyed: King Asa, for example, cut down the Asherah (Astarte) image "and burned it at the brook Kidron" (1 Kgs. 15:13). It is thus a liminal location between the sacred and the profane, leaning toward the latter—an association bolstered by the fact that the actual valley is surrounded by cemeteries more than two millennia old.

Potash's choice of Timna for the title of her 1960 book is also highly equivocal. Timna is located north of Eilat, at the tip of Israel's southern desert (the name was bestowed on Wadi Mune'iye by the Israeli govern-ment's Negev Names Committee as part of the symbolic renaming of sites in order to bolster legitimacy [Benvenisti 2000, 19]).[9] Although some scholars

9. Benvenisti discusses renaming as a statement of ownership: for Israelis during the 1950s, giving Hebrew names to sites with non-Hebrew (Arabic or European) names meant "erasing the two thousand years of our absence from the country and all the alien tradition that existed in it"

connected the ancient copper mines found at Timna with the reign of King Solomon—a period idealized as that of greatest Israelite wealth and national sovereignty—no ancient Israelite presence has been decisively established there.[10] The biblical associations of the name "Timna" not only antedate Judaism but are linked with Esau, a name that in Jewish tradition signifies any non-Jewish, hostile entity: Timna was a concubine of Eliphaz, Esau's son (Gen. 36:12). Potash's conjunction of Timna in the title with the moon, an ancient, non-Israelite Near Eastern deity, strengthens her link with "Canaanite" thematics.

Significantly, of the eighteen poems in the section "Funem Tatens Khumeshl" (From my father's little Pentateuch) in *From Kidron Valley* (1952, 29–60), only five deal with biblical figures given positive valence by conventional Judaism (Abraham, Jacob, and Jephthah's daughter). Underscoring the individualism of Potash's approach, the poem devoted to Abraham emphasizes a conjectured warm relationship between the patriarch and his rejected son, whom he visits without Sarah's knowledge. The remainder focus on pre-Israelite characters from Genesis (Cain, his descendants Tubal-Cain and Naama, Lot's wife, and Ishmael), who figure in "Canaanite"-influenced thematics of Yishuv literature.[11] The section's title, "From My Father's Little Pentateuch," thus carries considerable irony for Yiddish readers because these figures are, at best, ignored in traditional eastern European Jewish culture. The irony is intensified by the use of the endearing diminutive *khumeshl* (created by adding the suffix *l* to *khumesh*, the Yiddish term for the Pentateuch) for the sacred book that is identified by its possessor, her father. The Bible is familiarized and domesticated, depicted as a small, well-thumbed book that is part of the home, rather than as the formal synagogue scroll. It is therefore all the more striking that most of the biblical figures in

---

(1988, 136). For an expanded account of the politics and process of hebraizing the landscape, see Benvenisti 2000.

10. Archaeological excavations at Timna revealed the remains of copper mining and production facilities dating from the fifteenth century to the eleventh century B.C.E., a period that, according to most historical reconstructions, antedates the arrival of the Israelites in the country. One of the major finds at Timna is a temple of the Egyptian goddess Hathor, dating to the fourteenth century B.C.E. (Stern 1992, 4: 1587–99).

11. In another example of Potash's idiosyncratic vision, two of the poems (1952, 45–49) focus on the rebel angels Aza and Azael. According to the Zohar, they are instructors of sorcery (Scholem 1974, 184).

these "Bible" poems are outcasts who are driven out of home to wander or be killed.

One poem in the "Biblishe Motivn" (Biblical motifs) section in *Poems* (1967, 163–71) depicts perhaps the most problematic female pre-Jewish "other": Hagar, Abraham's concubine who was cast out with her child Ishmael (Gen. 21). Potash's poem "Hagar" is ostensibly in the tradition of Itzik Manger's well-known Yiddish ballads based on Pentateuchal characters ("Khumesh-Lider" [Pentateuch songs/poems, written in the 1930s and 1940s), but it differs from the neofolkist settings and rhythms of Manger's three poems on the biblical Hagar, which echo the style of Yiddish reworkings of biblical tales dating to the fourteenth century.[12] Unlike Manger, who familiarizes the characters in two of his Hagar poems by setting them in an eastern European Jewish environment complete with Slavic cart drivers and railroad trains (1984, 29–32), Potash situates her Hagar in a red-hued stony desert and characterizes Hagar's son, Ishmael, as a "prophet," echoing Islamic tradition and thus distancing the characters from the conventional cultural background of Yiddish readers. Such separation from the Diaspora is consistent with the goals of contemporaneous mainstream Hebrew culture, yet Potash deepens the paradox by presenting Hagar, the outcast, in the paradigmatic Jewish diasporic language.

An especially multilayered recontextualization that also continues the dialogue with Manger occurs in the title poem of *Kidron,* "In Nachal Kidron" (In the Kidron Valley [1952, 40–41]). The refiguring is clear at the outset: unlike Manger's two poems about Eve (1984, 9–12), Potash's title does not mention the protagonist of the poem. Rather, the focus is on the location, using the biblical Hebrew *nachal* (riverbed or valley), adopted by modern Hebrew, rather than its Yiddish counterpart *tol* (which appears in the book's Yiddish title, *Fun Kidron Tol).* The use of a biblical/modern Hebrew word to replace a common Yiddish term creates a unique linguistic and temporal location: neither Hebrew nor Yiddish, neither biblical nor modern. This is where Potash situates the primordial woman, Eve, sitting alone and embittered after the expulsion from Eden (Gen. 3). In effect, she creates an alternative version to Genesis 3:23, in which Adam is banished from Eden and sent to till the earth, and Eve is not mentioned at all.

12. For a discussion of early Yiddish reworkings of the Bible, see Shmeruk 1978, 105–46.

<u>אין נחל קדרון</u>

אין נחל קדרון
אויף אַ טרעפּ,
זיצט חוה
אין אַ קרוין
פון צעפּ - -

קומט אַ ווינט
און רייסט זי
פאַר די האָר:
- "זאָג חוה - -
איז דאָס וואָר - -
דו ביסט אַליין
געבליבן? - -
אדמען פֿאַרטריבן?"

חוה שווייגט פֿאַרביטערט - -
ס'האָט דער ווינט,
פון חוה'ס שווייגן
אויפֿגעציטערט - -

ס'איז ניט געווען
פאַר ביידן - -
ארויסגעטריבן זיי
פון גן-עדן - -

חוה שאָקלט
מיטן קעפּל;
ווערעמדיק געווען
דער עפּל - -

אין נחל קדרון
אויף אַ טרעפּ,
זיצט חוה
אין אַ קרוין
פון צעפּ - -

In Nachal Kidron

In Kidron Valley
on a step,
sits Eve
in a crown
of braids—

A wind comes
and pulls her
by the hair:
"Tell me, Eve—
is it true—
you've been left
alone?—
Drove away Adam?"

Eve is silent, embittered—
the wind
shuddered
because of Eve's silence.

It wasn't
for the two of them—
driven out
of Eden—

Eve shakes
her head;
wormy was
the apple—

In Kidron Valley
on a step,
sits Eve
in a crown
of braids—

12. "In Nachal Kidron" (In the
Kidron Valley), poem
by Rikuda Potash.

The Kidron Valley, where idols were incinerated during the reign of the kings of Judah, is domesticated in the pre-Judaic setting of the poem: Eve, crowned with her braids in a conventional literary depiction of a young unmarried Jewish woman,[13] sits on a step. Yet this is no sentimental scene of eager, youthful anticipation; Eve's adventure is behind her as she sits solitary and disillusioned. In a modernist reversal of the biblical account, we are informed, through the agency of the wind, that it was she who drove Adam away. Eve herself does not speak but shakes her head despondently: the apple was wormy. Her crown of braids—perhaps a feminine equivalent of Jesus' crown of thorns—is unraveled by the wind, which is terrified in the face of Eve's silence. As the opening stanza is repeated at the poem's close, Eve seems to be sentenced to eternal liminality. In a travesty of domesticity, this woman with the braids of a Jewish virgin, perched on a man-made step, is part of the ominous Kidron landscape. Bezalel Narkiss (1997) suggests that some of Potash's poems be read together with Mordecai Ardon's paintings; and indeed the work of the two often seems complementary. Ardon's 1939 painting *Kidron Valley,* for example, depicts a hilly landscape that extends nearly up to the sky and is divided symmetrically by a valley, with low stone huts on one side and bare rock terraces on the other side. The location of Potash's Eve expresses a similar sense of desolation.

Potash's dialogue with Manger in this poem is signaled by the insertion of *inclusio* stanzas at the beginning and end of the poem, following his pseudofolk style. Coming from a different poetic position—that of modernist iconoclasm—she takes up his model where he leaves off, and then she refashions it. The second of Manger's "Eve" poems (1984, 11–12) presents a bewildered Adam, tempted by the fragrant apple shimmering magically in Eve's hand. Potash's Eve, in contrast, is on her own after the expulsion. Eden is set up as synonymous with togetherness, as the Yiddish *beydn* (the two of them) is rhymed with *eydn* (Eden); Eve's loneliness is her true punishment. Her implied final observation, "wormy was the apple," provides a dramatic opposition to Manger's sparkling scarlet apple *("der epl . . . finklt vi sharlakh royt"* [1984, 12]) and exposes the fallacy of its promise. The biblical Eve—and Manger's Eve—will be solaced by having children; in fact, she is the mother of all humans. But Potash's Eve is condemned to sit on her step alone in her virgin's braids, a fate ironized by the *inclusio* structure that serves as a mock-folk refrain.

13. Traditionally observant Jewish women have their hair cut off after marriage.

The physical landscape of Jerusalem, the traditional focal point of Jewish longing, was the locus of much of Potash's poetic expression, and the city is perhaps the place most commonly named in her poems. In fact, the Yiddish literary community of the Yishuv found it easiest to categorize her as "the celebrant [*bazingerin*] of Jerusalem" (Shargel 1977b, 74). Yet a pervasive sense of alienation from this affiliation is evident in the first section of Potash's "In Shotn fun Kikoyon" (In the shadow of the castor bush [1967, 121]). The speaker, though physically in Jerusalem, is estranged from it and is located in the domain of the surreal.

In the Shadow of the Castor Bush (a)

In the white nights a blue dream lies upon Jerusalem;
around a green glow fly the houses,
transparency cracks open, like a pomegranate,
I can't find the way back to my house.

So I wander on an alien shadow
of a house, or perhaps a tree,
maybe in fact the reincarnation of a tune
or indeed an old overgrown stone.

Seven times the whiteness lifts up its hands
and asks whether the reincarnation is I myself
—where to, where to, you, unknown one,
where do you want to go to now?

The title of the poem alludes to the biblical Jonah, the wandering prophet who sought in vain to flee his fate, eventually finding refuge in the shade of a wild castor bush only to have God destroy it as a warning (Jon. 4). Jerusalem, emblem of Jewish homecoming, is initially located in a white night, evoking the "white nights" of northern Europe,[14] but is immediately subsumed by the

14. This trope figures in the work of the Hebrew poet Leah Goldberg; her poem "Tel-Aviv 1935," for example, is suffused with elegiac, nostalgic images of night in European urban settings: "Like blackening pictures inside a camera / pure winter nights were reversed, / rainy summer nights overseas / and dark mornings of capital cities" (1981, 8). Other poems in Goldberg's volume represent different aspects of the immigrant experience, yet the volume is titled *Im ha-Laylah ha-Zeh* (With this night).

אין שאָטן פֿון קיקיון (א)

;אין די װײַסע נעכט ליגט אַ בלױער חלום אױף ירושלים
,פֿליִען די הײַזער אַרום אַ גרינער שײַן
,שפּאַלט זיך אױף װי אַ מילגרױם די ליטערקײט
.כ'געפֿין נישט דעם װעג אין מײַן הױז צוריק צו גײן

בלאָנדזשע איך אױף אַ פֿרעמדן שאָטן
,פֿון אַ הױז, אָדער גאָר אַ בױם
אפֿשר איז דאָס גאָר אַ גילגול פֿון אַ ניגון
.אָדער גאָר אַן אַלט-באַװאַקסענער שטײַן

זיבן מאָל הײבט אױף די װײַסקײט אירע הענט
און פֿרעגט אױב ס'איז דער גילגול איך אַלײן
--,װוּ אַהין, װוּ אַהין דו, אומבאַקאַנטע
?װוּ אַהין װילסטו איצטער גײן

13. "In shotn fun kikoyon" (In the shadow
of the castor bush), poem by Rikuda Potash.

"blue dream" that overlies it, a vision recalling the luminous dark blue of the night sky in many of Ardon's paintings. In this surreal vision, even the houses take to the air (in an image reminiscent of Marc Chagall's work, which Potash admired) as the speaker strays from one patch of shade to another. The pomegranate, its fruit tightly packed with shiny red, juicy seeds, is a complex traditional metaphor for fertility, beauty, and God's blessings in the Promised Land.[15] Yet here it becomes a mirror image of the dusty castor bush with its inedible beans, unwelcome yet ubiquitous in the Middle East. The symbol of plenty is refigured as a simile for a brilliant, barren void. The whiteness is now personified as an interrogator, asking the nameless speaker where she wants to go, in an echo of the paradigmatic *talush* question. Potash employs the formulaic "seven times" to create an even more powerful sense of the legendary combined with a sense of the inevitable: if this is an alternative reality, as the poem intimates, it is no less inescapable.

In a metaphoric progression, the speaker is transformed: the shadow is successively construed as a house, a tree (perhaps the castor bush itself), a tune—in a continuation of Potash's intriguing dialogue with Perets's "The

15. "Your cheeks are like halves of a pomegranate" (Song of Songs 4:3, 6:7); the fruit is one of the seven agricultural plant species of the Promised Land that ensure sustenance (Deut. 8:8).

Reincarnation of a Tune"—or a grass-covered stone. Finally, the speaker is revealed as the nomadic subject, a variation on the "wandering Jew" trope. Even Jerusalem cannot satisfy her need for a home; like Jonah, she is estranged and adrift. Potash uses the flexibility of Yiddish syntax to intensify the speaker's modernist dislocation and alienation. Following the initial dreamlike portrayal of the houses floating in the sky in the first two lines, the reflexive verb form *shpalt zikh* (cracks open) creates an ominous fissure at the beginning of the third line. The tension thus established is resolved at the end of the line when the subject, "transparency," is finally revealed. A subtle sound pattern joining lines 1 and 4 of the second stanza creates a paradoxical parallel between the insubstantiality of *shotn* (shadow) and the physicality of *shteyn* (stone). This Jerusalem wavers between reality and mirage, as the European "white night" dominates the scene; it is far from being the ultimate Jewish home, though it is haunted by a Jewish/Yiddish past.

Potash's mythology and poetic credo begin to emerge in the very first poem of the "Father's Pentateuch" section of *Kidron*, "Bereshis-Bild" (Genesis picture [Potash 1952, 31]), in a highly personal primeval scene. The vision reverses the biblical accounts of Creation (Gen. 1–2), in which God is the agent who carries out a plan. In Potash's cosmogony, God is an aimless wanderer who has no place in a preexisting world. Moreover, although the poem's

בראשית-בילד (א)

פיאָלעטער-גרינפֿאַרגאַסענער
פֿלעקיקער גרוייער הימל –

אין יַמישן-בעט שלאָפֿן שטערן
לייבן צעשוייבערטע און בערן.

אויף שטיינערנע וועגט,
גייט אויף די יצירה און ברענט -- --

אן אַלטאַמירא מאַלעריַי דער אַרום
ביימער מיט גרינע האַריקע קעפ -- --
פֿעלזן, שטיינער מאַזאַאיק טרעפ -- --

14. "Bereshis-bild" (Genesis picture), poem by Rikuda Potash.

גאָט גייט אַרום אין אַ לייבן-פֿעל געהילט
ער נעמט דעם שטעגן און ער גייט
ווּ אַהין? ווּ אַהין?

title incorporates the Hebrew name of the biblical book of Genesis (in Yiddish pronunciation *bereshis*), the poem is also defined as a "picture," a work of art created by human hands—a definition borne out by the poem's imagery. This is an especially discordant transgression of the Second Commandment: "You shall not make for yourself . . . any likeness of anything that is in heaven above, or that is in the earth beneath, or that is in the water under the earth" (Ex. 20:4). A tone of irony can be detected, evoking Potash's early *ars*-poetic credo of all art as illusion, established in "Illusionists."

Genesis Picture

Violet-greenwashed
blotchy gray sky—

In an ocean bed sleep stars,
disheveled lions and bears;

on stone walls
Creation rises and burns—

An Altamira painting are the surroundings
trees with green hairy heads—
cliffs, stone mosaic steps—

God walks about robed in a lion-skin
he takes the stick and goes
where to? where to?

This mythology presupposes the existence of sky, sea, stars, animals, and walls before ever introducing the concept of Creation *(yetsire)*. Though it evokes ancient Near Eastern creation stories, it is unlike both the Mesopotamian epics in which water is the primeval substance and the biblical account in which the sky and earth are the first creation. Here the sky is separated from the sea. The stars as well as the great carnivorous animals (who lend their names to the constellations Leo and Ursa) sleep in the depths. "Creation" appears as an independent entity when it is likened to the rising sun (the Yiddish *oyfgeyn* in line 6, which is the infinitive of the present-tense *geyt oyf*, is used exclusively for "sunrise"). This version of Creation harbors danger: rather than shedding light and providing warmth, it burns.

Potash has been described as a visual artist manqué (Narkiss 1997); she liked to decorate her personal letters with sketches (Fuchs 2003) and was clearly familiar with modernist European art, especially that created by Jewish artists such as Chaim Soutine and Marc Chagall.[16] She was also profoundly concerned with issues of verbal representation of the visual. Many of her poems can be described as intense verbal paintings, in which visual images are translated into words as the "real" image is represented as a work of art, highlighting the constructedness of art. In this approach, she joins in the Jewish modernist interrogation of a basic feature of Jewish culture rooted in the Second Commandment: the separation of image and voice. It was also a feature of the modernist attempt to redefine the boundaries between image and text (Mann 1997, 9). She expands her vision beyond Jewish tradition when, in a modernist stroke, she draws on European prehistoric cave art tens of thousands of years earlier than the ancient Near Eastern civilizations.

The multicolored rock art of Altamira, Spain, had exerted a profound influence on the European artistic sensibility since its discovery in the late nineteenth century and was especially significant in the primitivist bent of modernist painting. As Hugh Kenner points out, the art of a culture about whose artists there is no information exists "outside of history" (1971, 30) and thus has an immediacy that can endow it with profound personal significance. Potash reworks the prehistoric art in this spirit: whereas lifelike cave art almost exclusively depicts animals and humans painted in red ochre and is interpreted as connected with hunting rituals, her "Altamira painting" departs from warm earth tones. The color combinations are more subtle: violet washed over with green, a gray-flecked sky—colors that evoke some of Ardon's abstract expressionist paintings, such as *Valley of the Cross* (1939) and *Bethlehem* (1943), in which the sky is depicted in blotches of blue, violet, pale green, and gray.

In Potash's poem, green trees and boulders incongruously combine with man-made stone mosaic steps. The instant of artistic creation is brought into the range of human capacity.[17] When God appears, almost as an afterthought, he is not the all-powerful deity of Genesis. He materializes as a pri-

---

16. The important topics of Potash's modernist palette (which seems to follow the guidelines laid down by Kandinsky in 1912 [Kandinsky 1947]) and her connections with European visual art and artists merit careful analysis but are beyond the scope of this project.

17. A concept akin to that of Else Lasker-Schüler, who is described as believing that "art is a continuation of the first Creation" (Durchslag and Demeestere, in Lasker-Schüler 1980, xviii).

mordial human figure, dependent on animal skins for warmth, taking up his stick and going off aimlessly. In this retelling of Genesis, it is God himself who has been banished from some unknown Eden not of his making, sentenced to wander the earth in yet another permutation of the "wandering Jew" image that Potash reworks in "In the Shadow of the Castor Bush."[18] The Creation story is refigured as a prehistoric cave painting with overtones of the Babylonian Gilgamesh legend in which the hero is wrapped in a lion pelt and wields a heavy tool (Dalley 1989, 39–153), an image that recurs in the Greek mythological figure of Hercules. Dissonant notes are struck by the incongruous juxtapositions of natural features, mythology, human artifacts, and art.

The dissonance is intensified by interpolating Hebrew, Spanish, and Latin into Yiddish. Potash conventionally uses the Yiddish Hebrew-derived *yam* for "sea." But whereas in Genesis the sea is initially uninhabited—only on the fifth day does the water "bring forth swarms of living creatures" (Gen. 1:20)—Potash's *yam* is from the outset populated with stars as well as carnivores, imagery that again seems to be informed by ancient Near Eastern mythology.[19] Most crucial is her introduction of the freighted Hebrew-derived word *yetsire* (Creation), shattering the vision of a static, silent world with contrived colors and dormant creatures. The Hebrew root *y'ts'r'* (to create) is initially linked in the Bible almost exclusively with God's actions; as a verb, it first refers to God's creation of man from the earth (Gen. 2:7, 19) and later often denotes the craft of the potter. The vibrant *yetsire,* with its divine connotations, here seems caged within the stone walls on which it rises like the sun.

The word carries an additional valence for the Jewish reader; it is part of the title of the *Sefer Yetzirah* (Book of Creation), a Hebrew mystical discourse on cosmology and cosmogony composed between the second and sixth centuries C.E. and incorporated into the Kabbalah. According to the *Sefer Yetzirah,* Creation is a product of language: it was implemented through the unlimited interconnections of the twenty-two letters in the Hebrew alphabet, which in its entirety is considered a mystical name. The exis-

18. This image is powerfully revisited yet again in "Babylonian Gods."

19. Potash's version evokes the Ugaritic creation myth in which *yam* is the home of great monsters such as *tannin* and *nachash*. In the Anath texts that form part of that myth, the sea god, ruler of *yam*, challenges the authority of the storm god Ba'al and is eventually overcome by the goddess Anath, Ba'al's sister (Cassuto 1971, 93). Cassuto considers the biblical and postbiblical Jewish tradition of terrible conflict between God and *yam* with its resident monsters *tannin* and *nachash* (such as in Is. 27:1)—a tradition that poses a counterversion to the account in Genesis 1—to be rooted in this ancient epic (1971, 49—50).

tence of everything depends on its particular combination of letters (Scholem 1974, 23–25). Thus, Potash's entire cosmogony is rooted in human creativity and excludes God; indeed, language and art combine to drive God out. In fact, interpolating the Spanish place name "Altamira" as an adjective for *painting* in the very next line expropriates the scene from the mystical Jewish context, removing it from the realm of language altogether and situating it in the domain of the senses. The vision now seems to be relocated in a museum; the sense of artifice is intensified when she inserts the Latinate technical term *mosaic* in addition to the word *painting*. Indeed, neither biblical Creation nor God has a place in this contrived universe: the first is transmuted, whereas the second—though he "walks" like God in the Garden of Eden (using the same Yiddish phrase, *geyt arum,* as in Yehoyesh's translation of Gen. 3, 8)—takes up the wanderer's staff and leaves with no clear destination. God is now the *talush.*

Potash subscribes to the modernist principle of conflating different artistic media and combining sensory experiences such as sight, sound, and touch. In "Illusionists," the plaintive "didl-didl," the childlike repetition of the street organ's tone during the horrific street show, lends a deceptive air of innocence. The poems that apostrophize and celebrate the Israeli desert region of Timna are rich in warm shades of red and brown and coruscate with bright metallic tones and ringing sound as the immediacy of sight and sound are melded through innovative syntactic reworking to evoke personal visions. In "A Tfile fun an Odler" (An eagle's prayer [Potash 1952, 13]), for example, the magical transmutation of substances is manifested by refashioning a noun into a verb: "The copper [*kuper*] from underneath / coppers [*kupert*] a prayer." Her language mimics the metallurgic process in which human agency transforms raw ore into workable metal. The protector of the mine in "Der letster Shoymer" (The last watchman [1952, 18–21]) is subsumed into the metal he is guarding: "Slowly copper themselves [*es kupert zikh*] / the head and the hair; / the eyes, the neck / and the ears as well— /slowly [*pamelekh*] the watchman [*shoymer*] becomes / lost in copper [*kuper*]" (20). The recurring harsh consonants *k* and *p* in *kuper* reproduce the clang of metal, until the softer *sh* and *m* of *shoymer,* further muted by the gentle *m* and *l* that follow the initial hard *p* of *pamelekh,* disappear into the final repetition of the metallic *kuper.*

Potash refracts "Canaanite" themes such as pagan gods and traditions selectively through the prism of her particular sensibility. In Shamri's "Leyzer Tsipress," a celebration of the communal ethos, the land of Canaan begs the

Jewish protagonist who has come from the Diaspora to plow it as soon as possible in order to fulfil the communal goal (1970, 39). Potash, in contrast, invests the land and its gods with purely personal significance. Perhaps the most striking expression of her idiosyncratic construction of the local is manifested in "In Tammuz" (1967, 218–19).

In Tammuz

Old Tammuzes with gray beards
sink and pass away on the dark earth.
Old Tammuzes with folds over their eyes
I escorted into the hill,
bowed my head before them—
now comes toward me
a young Tammuz,
his eyes like a grape,
on an eagle he flew
down to the Judean mountains,
I presented him with
a red cherry-tree a dream.

Tammuz!
Wondrous Tammuz!
Seduce me not!
As you seduce
the young moon— —
Although the dovecote is empty
the pigeon couple flew away
into the avenue of pines [oren],
the pine-tree [zhivitse-boym] is fragrant
somewhere with a lost day
of an unwritten poem,
and a large watermelon head
thinks about my tired hands—

the knife lies concealed . . .
Will I then be as cruel
as Judith with Holofernes's head?
Wondrous Tammuz!
Seduce me not!

אין תמוז

אַלטע תמוזן מיט גרויע בערד,
זינגען און פֿאַרגייען אויף דער טונקעלער ערד.
אַלטע תמוזן מיט פֿאַלדן אויף די אויגן
האָב איך באַגלייט אין באַרג אַריַין,
מײַן קאָפּ פֿאַר זיי געבויגן —
איצטער קומט מיר אַנטקעגן
אַ יונגער תמוז,
ווי אַ ווײַנטרויב זײַנע אויגן,
ער איז מיט אַן אָדלער
אין די הרי-יהודה אַראָפּגעפֿלויגן,
איך האָב אים אַנטקעגנגעטראָגן
אַ רויטן קערשנבוים אַ חלום.

תמוז!
אויסטערלישער תמוז!
פֿאַרפֿיר מיך נישט!
ווי דו פֿאַרפֿירסט
די יונגע לבֿנה -- --
כאַטש דער טויבנשלאַק איז לײדיק
דאָס טויבן-פֿאָר איז געפֿלויגן
אין דער אורן-אָלעע,
דער זשוויווצע-בוים שמעקט
ערגעץ מיט אַ פֿאַרלוירענעם טאָג
פֿון אַ נישט-דערשריבן ליד,
און אַ גרויסער אַרבוזן-קאָפּ
טראַכט וועגן מײַנע מידע הענט —

ס'מעסער ליגט באַהאַלטן...
וועל' איך דען זײַן אַזוי אכזריותדיק
ווי יהודית מיט הליפֿרנסנס קאָפּ?
אויסטערלישער תמוז!
פֿאַרפֿיר מיך נישט!

15. "In Tammuz" (In Tammuz), poem by Rikuda Potash.

The title, "In Tammuz," carries a primarily temporal valence. "Tammuz" is the name of a month in the Jewish calendar, yet this name, which epitomizes national and religious disaster in traditional Judaism (the sieges of both the First and Second Temples are said to have begun on the seventeenth day of Tammuz), is itself a relict of Near Eastern antiquity, before the cultures diverged, when terms common to regional languages were widely current.[20] The expectation of "Tammuz" as a month, promised by the title, is immediately subverted by the reference to multiple figures. The Babylonian variation of the Sumerian god Dumuzi is the god of fertility and the harvest, as well as the lover of the goddess Ishtar (Astarte). In this mythology, Tammuz dies for the sin of trying to usurp Ishtar's rule and is reborn every year; women mourn the death of the god who emblematizes virility.[21] In the Bible, the Tammuz cult, practiced by women, is part of

20. The names of all the Jewish months are derived from the ancient Akkadian.

21. The myth is ubiquitous in the ancient Near East and is reflected, for example, in the Egyptian cults of the male god Osiris and his female consort Isis. Gertz (1985) uses the seminal Tammuz myth, appropriated by Yonatan Ratosh, for the title of her essay on Ratosh, denoting the entire complex and function of ancient Near Eastern mythology in his poetry.

Ezekiel's denunciation of those who profane the house of the Lord: "[The angel] said also to me, 'You will see still greater abominations which they commit.' And he brought me to the entrance of the north gate of the house of the lord, and behold, there sat women weeping for Tammuz" (Ez. 8:13–14). Thus, biblical Jewish tradition marks Tammuz as the emblem of undesirable pagan practices. The speaker's personal construct of "Tammuz" evolves in the course of Potash's poem: the first line presents the dying manifestations of an aged god, followed halfway through the poem by the appearance of a vigorous young divinity, who is then threatened by an increasingly powerful female speaker.

The poem may be read in dialogue with two of Shaul Tchernichovsky's Hebrew poems: the 1909 "Mot ha-Tamuz" (The death of the Tammuz [1990, 74–76]), which introduces the Tammuz myth into a biblical context, and the 1936 "Ayit! Ayit al Harayikh!" (Eagle! Eagle over your hills! [1990, 384]), in which a supernaturally huge eagle is depicted as casting a permanent menacing shadow over the land.[22] Even more significant, Potash's poem sounds an antiphonal note to Ardon's 1962 painting *Tammuz*.[23] Ardon's painting depicts an ethereal androgynous Tammuz, floating in a luminous blue night sky next to a crescent moon, holding a stringed instrument. The instrument, held at the pelvic region, has been invested with the "deeper significance of creativity" as well as with femininity (Vishny 1974, 43).[24] Potash literally brings the pagan Tammuz myth back to earth, first resituating it in a diasporic Jewish setting: she invests the old incarnations of the god with a stereotypical Jewish appearance, gray-bearded and hooded-eyed. Contradictory images create an ambivalence: whereas her title dissociates the god from his tangible image and hints at a temporal location, the apparition of the young god is instantly physicalized and now locally situated. He is borne on eagle's wings to the geographic setting of the Judean Mountains around Jerusalem, and his eyes are grapelike—the paradigmatic local fruit, which

22. "Eagle! Eagle over Your Hills" is usually interpreted in the context of the 1936–39 Arab uprising, in the course of which many Jewish settlements were attacked. It is interesting that Potash and Tchernichovsky were both members of the cultural salon in the Narkiss home (Narkiss 1997).

23. Based on its location in the last section of *Poems,* the poem could be roughly contemporaneous with Ardon's painting. However, as noted, hardly any of Potash's work is dated.

24. The moon symbolizes a pagan goddess in the pantheons of some ancient Near Eastern cultures, such as that of the Nabateans, among the forerunners of the Arabs.

16. Mordecai Ardon, *Tammuz* (1962), oil on canvas; photograph by Avraham Chai, courtesy of Michael Ardon.

ripens in late summer and produces intoxicating wine. This Tammuz is of both sky and earth.

The speaker reverses the geographical and cultural context once again as she presents Tammuz with a red cherry tree, a traditional European symbol of spring. Cherries hold special significance in Potash's lexicon of images: she refers to her girlhood as *"mayn kershn-tsayt"* (my cherry time) in a group of poems devoted to memories of her youth and family (Potash 1967, 33–67). The vivid sensuality of the red cherry dream stands in strong contrast to the nostalgic, ephemeral images of her European youth, such as the aromatic pine tree, with its inedible fruit and unfulfilled promise. The cultural dissonance of the local versus the nonlocal is jarringly expressed through the interpolation of modern Hebrew. In successive lines, the Jerusalem pine (modern Hebrew *oren*)[25] and the European pine (Slavic Yiddish *zhivitse*) produce opposing associations: although the pigeon "couple," a symbol of domesticity, has disappeared into the Jerusalem pines planted in a man-made avenue, the wild European pine emits its evocative fragrance of lost opportunities. The watermelon "head," earthy emblem of summer, is antithetical to the soaring Tammuz. These images counter the semiabstract figure in Ardon's painting, which is suspended at a distance from the earth and does not attain a grounded materiality. Yet both Ardon and Potash represent the metapoetic as problematic: Ardon's musician has arms but no hands, whereas Potash's speaker mourns an unwritten poem.

Fiercely declaring her independence, Potash subverts the Tammuz myth, which posits the god as a procreative life force, when she represents him as a threat to her own creativity. This Tammuz is outlandish and alien and intensifies the sense of poetic frustration brought on by the fragrance of a "lost day / of an unwritten poem." Yet she refuses to be seduced away from her art, unlike the young moon (feminine-gendered in the Yiddish-inflected Hebrew word *levone*), who becomes invisible as the lunar month begins. Powerfully fusing cultures and traditions, Potash threatens Tammuz with the fate of Holofernes (in the apocryphal Book of Judith, the Assyrian commander who endangers the people of Israel and is beheaded by the beautiful Jewish widow Judith, whom he tried to seduce). This reference to the ultimate aggressive act upon an enemy in an erotic setting, specifically by a Jewish woman who is held up (mostly by non-Jews) as a model of feminine valor, has radical implications.[26] The poetic speaker, attracted to the eroticism embodied in Tammuz's grape eyes and seductive powers, rebels against the inevitable course of events dictated by the myth. She is ready to slay Tammuz—the artist who lacks hands—in order to complete her own work of art.

25. The fast-growing, native Jerusalem pine *(Pinus halepensis)* has been ubiquitous in Israel since it was introduced for reforestation by the British Mandate authorities in the 1920s.

26. Potash's speaker differs from that in "Ikh bin a Tsirkus-dame" (I am a circus lady) by the modernist female Yiddish poet Celia Dropkin (Korman 1928, 163–64). Dropkin's first-person protagonist is aware of the magnetism of danger as she longs to fall onto the daggers of her circus act yet does nothing to ward off the danger.

The complexity of Potash's dual location in European and Near Eastern cultures and the innovativeness of her particular vision are clearer if we realize that the story of Judith and Holofernes, prefigured in the poem by the image of a severed "watermelon head," is a staple of Renaissance and Baroque art. The Book of Judith is not included in the Hebrew Bible, nor is it part of the Jewish imaginary. Potash, with her expertise in European art, would have been familiar with the "Judith and Holofernes" depictions by painters such as the fifteenth-century Andrea Mantegna, Donatello, and Botticelli, and the seventeenth-century Caravaggio, to name the best known. A more conventional Jewish poem with the same thematics would probably have alluded to the Jael and Sisera episode (Jud. 4), on which the Judith story is clearly patterned. "In Tammuz" fuses the disparate cultural elements of Potash's integrative poetic world. The prebiblical Tammuz and the postbiblical Judith (ignoring the biblical stratum, which figured so largely in Yishuv culture) are effectively combined with Near Eastern and European landscapes to voice Potash's particular credo.

Potash's problematics are poignantly expressed in "Bovlishe Geter" (Babylonian gods [1967, 162]), which juxtaposes ancient regional gods with the speaker's personal deity. Reflecting Potash's location at a nexus of traditional Jewish culture and modernism, the poem engages in dialogue with traditional Yiddish imagery as well as with key thematics of premodern and modernist Hebrew poetry.

The non-Jewish gods are simultaneously endowed with life and lifeless. The speaker evokes and refashions biting biblical satire, such as that in Psalms 115:3–8, which is chanted every year as part of the Passover Haggadah.[27] The foreign gods combine artificial and natural substances: bronze, manufactured in antiquity out of copper and tin, with granite, one of the most durable rock materials used in the ancient Near East. In a paraphrase of the biblical description, the Babylonian gods are lifeless. For all their sheen

---

27. "Our God is in the heavens; he does whatever he pleases. / Their idols are silver and gold, the work of men's hands. / They have mouths, but do not speak; eyes, but do not see. / They have ears, but do not hear; noses, but do not smell. / They have hands, but do not feel; feet, but do not walk; and they do not make a sound in their throat. / Those who make them are like them; so are all who trust in them." The trope, with variations, recurs elsewhere in the Bible, perhaps most notably in Isaiah 40:19–20 and 44:9–20. It was reworked in Yiddish as a mocking song, with more than one version. Thus, a 1901 text reads, "Eyes have they / but cannot see / Oy and vey is their lot / blind Gods have they" (Ginzburg and Marek 1991, 35 and a different version on 36). Yet another version appears in Kotylansky 1954, 53–57.

and strength, they cannot feel or express emotion, although they were created in the process that emblematizes life: they were born of their goddess-
mother. The speaker's god, in contrast, is a powerless infant, an orphan who
is secured—or imprisoned—by Jewish ritual accessories of a sacred, protec-
tive nature: he is swaddled in phylactery straps *(rets'ues)* and falls asleep on
a bed of parchment lettering *(parmet-oysyes)*.[28]

בבֿלישע געטער

זייער מאַמע-גאָט
האָט זיי געבוירן
פֿון בראָנדז און גראַניט.
זייערע פּנימער
האָבן נישט קיין שמייכל,
קיין געוויין.

מײַן גאָט
איז געוויקלט אין רצועות
פֿון ייִדישער פּײַן.

ער גייט שלאָפֿן
אויף אַ בעט פֿון פּאַרמעט-אותיות –
ווײַל זיי ליגן געשענדט.

בבֿלישע געטער
קאָנען נישט געבוירן
קיין געוויין.

מײַן גאָט איז אַ יתום
צווישן פֿײַער,
שטורעם,
אין קיינעמס לאַנד.

Babylonian Gods

Their mother-god
bore them
out of bronze and granite.
Their faces
have no smile,
no crying.

My god
is swaddled in straps
of Jewish anguish.

He goes to sleep
on a bed of parchment-letters—
because they lie violated.

Babylonian gods
cannot give birth
to crying.

My god is an orphan
amid fire,
storm,
in no one's land.

17. "Bovlishe Geter" (Babylonian
gods), poem by Rikuda Potash.

Potash's use of the Yiddish-inflected Hebrew words *retsu'es* (Hebrew
retzu'ot, "thongs") and *oysyes* (Hebrew *otiyot,* "letters") constitutes a multiple transgression. In traditional Jewish culture, only men wear the phylac-

28. Copies of the Jewish Bible meant for reading during synagogue services are handwrit-
ten on parchment.

teries and read the Bible; a female poet incorporating these sacred attributes into her poetry is infringing on social convention. The violation is compounded when she introduces these masculine emblems of religious ritual into the domain of the domestic, traditionally reserved for women: the phylactery straps, used to secure holy texts, here serve as swaddling for an infant, and the parchment inscribed with sacred letters is the infant's bed. The image of the Jewish god swaddled—or confined—in phylactery straps has significant antecedents in modern Hebrew poetry. Tchernichovsky incorporated it into his "Le-nokhach Pesel Apolo" (Facing a statue of Apollo), written in 1899, when Hebrew was being revived as a modern language. The poem was revolutionary for its time and shocking in its explicit admiration of Greek culture (anathema to religious Jewish tradition) and prerabbinic Jewish religion. In the closing phrase of Tchernichovsky's poem, the speaker comments wryly on the decline of the Jewish God: "The God of those who conquered Canaan by storm—/was imprisoned in phylactery straps" (1990, 87). Thirty years later Avraham Shlonsky reworked the image in clear dialogue with Tchernichovsky in his 1927 poem "Amal" (Toil), in which the Zionist "rebuilding" of the land is figured as religious worship and the land itself is the worshiper. In Shlonsky's depiction, "my country wears light like a prayer shawl [*tallit*]. / Houses stand like phylacteries [*totafot*]. / And like phylactery straps roads stretch down, paved by hands" (1927b, 88). Thus, the image of phylactery straps, firmly anchored in the Jewish symbolic lexicon, was differently appropriated by different writers; Potash was perhaps the only female poet of her time, however, who incorporated it so definitively into the feminine poetic domain.

In her final appropriation of God, he is far removed from the majestic figure linked with the fire and storm of the Mount Sinai revelation ("And Mount Sinai was wrapped in smoke, because the Lord descended upon it in fire . . . and the whole mountain quaked greatly" [Ex. 16:18]). Here, God is a pathetic orphaned figure, an intensification of the divine wanderer in "Genesis Picture," cast in the image of the paradigmatic exile, Cain, or by implication the "wandering Jew." Potash achieves this startling association by using the Yiddish words *keyn* (none), *keynem* (no one), and their derivatives four times to resonate with the similar sound pattern of *kayins* (Cain's). Yet, by the same token, becoming free from (literally) binding tradition and sallying out into "no one's land" *(keynems land)* incorporate great potential for self-expression. Neither the Jewish god nor the "Babylonian gods" can provide fulfillment.

A keen artistic presence is filtered through a strong attachment to the landscape in Potash's "Timna" poems. Barbara Mann notes that "the representation of landscape is always tied to larger questions concerning culture and identity" (1999, 236). Potash's artistic sensibility was powerfully drawn to the desert, which the nativist perception—following the biblical tradition that views the Israelites' desert period as a time of spiritual integrity—considered part of the nation's originary location.[29] The "Timna" section that constitutes one-third of *Moyled iber Timna* (New Moon over Timna [Potash 1960, 8–28]) resonates with the scenery and traditions of Israel's Negev Desert. Attraction to the desert as a link with the distant national past was so much a part of Israeli culture that the Yiddish poet Avrom Sutzkever, writing in Israel, identifies a piece of flint as the knife that slaughtered sacrifices to God (1968, 133). In a poetry collection titled *In Midber-Sinay* (In the Sinai Desert), a title that evokes the period that the Bible idealizes, Sutzkever carries on a dialogue both with the biblical vision of the dry bones (Ez. 37) and with Bialik's important 1902 *poema* "The Dead of the Desert," which implies that the nation is a giant slumbering in a desert yet capable of attaining glory (Bialik 1950, 354–63). In Sutzkever's vision, God blows the breath of life into "your dead nation, dead bones," whose veins are growing warmer in the granite and quartz desert rock (1957, 12).

Potash constructs a personal imagery as she incorporates the desert into the traditional feminine domain—that of home. In "Di Kuper-greber" (The copper miners), "a cradle stands on the path / and rocks and rocks / bygone days— / not the family / the cradle stands and rocks and rocks" (1960, 17). Here, the traditional Jewish cradle, so eminent in family life and lore, nurtures and safeguards the distant past. Tellingly, there are no biblical elements in the poems of *New Moon over Timna*. She combines pagan, premonotheistic deities and landscapes with postbiblical figures of Jewish thought, thereby negating Zionism's selective reconstruction of the Jewish past. In "Der Kuperner Melekh" (The copper king [1960, 25–26]), the demon Ashmedai (a postbiblical Jewish construct) travels the Milky Way (a name derived from Greek mythology) in company with the feminine-gendered young moon (the Yiddish-inflected Hebrew-derived *levone*, moon); and in "Der Letster Shoymer" (The last watchman [1960, 21]), the ancient Near Eastern god

---

29. This sense is perhaps most eloquently expressed in Jeremiah, as God addresses the nation: "Thus says the Lord, I remember the devotion of your youth . . . how you followed me in the wilderness, in a land not sown. / Israel was holy to the Lord" (Jer. 2.2–3).

Tammuz makes his first appearance in her corpus as he vanishes along with summer. Elements of folklore rhetoric are introduced in "Der Veg fun Timna" (The Timna road [1960, 11–12]), when the speaker sounds a call, couched in formulaic terms, to "cross seven strides / seven times seven / bow down before the copper-god / seven times seven" (11).

The poetic significance of the desert landscape and of Timna in particular is perhaps most explicit in the apostrophic poem that opens *New Moon over Timna*: "Gli Mikh Oys" (Glow me out [1960, 8–9]). Potash conflates divinities, domains, and locations in a prayer for integrity that is rendered more powerful by unusual and ambiguous linguistic usage.

In a breathless rhythm, conveyed by the brief lines often linked by enjambements, the speaker apostrophizes a changing entity. Jonathan Culler defines the act of apostrophizing as the act of "constituting the object as another subject with whom the poetic subject might hope to strike up a harmonious relationship" (1981, 143). As the poem begins, Potash's apostrophe seems to work toward constituting a single object. The initial addressee is God, but Timna—God's creation—joins its creator, as the addressee is doubled and the identities become conflated three lines before the end of the poem.

The imagery is an incongruous blend of domains: the divine, male sphere of artisanship that borders on both the magical and the artistic, and the domestic female sphere of housework, here also equated with the divine. First, God is portrayed as a metalworker, forging the copper-producing site of Timna out of the fiery universe through metallurgy, the craft universally perceived as mysterious because it results in what seems to be alchemy: materials and forms are transformed into other, seemingly unrelated materials and forms. Next, "Solomon's Pillars" (a natural sandstone formation of the Timna region, named in the same hebraizing spirit that invented the modern name of the region) are given volition and power in this world where the inanimate is endowed with life. At this point, the speaker resituates the theological and metapoetic apostrophe in a stereotypical feminine domestic scene, when she asks God to knead her in and mix her thoroughly, as though making bread—a transmutation of substances that recalls metallurgy. This image is abruptly confounded when one of the ingredients of this homely product is revealed to be quartz, a component of sandstone and one of the hardest substances in nature. The speaker wishes for her human blood to mix with the lifeless mineral in order to create the new compound that will sustain her individuality. The repeated references to heat and light evoke both smithy and kitchen, loci of human creativity that can be linked to the divine. Finally, the speaker combines the creation, Timna, with the creator, God, when she addresses both but closes abruptly with the latter. She has undergone a transmutation of purpose: whereas at the outset she asked the addressee to "glow" her into the copper, now she asks to be "coppered out" (recasting the noun *copper* as a verb).[30] Her closing wish is to be "glowed out" *(gli mikh oys),* made radiant.

גלי מיך אויס

אינעם פֿײַערדיקן יקום
אויס וואָס האָסט אויסגעגליט
ת מ נ ע
גלי מיך אינעם קופער
שטעמפל מײַן ליד
און לאָז אַרײַן מיך
אין דײַן יצירה
ווי איך האָב דיך אַרײַנגעלאָזט
איו מײַן שטומקייט —
גאָט
אין דער וויסטעניש
פֿון דײַנע מכרות
דאָ ווו די זײַלן פֿון שלמהן
שטורעמען מיט גבורה,
קנעט מיך אַרײַן
און מיש מיך אויס,
מיט זייער אוראַלטן קיזל
זאָל מײַן בלוט מיט שטיין
זיך ריזלען
מיט די אויסטערלישע
קיזלען —
לאָז מיך בלײַבן האַרטנעקיק
ע ק ש נ ו ת ד י ק
און קופער מיך אויס
אין דיר
ת מ נ ע
גלי דו מיך אויס
גאָט

18. "Gli Mikh Oys" (Glow me out), poem by Rikuda Potash.

Glow Me Out

In the fiery universe
from which you have glowed out
Timna
glow me into the copper
stamp my song
and admit me
into your creation
as I have admitted you
into my muteness—
God
in the desolation
of your mines,
here where Solomon's pillars
storm with might,
knead me in
and mix me through,
with their primeval quartz
let my blood with stone
trickle
with the outlandish quartzes—
let me remain
stubborn
obstinate
and copper me out
in you
Timna
you, glow me out [of]
God.

(emphases in the original)

Potash overturns normative Yiddish usage by interpolating high-register Hebrew words that are not part of traditional discourse but were adopted by modern Hebrew. *Yekum*, the biblical term that I have translated in the modern Hebrew sense of "universe," appears in Genesis 7:4, where it denotes "every living thing" that God plans to destroy in the Flood. *Yetsire*, "Creation," as noted, evokes an entire mystical semantic domain; *mikhres* (Hebrew *mikhrot*, "mines"), which occurs once in the Bible (Zeph. 2:9), is widely used in modern Hebrew; and the noun *gevura* (might), is part of literary usage. The juxtaposition of "might," offering connotations of God's majesty, with the homey request to "knead me in and mix me thoroughly" creates a keen opposition between the ineffable and the domestic. In a poem with no regular meter, Potash uses rhyme only once, to juxtapose opposites: the verb *rizlen* (trickle) is countered by *kizlen* (quartzes). The contrast between the flowing warm-hued liquid that metonymizes life and the inert glassy stone particles places in question the possibility of reconciling the two.

As in "In the Shadow of the Castor Bush," the inversion of Yiddish syntax results in subtle shifts in emphases. Initially the subject uses normal syntax: *"gli mikh oys"* (glow me out); *"shtempl mayn lid"* (stamp my song). The enhanced foregrounding of her presence is marked by syntactic dislocation. When she says *"loz arayn mikh / in dayn yetsire / vi ikh hob dikh arayngelozt / in mayn shtumkeyt"* (admit me / into your Creation / as I have admitted you / into my muteness), her repositioning of the subject *mikh* (me) at the end of the line and after the verb *loz arayn* (admit into)—rather than preserving normative order, which would be *loz mikh arayn*)—places it in apposition to *dikh* (you), God, located in the penultimate position in that line, and sets speaker and addressee on equal footing. Now she can propose the exchange: you let me into your Creation as I have let you into my muteness. In this modernist moment, the artist and God are equals. However, in both places where the addressee is named, his name is set off on a line by itself. The position of the last mention of God, in the final line following an address to Timna, makes possible both a kataphoric and an anaphoric reading: either Timna or God can be the "you" of the penultimate line. Thus is the boundary between creator and creation obscured.

---

30. A usage similar to Sutzkever's *"gefeldzikte vuksn"* (rockified heights [1952, 70]).

"My God Is an Orphan": Critical Reception

As her poems reveal, Potash is located in an ambivalent intercultural limbo, neither in the Diaspora nor in the homeland. Local contemporaneous critics largely focused on the single theme of Jerusalem in her work and portrayed her as predominantly attempting to reconcile the displacedness of Yiddish with the tangible aspects of the Zionist homeland. Yet her work is much more complex than this essentializing view concedes. Yiddish critics outside Palestine construed her local thematics as a betrayal of the cause of Yiddish: a Yiddish poet, by definition homeless and owing allegiance to the word alone, should not write so intimately about a landscape-even that of the ancestral homeland (for example, "copper me out in you, Timna" [Potash 1960, 9]).

Moreover, if the landscape is that of the Land of Israel, firmly linked in Jewish thought with the Jewish God, pagan gods such as Tammuz should not be personally and passionately apostrophized. Paradoxically, her linguistic praxis was condemned for an aspect that is fundamental in Yiddish: she was berated for incorporating too much of another language (Hebrew, considered a foreign language by many Yiddish purists), deviating from "true" Yiddish and thus delegitimizing her as a Yiddish writer. The difficulty of categorizing Potash was compounded by the fact that many literary critics usually characterized female poets separately as "private, vague, conventional, intuitive, romantic, and appropriately emotional" (Hellerstein 1994, 138).[31] A woman who wrote modernist poetry that simultaneously was historically informed and struck a strong primeval chord was certainly an aberration. Finally, the anomaly was intensified by her lingering solitariness within a Yiddish subculture that as a minority in a collective-exalting culture depended on close ties between its members.

The dichotomy between Potash's worlds underlies these different critical

31. Hellerstein (1994) offers an intriguing view of the role and politics of anthologizing as a major factor in establishing literary canons. Although Korman's 1928 ground-breaking anthology legitimized and preserved the tradition of Yiddish poetry written by women, dating to the beginnings of Yiddish literature (xxvii), the very inclusion of these writers in a collection of women's poetry meant that they were irretrievably relegated to the category of "women poets," circumscribing their significance in Yiddish letters. The categorization continues to apply. The 1987 anthology edited by Howe, Wisse, and Shmeruk, for example, includes the poems of thirty-four men but only five women (Potash is not among them).

responses, which avoided addressing the complex nature of her work.[32] Y. Z. Shargel subtitled his 1955 essay on Potash "Di Bazingerin fun Yerusholayim" (The celebrant of Jerusalem). Playing on the literal meaning of Potash's first name, "dance," Shargel constructed an elaborate gender-oriented metaphor in which her poems, "like her name, are so dancing [*rikudike*], so light-footed, full of hints" (1977b, 74). Limiting himself to her Jerusalem poems, he conceded that they are "not only the womanly prayer of a traditionally observant woman" (75), thereby betraying his preconceptions. He concluded: "Jerusalem calls and arouses *yiddishkeyt* in her, her poem dances a circle around Jerusalem, loved and hallowed for generations" (76).

The image of Potash as a female poet in the conventional mold, focusing on Judaism's timeless hub from a "feminine" perspective, set the tone for later critiques. Aryeh Shamri locates her in the stereotypical feminine domain of the home in his eulogy: "With the distinctive note of the Yiddish poem . . . in every stone on the hills—she sought a foundation for a home and a redress for lost domesticity [*heymishkeyt*]" (1965, 19). Introducing Potash's posthumous *Poems,* Yeshayahu Shpigl first characterizes her poetry as influenced by symbolist and romanticist writers and goes on to describe her as typically Jewish/Yiddish and feminine: "Her poetic prayer [*tfile*] grew out of the gray, stony loneliness of a Jewish woman poet" (1967, 8). Although Shpigl uses the Hebrew-derived *tfile,* he adopts the stereotypes attached to Jewish female poets, the earliest of whom are associated with a characteristic type of "poetic prayer": *tkhines,* prayers created for (though not necessarily by) and said exclusively by women. Because the subject matter of *tkhines* usually comes from the domain of domesticity, Shpigl locates Potash in that domain by association.

The critique by Yankev Glatshteyn (1963, 69–76) reveals other biases. Glatshteyn began as a leader of the introspectivist poetic group In Zikh (1919), a movement concerned with "the details of form and language . . . the right word in the right place, no superfluous similes or adjectives" (Har-

---

32. In much the same way, Esther Raab tended to be categorized as a landscape poet (Miron 1991, 23) and Dvora Baron to be defined by her shtetl stories (Miron 1987, 277). Needless to say, the work of both writers is considerably more multifaceted than these labels imply.

shav 1990, 184).[33] In his scathing 1960 review of *New Moon over Timna* (scathing but nonetheless spanning seven pages), Glatshteyn accuses Potash of lacking self-discipline: "One sees that the poet's breath was taken away. She wants to say something through seeing, but no longer has control over the words. . . . Many poems come out of Rikuda Potash's poem-smithy so hot and molten that they have no chance of becoming the word-instrument that poems must be, but are smelted poesy, where word, sound, momentum, mood, picture, meaning, everything bubbles and boils" (1963b, 70). This terminology evokes Uri Tsvi Grinberg's expressionist proclamation, which extols the chaotic in art: "We are in favor of the free, naked, blood-seething human expression" (1922a, 4). As an introspectivist, Glatshteyn's antipathy toward this maximalist version of expressionism apparently slants his opinion of Potash's work so that he sees it as a "babble" *(geplapl)* that lacks the reflectiveness admired by introspectivism (1963, 72). Potash, he says, "surrenders to her visions with a shuddering rhythm of the word" (70). Glatshteyn deprives her of agency and renders her a passive, helpless vehicle of inchoate impressions, less significant in his view even than Gertrude Stein, who consciously employed "automatic writing" (71). He singles out her interpolation of Hebrew words into the Yiddish text as especially heinous; one of his first comments is against her "hebraized Yiddish [*hebraizirten yidish*]" (69).[34] He stereotypes Potash as female in the classical fashion by saying that "even her calm poems are hysterical" (70). After effectively delegitimizing her art as hysteria, he speaks patronizingly about the fondness that "one can even develop for her charming defects [*kheynevdike khesroynos*], for the Oriental song [*orientalishe gezang*] of a Yiddish poetess [*poetese*] in the land of Israel" (75). Like the Israeli critics, Glatshteyn thus schematizes Potash's complex poetic vision to fit his own preconceptions.

Rikuda Potash is perhaps the paradigmatic example of a writer who resists classification. Although Jewish culture and language are obviously the principal elements of her multifaceted poetic world, her poetry is an amalgam of components from different spheres and semantic domains. Her concerns are not exclusively those of the community—neither of the

33. Introspectivism has been described as a reaction to the aestheticist neoromantic poetics of its predecessors, Di Yunge (the Young Generation), as well as to expressionism with its "coarse and pathetic expression" (Harshav 1990, 178).

34. Interestingly, Glatshteyn excoriates in Potash the same type of Hebrew-Yiddish interweaving and rhyming that he praises in the work of Rochl Fishman, an American-born Yiddish poet who lived on an Israeli kibbutz from 1954 until her death in 1984. The poems of Fishman,

"Canaanite" minority nor of the mainstream Yishuv, which appropriated "Canaanite" thematics, nor yet of the Yishuv's marginal Yiddish culture. Her language is often a personal construct that incorporates biblical and modern Hebrew as well as European and Near Eastern sources. Her work should be viewed as an example of a singular voice that developed in the face of cultural calls to uniformity, calls sounded even within the minority Yiddish culture, which was, because of its linguistic vehicle, a culture of dissent. Her statement "My god is an orphan in no one's land" creates the possibility that an original identity may be forged in unclaimed territory. Yiddish, the fusion language that accepts disparate elements, combined with Rikuda Potash's modernist sensibility to serve as the proper vehicle for her particular version of the Palestine experience. Her "Canaanizing" poems are unique in Yiddish modernism as well as in the cultural climate of the Yishuv and early Israel. They are at one and the same time profoundly Jewish (primarily, of course, through language) and pagan, Palestinian and European, situated in the present and in the past. Potash's oeuvre offers an intriguing option: the god of "Genesis Picture"—who takes up a stick and wanders "where to?"— is free to construct a new world, one open to diverse elements from widely differing locations.

---

whose speaker is a figurative daughter of Shamri's "Leyzer Tsipress," revel in the collective experience on the land. Glatshteyn characterizes her poetry as "free of Jewish worry " and approves of her "yiddishized Hebrew [*ayngeyidishten hebreish*]" (1963a, 134). It should be noted that Glatshteyn moderated his criticism of Potash in an essay written after her death, in which he characterizes her Hebrew-infused Yiddish, along with that of other Yiddish writers in Israel, as "fresh and fruitful" (1972, 141).

Epilogue

This book may be seen as the logical continuation of a personal process of cultural archaeology. My own culture has been predominantly Hebrew, shaped in the Zionist Yishuv and Israel, yet its roots lie deep in my family's "Yiddishlands" in Poland, the United States, and Palestine. The initial impetus for this project came from a personal return of the repressed—the resurfacing of long-forgotten turns of phrase, complete with beloved intonations and gestures. I was leafing through Mordecai Kosover's study of Palestinian Yiddish when Chaim Ben-Tziyon Segal's voice, gone for more than thirty years, suddenly became audible to me. My paternal grandfather Chaim was born in Turkish Ottoman Jerusalem in 1885 and was part of my life until his death in 1973. Always ready to amuse a child with tuneful songs and colorful drawings, his warm and engaging personality was conveyed primarily through a language that combined Arabic, Turkish, English, and Hebrew within the frame of Yiddish. This rich linguistic tapestry seemed perfectly natural because it was echoed in my parents' fluidity of movement between Hebrew, Yiddish, and English in their own speech. When this flexibility resurfaced as a legitimate part of my cultural foundations, I decided to examine the conventional assumptions about Yiddish in the Yishuv. After all, Yiddish was a component of the culture that had been incorporated in at least one product of the Yishuv—myself. Clearly, it had not disappeared as utterly as the history books implied.

Israel's academic community had adopted the mainstream Zionist attitude. The inauguration of a chair of Yiddish studies at the Hebrew University in September 1951 provided the language with the beginnings of legitimation in Israeli culture. In his speech for the inauguration, the newly appointed head of the chair, Dov Sadan, kept the discussion on an academic plane, quoting Bialik on one aspect of the relationship between Hebrew and Yiddish: by providing a colloquial medium, Yiddish and the other languages spoken by Jews helped to preserve Hebrew. In 1930, Bialik had said, "We owe a debt to the Yiddish language, for it warmed [preserved] the Hebrew language for a long time" (1935c, 155). Yiddish was thus relegated to the status of a minor cultural phenomenon that apparently functioned in the service of the major force, Hebrew. This account perpetuates the traditional metaphor of the Hebrew-Yiddish hierarchy, in which Hebrew is the mistress and Yiddish is its handmaiden, entrusted with the lady's well-being. Evoking Alexander Chashin's phrase about the danger of "making a historic leap to the point of breaking one's neck, from the First Temple period to the founding of Rishon le-Tziyon" (1914, cols. 1–2), Sadan then spoke out against a long-standing tendency to "abbreviate our history by abbreviating our culture. . . . We cannot help those leapfroggers, just because they would like to arrange a more convenient history for themselves; our history was as it was" (1952, 201).

However, as we have seen, the role of Yiddish in the lives of individuals in the Yishuv had implications that went far beyond the function of preserving the revival of Hebrew. I have attempted to locate, trace, and analyze the profound ambivalence that accompanied Yiddish. Although the far-ranging effects of Yiddish on the development of Israeli Hebrew have been documented and studied to some extent,[1] the fact existed that a Yiddish culture side by side with the Hebrew one has been repressed. This recovery of the considerable body of Yishuv Yiddish literature challenges the silencing of this literature. The amount and variety of the material as well as its literary and ideological scope require a reevaluation of Yishuv practices (as distinguished from officially sanctioned attitudes) with regard to the products of the Yiddish subculture.

Each of the writers discussed in this study represents a generational, ideological, and poetic variation within the Yishuv's Yiddish literary scene. Zalmen Brokhes ostensibly belongs to the generation of writers who romanticized and exoticized the Palestine experience of the Zionist Second Aliyah and so was inducted into the Hebrew canon as such, yet his characters are not bound by any ideology, Zionist or otherwise. The socialist-Zionist Avrom Rivess, writing during the period of the Yishuv's greatest expansion, brought his European expressionist poetic vision to the creation of a different perception of the Zionist project by depicting its Others in the

1. See, for example, Even-Zohar 1981, 1990a, 1990b, 1990c, 1990d; and Harshav 1993a, 81–180.

excommunicated language. Rikuda Potash, who continued to write well after Israeli independence, combined European imagery and poetics with ultralocal nativist components, successfully blending these features into an inclusivist cultural amalgam. It is precisely this hybridity, which thrives on pluralism, that offers new possibilities.

It is encouraging that the same Dov Sadan who in 1951 used Bialik's definition of Yiddish as a servant of Hebrew was able in 1970 to use different terms in order to acknowledge the existence of Yiddish in the Yishuv. Speaking about Jewish bilingualism to a Yiddishist audience in New York, Sadan described the unique vision of the Yishuv's Yiddish writers: "This particular group had a special significance—it unlocked a new horizon and a new land for Yiddish literature: the Land of Israel, not as childhood nostalgia or as a touristic theme, but as a tangible day-by-day experience in the very growth and struggle of the Yishuv" (1972b, 425). The contemporaneous dominant culture could not accept such a "new horizon" in the Land of Israel. Examination of the Yishuv's Yiddish literature reopens the possibility of admitting this new horizon and suggests an alternative version of the day-by-day experience that provided the basis for Yishuv—and, eventually, Israeli—identity.

My expedition of cultural and personal archaeology has also had the exhilarating result of reviving my own Yiddish, dormant for more than half a century. Once called up, Yiddish and its culture seemed to have been present always. More than simply a language for doing research, it became a living and infinitely pleasurable feature of my daily life. The recovery of these riches has been deeply rewarding and constitutes the true joy of this project.

GLOSSARY
REFERENCES
INDEX

Glossary

aliyah (pl. *aliyot*): literally "ascent," the traditional Hebrew term for immigration to Palestine. The waves of prestatehood Zionist immigration are numbered First Aliyah (1882–1903), Second Aliyah (1904–14), Third Aliyah (1919–23), Fourth Aliyah (1924–28), and Fifth Aliyah (1929–39). There was no official immigration during the two world wars.

Ashkenazis: a common term for Jews of European origin (Hebrew).

"Canaanites": a political and cultural movement of the Yishuv in the early 1940s that repudiated all late biblical and rabbinic Judaism and espoused premonotheistic regional traditions (Hebrew).

chalukah: a system of donations to the Old Yishuv from Jewish communities abroad (Hebrew-derived Yiddish).

chalutz (pl. *chalutzim*): in the Zionist lexicon, "pioneer" (Hebrew).

daytshmerish: pretentiously cultured, pseudo-German Yiddish (Yiddish).

efendi: a landowner (Arabic).

Haskalah: the European Jewish Enlightenment movement, roughly 1780 to 1885 (Hebrew)

heymishkeyt: a familiar and comfortable domesticity (Yiddish).

kapote: a long black outer garment worn by traditionally observant European Jewish men (Yiddish).

kefiyeh: an Arab headdress (Arabic).

khumesh: the Pentateuch (Hebrew-derived Yiddish).

mame-loshn: literally "mother tongue," a familiar Yiddish term for the language.

melitsah: the Hebrew prose style of the Enlightenment period, composed of a pastiche of biblical phrases.

moshav: a cooperative agricultural settlement in the Yishuv (Hebrew).

moshava: a farming village in which property is privately owned (Hebrew).

nusach: the normative Hebrew prose style of the late nineteenth century (Hebrew).

Old Yishuv: a Zionist term for the pre-Zionist Jewish community of Palestine.

Po'alei Zion: literally, "Workers of Zion," a major Labor Zionist political party in early-twentieth-century Palestine (Hebrew).

ha-Po'el ha-Tza'ir: literally "the Young Worker," a major Labor Zionist political party in early-twentieth-century Palestine (Hebrew).

poema: a subgenre of Yiddish and Hebrew poetry combining verse and narrative, derived from Russian literature (Russian).

Sephardis: Jews of Balkan, North African, and Near Eastern origin (Hebrew).

ha-Shomer: "the Watchman/Guard," a volunteer organization of young Zionists in Palestine who guarded and secured many Jewish settlements, 1909–20 (Hebrew).

shtetl: a small eastern European Jewish town (Yiddish).

talush: a young Jewish man who has cut himself off from tradition and family (Hebrew).

yarmulke: the skullcap that religiously observant male Jews wear constantly (Yiddish).

yeke: a pejorative term used by members of the Yishuv to denote new immigrants from Germany.

yiddishkeyt: the cultural and emotional quality associated with being Jewish (Yiddish).

Yiddishland: an imaginary territory constituted in the Yiddish language (Yiddish, coined by Chaim Zhitlovsky, 1937).

Yishuv: literally "settlement," the forming Zionist community in Palestine (Hebrew).

zhargon: pejorative non-Jewish term for Yiddish (French *jargon*).

Zhid: a Slavic pejorative term for Jew.

References

Abramovitch, S. Y. 1947. *Kol Kitvey Mendele Mokher Sfarim* (Collected works of Mendele Mokher Sfarim). Tel-Aviv: Devir.

Achad ha-Am (Asher Ginzberg). 1921. "Techiyat ha-Ru'ach" (Revival of the spirit). 1901. Reprinted in *Al parashat derakhim* (At the crossroads), 111–43. Berlin: Juedischer Ferlag.

Agnon, S. Y. 1960. "Giv'at ha-Chol" (The sand hill). 1919. Reprinted in *Al Kapot ha-Man'ul* (At the handles of the lock), 350–89. Tel-Aviv: Schocken.

———. 1967. "Iddo ve-Eynam" (Iddo and Eynam). In *Ad Hena* (Thus far), 343–95. Tel-Aviv: Schocken.

Alcalay, Ammiel. 1993. *After Jews and Arabs: Remaking Levantine Culture*. Minneapolis: Univ. of Minnesota Press.

Almog, Oz. 2000. *The Sabra: The Creation of the New Jew*. Berkeley: Univ. of California Press.

Almog, Shmuel. 1987. *Zionism and History*. New York: St. Martin's.

Alter, Robert. 1981. *The Art of Biblical Narrative*. New York: Basic.

———. 1988. *The Invention of Hebrew Prose*. Seattle: Washington Univ. Press.

———. 1996. *Genesis: Translation and Commentary*. New York: Norton.

Amichai, Yehuda. 1977. *Shirim, 1948–1962* (Poems, 1948–1962). Jerusalem: Schocken.

Amikam, Bezalel. 1979. "Hitrachavut ha-Yishuv ve-Tashtito ha-Kalkalit" (The expansion of the Yishuv and its economic infrastructure). In *ha-Yishuv bi-Yemey ha-Bayit ha-Le'umi, 1917–1948* (The Jewish national home from the Balfour Declaration to independence, 1917–1948), edited by Binyamin Eli'av, 285–392. Jerusalem: Keter.

Amrami, Tzvi. 1964. "Shana bi-Deganyah Bet" (A year in Deganyah Bet). In *Sefer ha-Aliyah ha-Shelishit* (The book of the Third Aliyah), edited by Yehuda Erez, 466–70. Tel-Aviv: Am Oved.

Anderson, Benedict. 1991. *Imagined Communities*. London: Verso.

Ardon, Michael. 2001. Conversation with the author, Jerusalem.

Ardon, Mordecai. 1988. "Untervegs—on a Veg" (On the way—without a path). *Di Goldene Keyt* 124: 96–105.

———. 1989. "Dray Froyen" (Three women). *Di Goldene Keyt* 127: 9–24.

Arikha, Yosef. 1988. "Shevilim ba-Galil ha-Elyon" (Paths in Upper Galilee). 1936. Reprinted in *Sifrut ve-Ideologiyah be-Eretz-yisra'el bi-Shenot ha-Sheloshim* (Literature and ideology in Palestine in the 1930s), edited by Nurith Gertz, 139–42. Tel-Aviv: Everyman's Univ.

Artists of Israel: 1920–1980. 1981. Susan Tumarkin Goodman, exhibition curator. Detroit: Wayne State Univ. Press.

Avi-Yonah, Michael. 1980. *bi-Yemey Roma u-Vizantiyon* (In the days of Rome and Byzantium). Jerusalem: Mossad Bialik.

Bachi, Roberto. 1956. "Techiyat ha-Lashon ha-Ivrit be-Aspaklariyah Statistit" (The revival of Hebrew: A statistical view). *Leshonenu* 20, no. 1: 65–82.

Bakhtin, Mikhail. 1973. *Problems of Dostoevsky's Poetics.* Translated by R. W. Rotsel. 1929. Reprint. N.p.: Ardis.

———. 1981. "Discourse in the Novel." 1934–35. Reprinted in *The Dialogic Imagination,* translated by Caryl Emerson, 259–422. Austin: Univ. of Texas Press.

Bal-Makhshoves. 1994. "One Literature in Two Languages." 1918. Reprinted in *What Is Jewish Literature?* edited by Hanna Wirth-Nesher, 69–77. Philadelphia: Jewish Publication Society.

Band, Arnold J. 1994. "Negotiating Jewish History." In *Tradition and Trauma: Studies in the Fiction of S. Y. Agnon,* edited by David Patterson and Glenda Abramson, 27–44. Boulder, Colo.: Westview.

Barasch, Moshe. 1981. "The Quest for Roots." In *Artists of Israel: 1920–1980,* Susan Tumarkin Goodman, exhibition curator, 21–25. Detroit: Wayne State Univ. Press.

Barlev, K. 1964. "Im Brener bi-Gedud ha-Avodah" (With Brenner in the Labor Battalion). In *Sefer ha-Aliyah ha-Shelishit* (The book of the Third Aliyah), edited by Yehuda Erez, 328–29. Tel-Aviv: Am Oved.

Ben-Ezer, Ehud. 1992. *be-Moledet ha-Ga'agu'im ha-Menugadim* (The Arab in Israeli fiction). Tel-Aviv: Zmora-Bitan.

Ben-Gurion, David. 1910. "Din ve-Cheshbon shel Mo'etzet ha-Miflagah be-Sukkot 5671" (Report of the party convention, Sukkot 1910). *ha-Achdut* 2, nos. 2–3: col. 30.

———. 1964. "ha-Aliyah ha-Chadashah be-Tzibur ha-Po'alim" (The new immigrants in the workers' community). 1923. Reprinted in *Sefer ha-Aliyah ha-Shelishit* (The book of the Third Aliyah), edited by Yehuda Erez, 95–101. Tel-Aviv: Am Oved.

Benvenisti, Meron. 1988. *ha-Kela ve-ha-Alah* (The sling and the club). Jerusalem: Keter.

———. 2000. *Sacred Landscape: The Buried History of the Holy Land since 1948.* Berkeley: Univ. of California Press.

Ben-Zvi, Yitzhak. 1910. "Din ve-Cheshbon shel Mo'etzet ha-Miflagah be-Sukkot 5671" (Report of the party convention, Sukkot 1910). *ha-Achdut* 2, nos. 2–3: col. 28.

———. 1911. "Li-She'elat yisud Iton be-Aravit" (On founding a newspaper in Arabic). *ha-Achdut* 3, no. 4: cols. 1–5; no. 5: cols. 5–7.

———. 1960. *Masa'ot bi-Sheviley ha-Aretz u-Shekhenotehah* (Travels along the paths of the land and its neighbors). Jerusalem: ha-Machon le-Hotza'ah la-Or.

———. 1966. *Zichronot u-Reshumot* (Reminiscences and notes). Jerusalem: Yad Ben Zvi.

Berger-Barzilai, Yitzchak. 1968. *ha-Tragedyah shel ha-Mahapekhah ha-Sovyetit* (The tragedy of the Soviet revolution). Tel-Aviv: Am Oved.

Berlowitz, Yaffa. 1996. *le-Hamtzi Am, le-Hamtzi Eretz* (Inventing a nation, inventing a land). Tel-Aviv: ha-Kibbutz ha-Me'uchad.

Bhabha, Homi K., ed. 1990. *Nation and Narration*. London: Routledge.

———. 1994. *The Location of Culture*. London: Routledge.

Biale, David. 1984. *Power and Powerlessness in Jewish History*. New York: Schocken.

———. 1992. *Eros and the Jews: From Biblical Israel to Contemporary America*. New York: Basic.

Bialik, Chaim Nachman. 1935a. "Al Shalom Ash u-Ferets Hirshbayn" (On Sholem Asch and Perets Hirshbein). 1927. Reprinted in *Devarim she-be'al-Peh* (Oral works), 212–14. Tel-Aviv: Devir.

———. 1935b. "Al ha-Universitah ha-Ivrit" (About the Hebrew University). In *Agudat Shocharey ha-Universitah ha-Ivrit* (Friends of the Hebrew University), 3: 3–25. Jerusalem: n.p.

———. 1935c. "She'elat ha-Leshonot be-Yisra'el" (The question of Jewish languages). 1930. Reprinted in *Devarim she-be'al-Peh* (Oral works), 142–57. Tel-Aviv: Devir.

———. 1950. "Metey Midbar" (The dead of the desert). 1902. Reprinted in *Kol Shirey Chaim Nachman Bialik* (Collected poems of Chaim Nachman Bialik), 354–63. Tel-Aviv: Devir.

———. 1965a. "Aryeh Ba'al-guf" (Aryeh the muscle-man). 1898. Reprinted in *Kol Kitvey Chaim Nachman Bialik* (Collected works of Chaim Nachman Bialik), 113–27. Tel-Aviv: Devir.

———. 1965b. "Chevley Lashon" (Language pangs). 1905. Reprinted in *Kol Kitvey Chaim Nachman Bialik* (Collected works of Chaim Nachman Bialik), 197–201. Tel-Aviv: Devir.

———. 1965c. "Giluy ve-Khisui ba-Lashon" (Revealment and concealment in language). 1915. Reprinted in *Kol Kitvey Chaim Nachman Bialik* (Collected works of Chaim Nachman Bialik), 202–4. Tel-Aviv: Devir.

———. 2001. *Ch. N. Bialik, Shirim be-Yidish, Shirey Yeladim, Shirey Hakdashah* (Ch. N. Bialik, Yiddish poems, childrens' poems, dedication poems). Edited by Dan Miron, Uriel Ofek, Chaya Hoffman, Shemuel Tartner, Ziva Shamir, Chone Shmeruk, and Ruth Shenfeld. Tel-Aviv: Tel-Aviv Univ.

Bistritsky, Nathan. 1978. *Yamim ve-Leylot* (Days and nights). 1940. Reprint. Tel-Aviv: Sifriyat Po'alim.

Blay, Avrom. 1931a. "A Kosherer Top un a Kosherer Lefl" (A kosher pot and a kosher spoon). *Dray:* cols. 34–35.

———. 1931b. "Di Likhtike Shayn vos Lozt nit Shlofn" (The bright light that prevents sleep). *Yuni:* 18–19.

Boyarin, Daniel. 1997. *Unheroic Conduct.* Berkeley: Univ. of California Press.

Bradbury, Malcolm, and James McFarlane, eds. 1991. *Modernism: A Guide to European Poetry 1890–1930.* London: Penguin.

Brandes, Yochi. 1997. *Gemar Tov* (Happy ending). Tel-Aviv: ha-Kibbutz ha-Me'uchad.

Brenner, Yosef Chaim. 1978. *Ketavim* (Collected works). Vols. 1–2. Tel-Aviv: ha-Kibbutz ha-Me'uchad.

———. 1985. *Ketavim* (Collected works). Vols. 3–4. Tel-Aviv: ha-Kibbutz ha-Me'uchad.

Brokhes, Zalmen. 1910. "Di Borvese" (The barefoot ones). *Der Fraynd* (Warsaw) 298 (31 December): 3–4.

———. 1911a. "Galoti et ha-Cherpa!" (I removed the shame!). *Moledet* 1, no. 2: 81–91.

———. 1911b. "ha-Matmon" (The treasure). *Moledet* 1, nos. 5–6: 351–60.

———. 1912. "Malach be-Yam ha-Melach" (A sailor on the Dead Sea). Part 1, *Moledet* 2, nos. 3–4: 180–95; part 2, *Moledet* 2, nos. 5–6: 306–32.

———. 1913. "ha-Kabarnit ha-Zaken" (The old captain). *Moledet* 4, nos. 4–5: 390–406.

———. 1918. *Untern Shotn fun Chermn* (In the shadow of the Hermon). New York: Assaf.

———. 1937. *Der Yardn Roysht* (The Jordan roars). Warsaw: Bzrzoza.

———. 1954. *be-Tzel ha-Chermon* (In the shadow of the Hermon). Tel-Aviv: Tversky.

———. 1973. "Der Shtekn" (The stick). In *Almanakh Yidishe Shrayber fun Yerusholayim* (Almanac of Yiddish writers of Jerusalem), 96–102. Jerusalem: Yidishn Shrayber un Zhurnalistn Fareyn in Yisroel.

———. 1974. *ha-Yarden So'en* (The Jordan roars). Tel-Aviv: Newman.

Cassuto, Umberto. 1971. *The Goddess Anath.* Translated by Israel Abrahams. Jerusalem: Magnes.

Chalamish, Mordechai, ed. 1990. *Yidish be-Yisra'el: Al Sofrim, Meshorerim, Omanim* (Yiddish in Israel: Writers, poets, artists). Tel-Aviv: Eked.

Chanani, Yosef. 1937. "Shalosh Etzba'ot" (Three fingers). *Gilyonot 5*, no. 2: 142–46.

Chankin, Chaya-Sarah. 1937. "ba-Nedudim" (Wandering). In *Kovetz ha-Shomer* (ha-Shomer collection), 108–20. Tel-Aviv: Archiyon ha-Avodah.

Charit, Y. 1937. "Kibush ha-Mir'eh" (Taking over the herding). In *Kovetz ha-Shomer* (ha-Shomer collection), 226–28. Tel-Aviv: Archiyon ha-Avodah.

Ch[ashin], Al[exander]. 1914. "Lamah Ragshu?" (Why were they excited?). *ha-Achdut 5*, no. 37: cols. 1–5.

Chorin, Yehuda. 1964. "be-Gan-Shmuel" (In Gan-Shmuel). In *Sefer ha-Aliyah ha-Shelishit* (The book of the Third Aliyah), edited by Yehuda Erez, 462–66. Tel-Aviv: Am Oved.

Cohen, Amnon, ed. 1981. *ha-Historiyah shel Eretz-yisra'el: Shilton ha-Mamlukim ve-ha-Otmanim* (The history of Palestine under Mamluk and Ottoman rule). Jerusalem: Yad Ben-Zvi.

Cohn, Dorrit. 1978. *Transparent Minds: Narrative Modes for Presenting Consciousness in Fiction*. Princeton, N.J.: Princeton Univ. Press.

Culler, Jonathan. 1981. "Apostrophe." In *The Pursuit of Signs: Semiotics, Literature, Deconstruction*, 135–54. Ithaca, N.Y.: Cornell Univ. Press.

Dalley, Stephanie. 1989. *Myths from Mesopotamia*. Oxford and New York: Oxford Univ. Press.

Dear, I. C. B., ed. 1995. *The Oxford Companion to World War II*. Oxford and New York: Oxford Univ. Press.

Deleuze, Gilles, and Felix Guattari. 1993. *The Deleuze Reader*. Edited and introduced by Constantin V. Boundas. New York: Columbia Univ. Press.

Diamond, James C. 1986. *Homeland or Holy Land? The Canaanite Critique of Israel*. Bloomington: Indiana Univ. Press.

Dor, Moshe. 1974. "Etzba Barak" (Finger of lightning). In *le-Galot le-Adam Acher* (Revealing to another), 10–19. Tel-Aviv: ha-Kibbutz ha-Me'uchad.

Elboim-Dror, Rachel. 1990. *ha-Chinukh ha-Ivri be-Eretz-yisra'el* (Hebrew education in Palestine). Vol. 1. Jerusalem: Yad Ben-Zvi.

———. 1996. "Hu Holekh u-Va, mi-Kirbenu Hu Ba, ha-Ivri he-Chadash" (He is coming from among us, the new Hebrew). *Alpayim* 12: 104–35.

Eli'av, Binyamin, ed. 1979. *ha-Yishuv bi-Yemey ha-Bayit ha-Le'umi, 1917–1948* (The Jewish national home, from the Balfour Declaration to independence, 1917–1948). Jerusalem: Keter.

Eli'av, Mordechai, ed. 1981. *Sefer ha-Aliyah ha-Rishonah* (The book of the First Aliyah). Jerusalem: Yad Ben Zvi.

Elon, Amos. 1971. *The Israelis: Founders and Sons*. London: Sphere.

Erez, Yehuda, ed. 1964. *Sefer ha-Aliyah ha-Shelishit* (The book of the Third Aliyah). Tel-Aviv: Am Oved.

Erik, Maks. 1922. "Di Shprakh funem Yidishn Eksprezionizm" (The language of Jewish expressionism). *Albatros* 2: 17.

Ettinger, Shmuel. 1969. *Toldot Am Yisra'el* (History of the Jewish people). Vol. 3. Tel-Aviv: Devir.

Even-Zohar, Itamar. 1981. "The Emergence of a Native Hebrew Culture in Palestine, 1882–1948." *Studies in Zionism* 4: 167–84.

———. 1990a. "Aspects of the Hebrew-Yiddish Polysystem: A Case of a Multilingual Polysystem." *Poetics Today* 11, no. 1: 121–30.

———. 1990b. "Authentic Language and Authentic Reported Speech: Hebrew vs. Yiddish." *Poetics Today* 11, no. 1: 155–63.

———. 1990c. "Polysystem Theory." *Poetics Today* 11, no. 1: 9–26.

———. 1990d. "The Role of Russian and Yiddish in the Making of Modern Hebrew." *Poetics Today* 11, no. 1: 111–20.

Ezrahi, Sidra DeKoven. 2000. *Booking Passage: Exile and Homecoming in the Modern Jewish Imagination.* Berkeley: Univ. of California Press.

Frakes, Jerold C. 1989. *The Politics of Interpretation: Alterity and Ideology in Old Yiddish Studies.* Albany: State Univ. of New York Press.

Frumkin, H. 1964. "ha-Yishuv ve-Khalkalato al Saf ha-Aliyah ha-Shelishit" (The Yishuv and its economy on the eve of the Third Aliyah). In *Sefer ha-Aliyah ha-Shelishit* (The book of the Third Aliyah), edited by Yehuda Erez, 72–78. Tel-Aviv: Am Oved.

Fuchs, Aviva. 2003. Conversation with the author, Philadelphia.

Fuchs, Esther. 1987. *Israeli Mythogynies.* Albany: State Univ. of New York.

Fuks, Chaim Leyb. 1972. *Lodzsh shel Mayle* (Lodz of the spirit). Tel-Aviv: Perets Farlag.

Furness, R. S. 1973. *Expressionism.* London: Methuen.

Garnczarska-Kadari, Bina. 1995. *be-Chipusey Derekh: Po'alei Zion Smol be-Folin ad Milchemet ha-Olam ha-Sheniyah* (Seeking a path: Left Po'alei Zion in Poland until the Second World War). Tel-Aviv: ha-Makhon le-Cheker ha-Tefutzot.

Garrett, Leah. 2003. *Journeys beyond the Pale: Yiddish Travel Writing in the Modern World.* Madison: Univ. of Wisconsin Press.

Gellner, Ernest. 1983. *Nations and Nationalism.* Ithaca, N.Y.: Cornell Univ. Press.

Gertz, Nurith. 1985. "Mitos ha-Tamuz: Modernizm, Le'umiyut ve-Kena'aniyut be-Shirat Ratosh" (The Tammuz myth: Modernism, nationalism, and Canaanism in the poetry of Ratosh). *ha-Sifrut* 34: 126–41.

———, ed. 1988. *Sifrut ve-Ideologiyah be-Eretz-yisra'el bi-Shenot ha-Sheloshim* (Literature and ideology in Palestine in the 1930s). Tel-Aviv: Everyman's Univ.

Ginzburg, S. M., and P. S. Marek. 1991. *Yiddish Folksongs in Russia.* 1901. Reprint. Ramat-Gan: Bar-Ilan Univ. Press.

Glatshteyn, Yankev. 1929. *Kredos* (Credos). New York: Farlag Yiddish Lebn.

——. 1963a. "Rochl Fishman." 1960. Reprinted in *Mit mayne Fartogbikher* (With my diaries), 133–38. Tel-Aviv: Perets Farlag.

——. 1963b. "A Yidishe Dikhterin in Medines Yisroel" (A Yiddish poetess in the State of Israel). 1960. Reprinted in *Mit mayne Fartogbikher* (With my diaries), 69–76. Tel-Aviv: Perets Farlag.

——. 1972. "Rikuda Potash." In *In der Velt mit Yidish* (In the world with Yiddish), 139–45. New York: Alveltlekhen Yidishn Kultur-Kongres.

Gluzman, Michael. 2002. *The Politics of Canonicity: Lines of Resistance in Modern Hebrew Poetry.* Stanford: Stanford Univ. Press.

Goldberg, Leah. 1981. *Im ha-Laylah ha-Zeh* (With this night). Tel-Aviv: Sifriyat Po'alim.

Goldsmith, Emanuel. 1976. *Architects of Yiddishism at the Beginning of the Twentieth Century.* London: Associated Univ. Presses.

Gonen, Jay. 1975. *A Psychohistory of Zionism.* New York: Mason-Charter.

Gorni, Yosef. 1971. "Yachasah shel Mifleget Po'aley-Tziyon ba-Aretz la-Golah (bi-Tekufat ha-Aliyah ha-Sheniyah)" (The attitude of Po'alei-Tziyon in Palestine to the Diaspora [during the Second Aliyah period]). *ha-Tziyonut* 2: 74–89.

ha-Gorni-Green, Avraham. 1981. "Gishot Yesod u-Fo'etikah Mutzheret" (Basic approaches and explicit poetics). In *Sefer Shlonsky* (The Shlonsky book), edited by Yisrael Levin, 1: 113–35. Merhavya: Sifriyat Poalim.

Govrin, Nurit. 1981. *Shorashim ve-Tsamarot: Rishumah shel ha-Aliyah ha-Rishonah ba-Sifrut ha-Ivrit* (Roots and tops: The imprint of the First Aliyah on Hebrew literature). Tel-Aviv: Tel-Aviv Univ. Student Association.

——. 1984. *Manifestim Sifrutiyim* (Literary manifestoes). Tel-Aviv: Tel-Aviv Univ.

——. 1985. *Telishut ve-Hitchadshut: ha-Siporet ha-Ivrit be-Reshit ha-Me'ah ha-Esrim ba-Golah u-ve-Eretz-yisra'el* (Alienation and regeneration: Hebrew fiction in the Diaspora and Palestine in the early twentieth century). Tel-Aviv: Ministry of Defense.

——. 1989. *Devash mi-Sela: Mechkarim be-Sifrut Eretz-yisra'el* (Honey from the rock: Studies in Palestinian literature). Tel-Aviv: Ministry of Defense.

Greenzweig, Michael. 1985. "Ma'amadah shel ha-Ivrit bi-Yemey ha-Aliyah ha-Sheniyah" (The status of Hebrew during the Second Aliyah). In *ha-Aliyah ha-Sheniyah* (The Second Aliyah), edited by Mordechai Na'or, 198–212. Jerusalem: Yad Ben Zvi.

Grinberg, Uri Tsvi. 1922a. "Proklamirung" (Proclamation) *Albatros* 1:3–4.

——. 1922b. "Uri Tsvi farn Tseylem" (Uri Tsvi in front of the cross). *Albatros* 2: 3–4.

———. 1927. "Kabbalat ha-Panim le-Asch ve-Hirschbein" (The reception for Asch and Hirschbein). *Ketuvim* 1, nos. 34–35: 6.

Grossman, David. 1986. *Ayen Erekh Ahavah* (See under: Love). Tel-Aviv: ha-Kibbutz ha-Me'uchad.

Guri, Yosef. 1997. *Vi kumt di Kats ibern Vaser?* (One thousand Yiddish idioms and their equivalents in Hebrew, English, and Russian). Jerusalem: Hebrew Univ.

Halkin, Hillel. 1987. Introduction to *Tevye the Dairyman and the Railroad Stories,* by Sholem Aleichem, translated by Hillel Halkin, ix–xli. New York: Schocken.

Harkavy, Alexander. 1928. *Yiddish-English-Hebrew Dictionary.* New York: Hebrew Publishing Company.

Harshav, Benjamin. 1990. *The Meaning of Yiddish.* Berkeley: Univ. of California Press.

———. 1993a. *Language in Time of Revolution.* Berkeley: Univ. of California Press.

———. 1993b. "Mark Shagal: Tsiyur, Teatron Olam" (Marc Chagall: Painting, World Theater). *Alpayim* 8:9–97.

———. 1994. "The Role of Language in Modern Art: On Texts and Subtexts in Chagall's Paintings." *Modernism/modernity* 1: 2, 51–87.

Hellerstein, Kathryn. 1994. "Canon and Gender: Women Poets in Two Modern Yiddish Anthologies." In *Women of the Word,* edited by Judith R. Baskin, 136–52. Detroit: Wayne State Univ. Press.

Hever, Hannan. 1994. "Guru Lakhem min ha-Galitza'im" (Beware of the Galitzians). *Teoriya u-vikoret* 5: 55–77.

———. 2002. *Producing the Modern Hebrew Canon: Nation Building and Minority Discourse.* New York: New York Univ. Press.

Hobsbawm, E. J. 1990. *Nations and Nationalism since 1780.* Cambridge: Cambridge Univ. Press.

Howe, Irving, Ruth Wisse, and Khone Shmeruk, eds. 1987. *The Penguin Book of Modern Yiddish Verse.* London: Penguin.

Huppert, Shmuel. 1979. "Bechinat ha-Galut u-Morashtah be-Shirato ha-Eretz-yisre'elit shel Uri Tsvi Grinberg" (Examining the Diaspora and its heritage in the Palestinian poetry of Uri Tzvi Grinberg). *ha-Sifrut* 29: 93–103.

Izban, Shmuel. 1988. "Sholem Ash in Erets-yisro'el—tsurik mit Zekhtsik Yor" (Sholem Asch in Palestine—sixty years ago). *Di Goldene Keyt* 124: 121–28.

Jabotinsky, Ze'ev (Vladimir). *Ketavim Tziyoniyim Rishonim* (First Zionist Writings). 1905. Jerusalem: Eri Jabotinsky.

Jusdanis, Gregory. 1991. *Belated Modernity.* Minneapolis: Univ. of Minnesota Press.

Kandinsky, Wassily. 1947. *Concerning the Spiritual in Art.* 1912. Reprint. New York: Wittenborn.

Kantsedikas, Alexander. 1994. *Semyon An-sky: The Jewish Artistic Heritage.* Moscow: RA.

Karmi, Shlomo. 1997. *Am Echad ve-Safah Achat: Techiyat ha-Safah ha-Ivrit be-*

Re'iyah Beyn-techumit (One nation and one language: The revival of the Hebrew language from an interdisciplinary perspective). Tel-Aviv: Ministry of Defense.

Katznelson, Rachel. 1918. "Nedudey Lashon" (Language wanderings). In *ba-Avoda*, 68–78. Jaffa: Organization of Agricultural Workers.

——— [as Rachel Katznelson-Rubashov], ed. 1931. *Vos Arbetorins Dertseyln: a* [sic] *Erets-yisro'el Bukh* (The woman worker speaks: Collected writings of Jewish women workers in Palestine). New York: Pioneer Women's Organization.

——— [as Rachel Katznelson-Shazar]. 1966. "Nedudey Lashon" (Language wanderings). In *Al Admat ha-Ivrit* (On the soil of Hebrew), 231–41. Tel-Aviv: Am Oved.

——— [as Rachel Katznelson-Shazar]. 1989. *Adam Kemo Shehu* (A person as he/she is). Tel-Aviv: Am Oved.

Kedar, B. Z., ed. 1988. *ha-Tzalbanim be-Mamlakhtam, 1099–1291* (The Crusaders in their kingdom, 1099–1291). Jerusalem: Yad Ben-Zvi.

Kena'ani, Ya'akov. 1989. *Milon Chidushey Shlonsky* (Dictionary of Shlonsky's neologisms). Tel-Aviv: Sifriyat Po'alim.

Kenner, Hugh. 1971. *The Pound Era*. Berkeley: Univ. of California Press.

Keshet, Shula. 1994. "Beyn Historiyah le-Sifrut: ha-Tsenzurah ha-Ideologit al 'Yamim ve-Leylot'" (Between history and literature: The ideological censorship of *Yamim ve-Leylot*). *ha-Tziyonut* 18: 187–212.

Kohen, Berl. 1986. *Leksikon fun Yidish-shraybers* (Lexicon of Yiddish writers). New York: Rayah Ilman-Kohen.

Kohen, Berl, Azriel Naks, and Eliahu Shulman, eds. 1981. *Leksikon fun der Nayer Yidisher Literatur* (Lexicon of new Yiddish literature). Vol. 8. New York: World Jewish Congress.

Korman, Ezra, ed. 1928. *Yidishe Dikhterins Antologye* (Anthology of Yiddish women poets). Chicago: L. Stein.

Kosover, Mordecai. 1966. *Arabic Elements in Palestinian Yiddish*. Jerusalem: Achva.

Kotylansky, Chaim. 1954. *Folksgezangen*. New York: Yidishn Kultur-Farband.

Krivorochka, Avraham. 1926. "Dechi Ganges" (Waves of the Ganges). In *Bereshit*, 173–77. Moscow: n.p.

Kronfeld, Chana. 1993. "Subverting Gender: The Poetry of Esther Raab." Unpublished manuscript.

———. 1996. *On the Margins of Modernism*. Berkeley: Univ. of California Press.

———. 1997. Conversation with the author, Berkeley, Calif.

———. 1999. Conversation with the author, Berkeley, Calif.

Lasker-Schüler, Else. 1980. *Hebrew Ballads and Other Poems*. Translated by Audri Durchslag and Jeanette Litman-Demeestere. Philadelphia: Jewish Publication Society.

Lefevere, André. 1992. *Translation, Rewriting, and the Manipulation of Literary Fame*. London: Routledge.

Leviteh, Lyova. 1978. *Bereshit va-Sa'ar* (Beginning and storm). Tel-Aviv: ha-Kibbutz ha-Me'uchad.

Leybl, Daniel. 1931. "May, Yuni" (May, June). *Dray:* col. 34.

Liebman, Charles, and Eliezer Don-Yehiya. 1983. *Civil Religion in Israel.* Berkeley: Univ. of California Press.

Lincoln, Bruce. 1989. *Discourse and the Construction of Society: Comparative Studies of Myth, Ritual, and Classification.* New York: Oxford Univ. Press.

Lipsker, Avidov. 1991. Introduction to *ha-Siporet shel Shenot ha-Esrim be-Eretz-yisra'el* (Palestinian prose in the twenties), by Nilli Sadan-Loebenstein, edited by Avidov Lipsker, 7–15. Tel-Aviv: Sifriyat Poalim.

Litvak, L. 1928. "Undzerer Kultur-problemen" (Our cultural problems). *Onheyb:* 26–29.

Luncz, Avraham Moshe. 1918. *Kinor Tziyon* (Lyre of Zion). Jerusalem: n.p.

Magen, Mira. 1994. *Kaftorim Rekhusim Heytev* (Well-fastened buttons). Jerusalem: Keter.

Mahalo, Aviva. 1991. *Beyn Shney Nofim: Siporet ha-Aliyah ha-Shelishit beyn Nofey ha-Golah le-Nofey Eretz-yisra'el* (Between two landscapes: Fiction of the Third Aliyah between landscapes of the Diaspora and landscapes of the Land of Israel). Jerusalem: Rubin Mass.

Manger, Itzik. 1984. *Medresh-Itzik* (Itzik's midrash). Edited by Khone Shmeruk. 1951. Reprint. Jerusalem: Magnes.

Mann, Barbara. 1997. "Icons and Iconoclasts: Visual Poetics in Hebrew and Yiddish Modernisms." Ph.D. diss., Univ. of California, Berkeley.

———. 1999. "Framing the Native: Esther Raab's Visual Poetics." *Israel Studies* 4: 1, 234–57.

Markish, Perets. 1921. *Di Kupe* (The pile). Kiev: Kultur-lige.

———. 1924. "Yom mi Yagi'a" (Whose day will come). Translated by Avraham Shlonsky. *Hedim* 2, no. 1: 82.

Matisoff, James A. 2000. *Blessings, Curses, Hopes, and Fears: Psycho-ostensive Expressions in Yiddish.* 1979. Reprint. Stanford, Calif.: Stanford Univ. Press.

Miron, Dan. 1987. *Bodedim be-Mo'adam* (When loners come together: A portrait of Hebrew literature at the turn of the century). Tel-Aviv: Am Oved.

———. 1991. *Imahot Meyasdot, Achayot Chorgot* (Founding mothers, stepsisters). Tel-Aviv: ha-Kibbutz ha-Me'uchad.

———. 1996. *A Traveller Disguised: The Rise of Modern Yiddish Fiction in the Nineteenth Century.* 1973. Reprint. Syracuse, N.Y.: Syracuse Univ. Press.

Mitbonen, Y. 1934. "ha-Mishmar ha-Ivri, Kumah!" (The Hebrew guard, rise!). *Gilyonot* 2, no. 10: 289–93.

Mitchell, W. J. T., ed. 1994. *Landscape and Power.* Chicago: Univ. of Chicago Press.

Myers, David N. 1995. *Re-inventing the Jewish Past: European Jewish Intellectuals and the Return to History.* New York: Oxford Univ. Press.

Nachmani, Yosef. 1910. *ha-Achdut* 2, nos. 2–3: cols. 27, 30.

Na'or, Mordechai, ed. 1985a. *ha-Aliyah ha-Sheniyah* (The Second Aliyah). Jerusalem: Yad Ben Zvi.

——. 1985b. "ha-Mitos Nolad kevar ba-Aliyah ha-Sheniyah" (The myth was already born during the Second Aliyah). In *ha-Aliyah ha-Sheniyah* (The Second Aliyah), edited by Mordechai Na'or, 101–10. Jerusalem: Yad Ben Zvi.

Narkiss, Bezalel. 1997. Conversation with the author, Jerusalem.

The New Oxford Annotated Bible with the Apocrypha. 1977. New York: Oxford Univ. Press.

Niger, S. 1985. "Di Yidishe Literatur un di Lezerin" (Yiddish literature and the female reader). 1913. Reprinted in *Bleter geshikhte fun der yidisher literatur* (Studies in the history of Yiddish literature), 35–107. New York: S. Niger Bukh Komitet.

Niger, Shmuel, and Ya'akov Shatsky, eds. 1956. *Leksikon fun der Nayer Yidisher Literatur* (Lexicon of new Yiddish literature). Vol. 1. New York: World Jewish Congress.

Nordau, Max. 1909. *Zionistische Schriften.* Cologne: Jüdischer Verlag.

Novershtern, Abraham. 1991. "Who Would Have Believed That a Bronze Statue Can Weep?" Introduction to *Anna Margolin, Poems,* v–lviii. Jerusalem: Magnes.

Oyerbakh, Ephraim, Ya'akov Birnboym, Eliahu Shulman, and Moyshe Shtarkman, eds. 1968. *Leksikon fun der Nayer Yidisher Literatur* (Lexicon of new Yiddish literature). Vol. 7. New York: World Jewish Congress.

Oz, Amos. 1965. *Artzot ha-Tan* (The lands of the jackal). Tel-Aviv: Masada.

——. 1993. "ha-Gevirah ve-ha-Shifchah" (The lady and the maid). *Iyunim bi-Tekumat Yisra'el* 3: 10–19.

Pagis, Dan. 1991. *Hebrew Poetry of the Middle Ages and the Renaissance.* Berkeley: Univ. of California Press.

Palmon, Moshe. 1964. "Silikat" (Silicate). In *Sefer ha-Aliyah ha-Shelishit* (The book of the Third Aliyah), edited by Yehuda Erez, 573–78. Tel-Aviv: Am Oved.

Papiernikov, Yosef. 1938. *Onvuks* (Growth). Tel-Aviv: Eygns.

Perets, I. L. 1930. "Der Gilgl fun a Nign" (The reincarnation of a melody). In *Chasidish* (Chasidic), 2: 116–35. New York: Morgn Frayhayt.

Pilowsky, Aryeh. 1980. "Yidish ve-Sifrutah be-Eretz-yisra'el, 1907–1948" (Yiddish and its literature in Palestine, 1907–1948). Ph.D. diss., Hebrew Univ., Jerusalem.

——. 1981. "Lashon, Tarbut u-Le'umiyut ba-Yishuv he-Chadash: ha-Diyun ha-Tsiburi ba-Tokhnit le-Hakamat Katedrah le-Yidish be-Shilhey 1927" (Language, culture, and nationalism in the new Yishuv: The public debate over the establishment of a Yiddish chair in late 1927). *Katedrah* 21: 103–34.

——. 1986. *Tsvishn Yo un Neyn, Yidish un Yidish-literatur in Erets-yisro'el, 1907–1948* (Between yes and no: Yiddish and Yiddish literature in Palestine, 1907–1948). Tel-Aviv: World Organization for Yiddish and Yiddish Culture.

———. 1991. "Yetsirato ha-Sipurit shel Aharon Re'uveni be-Yidish" (The Yiddish fiction of Aharon Re'uveni). In *Aharon Re'uveni, gezamlte Dertseylungen* (Aharon Re'uveni, collected stories), 7–40. Jerusalem: Magnes.

Podriatshik, Leyzer. 1986. "A Vort vegn Perets Markish" (A word about Perets Markish). *Yisro'el Shtime,* 11 February; 25 February; 11 March.

———. 1991. *In Heykhl fun Vort* (In the palace of the word). Tel-Aviv: Perets Farlag.

Potash, Rikuda. 1934. *Vint oyf Klavishn* (Wind on keyboard). Lodz: n.p.

———. 1952. *Fun Kidron Tol* (From Kidron Valley). London: Moshe Oyved.

———. 1960. *Moyled iber Timna* (New moon over Timna). Tel Aviv: Tarshish.

———. 1967. *Lider* (Poems). Tel Aviv: Yidishn Literatn un Zhurnalistn Fareyn in Yisro'el.

———. 1968. *In Geslekh fun Yerusholayim* (In the alleys of Jerusalem). Tel-Aviv: Yisro'el-Bukh.

Raab, Esther. 1978. Interview. *Iton 77* (November–December): 14–15.

———. 1981. "Ne'urey ha-Shirah be-Eretz lo Zru'ah" (The youth of poetry in an un-sown land). *Chadarim* 1 (spring): 101–13.

———. 2001. *Kol ha-Prozah* (All the prose). Edited by Ehud Ben-Ezer. Petach-Tik-vah, Israel: Astrolog.

Rabin, Chaim. 1985. "The Continuum of Modern Literary Hebrew." In *The Great Transition: The Recovery of the Lost Centers of Modern Hebrew Literature,* ed-ited by Glenda Abramson and Tudor Parfitt, 11–25. Totowa, N.J.: Rowland and Allenfeld.

Rachel. 1910. "Din ve-Cheshbon shel Mo'etzet ha-Miflagah be-Sukkot 5671" (Re-port of the party convention, Sukkot 1910). *ha-Achdut* 2, nos. 2–3: col. 28.

ha-Ramati, Shlomo. 1981. "Techiyat ha-Dibur ha-Ivri ba-Moshavot" (The revival of Hebrew speech in the settlements). In *Sefer ha-Aliyah ha-Rishonah* (The book of the First Aliyah), edited by Mordechai Eli'av, 427–46. Jerusalem: Yad Ben Zvi.

———. 1997. *Ivrit mi-Si'ach Sefatayim le-Lashon Le'umit* (Hebrew from oral dis-course to national language). Tel-Aviv: Golan.

Ramras-Rauch, Gila. 1989. *The Arab in Israeli Literature.* Bloomington: Indiana Univ. Press.

Ratosh, Yonatan. 1982. *Sifrut Yehudit ba-Lashon ha-Ivrit* (Jewish literature in the Hebrew language). Tel-Aviv: Hadar.

Reichenstein, Avraham. 1943. *Reshit* (Beginning). Tel-Aviv: Am Oved.

Renan, Ernest. 1990. "Qu'est-ce que une nation?" (What is a nation?). 1882. Reprinted in *Nation and Narration,* edited by Homi K. Bhabha, 8–22. London: Routledge.

Re'uveni, Aharon. 1910. "Din ve-Cheshbon shel Mo'etzet ha-Miflagah be-Sukkot 5671" (Report of the party convention, Sukkot 1910). *ha-Achdut* 2, nos. 2–3: col. 29.

Reyzen, Zalmen. 1928. *Leksikon fun der Yidisher Literatur, Prese, un Filologye* (Lexicon of Yiddish literature, journalism, and philology). Vilna: Kletzkin.

Rivess, Avrom. 1923. "Bloye Royb-foygl" (Blue birds of prey). *Tayfun:* 28–30.

———. 1929a. "Iberflants" (Transplant). *Eyns:* 30–34.

———. 1929b. "In der Machne" (In the camp). *Tsvishn Tsvey un Dray:* cols. 3–8.

———. 1929c. "Zhukess" (Bugs). *Tsvey:* 2–11.

———. 1936. "Tayve" (Lust). *Bleter tsum Ondenk fun L. Malakh:* 40–45.

———. 1947a. "Der Bal-tshuve" (The penitent). 1932. Reprinted in *Iberflants,* 84–106. Tel-Aviv: Yidishn Literatn un Zhurnalistn-klub in Erets-Yisro'el.

———. 1947b. "Iberflants" (Transplant). 1929. Reprinted in *Iberflants,* 119–207. Tel-Aviv: Yidishn Literatn un Zhurnalistn-klub in Erets-Yisro'el.

———. 1947c. "In Klem" (In straits). 1944. Reprinted in *Iberflants,* 36–48. Tel-Aviv: Yidishn Literatn un Zhurnalistn-klub in Erets-Yisro'el.

———. 1952. "Chugenu ha-Sifruti" (Our literary circle). In *Sefer Zikaron le-Kehillat Lomza,* edited by Yom-Tov Levinsky, 165–67. Tel-Aviv: Irgun Oley Kehillat Lomza be-Yisra'el.

Roskies, David G. 1985. *Against the Apocalypse: Responses to Catastrophe in Modern Jewish Culture.* Cambridge, Mass.: Harvard Univ. Press.

———. 1995. *A Bridge of Longing: The Lost Art of Yiddish Storytelling.* Cambridge, Mass.: Harvard Univ. Press.

Rubinstein, Amnon. 1997. *me-Hertsl ad Rabin: Me'ah Shenot Tziyonut* (From Herzl to Rabin: One hundred years of Zionism). Jerusalem: Schocken.

Rubinstein, Elyakim. 1979. "mi-Yishuv le-Medina: Mosadot u-Miflagot" (From Yishuv to state: Institutions and political parties). In *ha-Yishuv bi-Yemey ha-Bayit ha-Le'umi, 1917–1948* (The Jewish national home from the Balfour Declaration to independence, 1917–1948), edited by Binyamin Eli'av, 129–281. Jerusalem: Keter.

Sadan, Dov. 1952. "Tsu der Efenung fun der Yidish-katedre in Yerusholaymer Universitet" (On the inauguration of the Yiddish chair in the Jerusalem University). *Di Goldene Keyt* 11: 187–202.

———. 1966. Introduction to *Mi-kan u-mi-Karov* (From here and from close by), edited by Mordekhai Chalamish, 13–15. Tel-Aviv: Sifriyat Po'alim.

———. 1972a. "Dray Aspektn" (Three aspects). 1951. Reprinted in *Heymishe Ksovim* (Familiar writings), 2: 387–92. Tel-Aviv: Menorah Farlag.

———. 1972b. "Vegn Tsveyshprakhikeyt" (On bilingualism). 1969. Reprinted in *Heymishe Ksovim* (Familiar writings), 2: 417–27. Tel-Aviv: Menorah Farlag.

———. 1978. "Der Colonist" (The colonist). In *A Vort Bashteyt,* 66–72. Tel-Aviv: Perets Farlag.

———. 1979. *Orachot u-Shevilim* (Ways and paths). Vol. 3. Tel-Aviv: Am Oved.

Sadan-Loebenstein, Nilli. 1991. *ha-Siporet shel Shenot ha-Esrim be-Eretz-yisra'el*

(Palestinian prose in the twenties). Edited by Avidov Lipsker. Tel-Aviv: Sifriyat Poalim.

———. 1994. *Aharon Re'uveni*. Tel-Aviv: Sifriyat Po'alim.

Scholem, Gershom. 1974. *Kabbalah*. New York: Quadrangle.

Schuster, Peter-Klaus, ed. 1987. *Der blaue Reiter praesentiert Eurer Hoheit sein Blaues Pferd, Karten, und Briefe* (The blue rider presents Her Highness with his blue horses, postcards, and letters). Munich: Prestel.

Schwarz, Arturo. 2003. *Mordecai Ardon: The Colors of Time*. Jerusalem: Israel Museum.

Scott, Clive. 1991. "Symbolism, Decadence, and Impressionism." In *Modernism: A Guide to European Literature 1890–1930*, edited by Malcolm Bradbury and James McFarlane, 206–27. London: Penguin.

Segal, Chaya. 1990. Conversation with the author, Jerusalem.

Segal, Yisra'el. 1990. *Ne'ilah* (Locking-up). Jerusalem: Keter.

Segal, Zev. 1934–69. Notebook of popular Yishuv songs. Author's collection.

Segev, Tom. 1993. *The Seventh Million*. Translated by Haim Watzman. New York: Hill and Wang.

———. 2001. *One Palestine, Complete*. Translated by Haim Watzman. New York: Henry Holt.

Seh-Lavan, Yosef. 1964. "ha-Aliyah ha-Shelishit u-Vituyah ba-Sifrut" (The Third Aliyah and its expression in literature). In *Sefer ha-Aliyah ha-Shelishit* (The book of the Third Aliyah), edited by Yehuda Erez, 846–67. Tel-Aviv: Am Oved.

Seidman, Naomi. 1997. *A Marriage Made in Heaven: The Sexual Politics of Hebrew and Yiddish*. Berkeley: Univ. of California Press.

———. 2000. Conversation with the author, Berkeley, Calif.

Shachar, Natan. 1999. "ha-Shir ha-Eretz-yisre'eli: Hithavuto, Tzmichato ve-Hit-patchuto ba-Shanim 1882–1949" (The Eretz-Israeli song: Its formation, growth, and development in 1882–1949). In *Toldot ha-Yishuv ha-Yehudi be-Eretz-yis-ra'el me-az ha-Aliyah ha-Rishonah: Bniyatah shel Tarbut Ivrit* (The history of the Jewish community in Palestine since 1882: The construction of Hebrew culture in Palestine), edited by Zohar Shavit, 495–528. Jerusalem: Mossad Bialik.

Shaked, Gershon. 1983. *ha-Siporet ha-Ivrit 1880–1980* (Hebrew narrative fiction 1880–1980). Vol. 2. Tel-Aviv: ha-Kibbutz ha-Me'uchad.

———. 1988. *ha-Siporet ha-Ivrit 1880–1980* (Hebrew narrative fiction 1880–1980). Vol. 3. Tel-Aviv: ha-Kibbutz ha-Me'uchad.

———. 2000. *Modern Hebrew Fiction*. Bloomington: Indiana Univ. Press.

Shalev, Meir. 1988. *Roman Rusi* (Russian novel). Tel-Aviv: Am Oved. (Translated as *The Blue Mountain*. Translation by Hillel Halkin. New York: Aaron Asher, 1991.)

Shamri, Aryeh. 1965. "Rikuda Potash: Di Zingerin fun Yerusholayim" (Rikuda Potash: The singer of/from Jerusalem). *Di Goldene Keyt* 53: 18–24.

———. 1970. "Leyzer Tsipress." 1936. Reprinted in *Gezangen in Shayer* (Songs in the barn), 11–46. Tel-Aviv: Yisro'el Bukh.

Shapira, Anita. 1992. *Land and Power: The Zionist Resort to Force*. New York: Oxford Univ. Press.

Shargel, Y. Z. 1977a. *Fun Onheyb On* (From the beginning). Tel-Aviv: Farlag Yisroel Bukh.

———. 1977b. "Rikuda Potash, di Bazingerin fun Yerusholayim" (Rikuda Potash, the celebrant of Jerusalem). 1955. Reprinted in *Fun Onheyb On* (From the beginning), 74–76. Tel-Aviv: Farlag Yisroel Bukh.

Shavit, Ya'akov. 1984. *me-Ivri ad Kena'ani* (From Hebrew to Canaanite). Tel-Aviv: Domino.

Shavit, Zohar. 1982. *ha-Chayim ha-Sifrutiyim be-Eretz-yisra'el 1910–1933* (Literary life in Palestine 1910–1933). Tel Aviv: ha-Kibbutz ha-Me'uchad.

———, ed. 1999. *Toldot ha-Yishuv ha-Yehudi be-Eretz-yisra'el me-az ha-Aliyah ha-Rishonah: Bniyatah shel Tarbut Ivrit* (The history of the Jewish community in Palestine since 1882: The construction of Hebrew culture in Palestine). Jerusalem: Mossad Bialik.

Sheppard, Richard. 1991a. "German Expressionism." In *Modernism: A Guide to European Poetry 1890–1930*, edited by Malcolm Bradbury and James McFarlane, 274–91. London: Penguin.

———. 1991b. "German Expressionist Poetry." In *Modernism: A Guide to European Poetry 1890–1930*, edited by Malcolm Bradbury and James McFarlane, 383–92. London: Penguin.

Shimoni, Gideon. 1995. *The Zionist Ideology*. Hanover, N.H.: Brandeis Univ. Press.

Shlonsky, Avraham. 1927a. "Al ha-Shalom" (On the peace). *Ketuvim* 1, nos. 34–35: 1.

———. 1927b. "Amal" (Toil). In *ba-Galgal* (In the wheel), 96–103. Tel-Aviv: Davar.

Shlonsky, Avraham, and Leah Goldberg, eds. 1942. *Shirat Rusiyah* (Poetry/song of Russia). Tel-Aviv: Sifriyat Po'alim.

Shmeruk, Khone. 1978. *Sifrut Yidish: Perakim le-Toldotehah* (Chapters in the history of Yiddish literature). Tel-Aviv: Tel-Aviv Univ.

———. 1999. "Yetsirato shel Uri Tsvi Grinberg be-Eretz-yisra'el u-ve-Polin be-Sof Shenot ha-Esrim u-vi-Shenot ha-Sheloshim" (The creative work of Uri Tsvi Grinberg in Palestine and in Poland in the late 1920s and the 1930s). 1978. Reprinted in *ha-Keri'ah le-Navi: Mechkerey Historiyah ve-Sifrut* (The call for a prophet: Studies in history and literature), edited by Israel Bartal, 175–97. Jerusalem: Hebrew Univ.

Shmeterling, David. 1935. "Mar'ot Kayitz" (Summer visions). *Gilyonot* 2, no. 9: 234–38.

Sholem Aleichem. 1987. *Tevye the Dairyman and the Railroad Stories*. Translated and with an introduction by Hillel Halkin. New York: Schocken.

Shoshani, Moshe. 1964. "Ganigar" (Ganigar). In *Sefer ha-Aliyah ha-Shelishit* (The book of the Third Aliyah), edited by Yehuda Erez, 473–76. Tel-Aviv: Am Oved.

Shpigl, Yeshayahu. 1967. "Rikuda Potash un ir Lid" (Rikuda Potash and her poem). In *Lider* (Poems), by Rikuda Potash, 7–8. Tel Aviv: Yidishn Literatn un Zhurnalistn Fareyn in Yisro'el.

Shteynman, Eliezer. 1927. "Milu'im" (Addenda). *Ketuvim* 1, nos. 34–35: 2.

Shturem, Mark. 1923. "Oyf Sheyd-veg" (At the crossroads). *Tayfun:* 25–27.

Stavi, Moshe. 1930. *ha-Boker Or* (At morning light). Be'er-Tuvia: N.p.

Steiner, George. 1985. "Our Homeland, the Text." *Salmagundi* 66: 4–25.

Stern, Efraim, ed. 1992. *ha-Entsiklopediyah ha-Chadashah le-Chafirot Arkheologiyot be-Eretz-yisra'el* (The new encyclopedia of archaeological excavations in the Holy Land). Jerusalem: Israel Exploration Society.

Sternhell, Zeev. 1998. *The Founding Myths of Israel: Nationalism, Socialism, and the Making of the Jewish State.* Translated by David Maisel. Princeton, N.J.: Princeton Univ. Press.

Sutzkever, Avrom. 1952. *In Fayer-vogn* (In the chariot of fire). Tel-Aviv: Di Goldene Keyt.

———. 1957. *In Midber Sinay* (In the Sinai Desert). Tel-Aviv: Farlag Perets Bibliotek.

———. 1968. *Firkantike Oysyes u-Mofsim* (Square letters and miracles). Tel-Aviv: Perets Farlag.

Tabenkin, Yitzchak. 1977. "Brenner be-Eyney Doro" (Brenner through the eyes of his contemporaries). In *Machbarot Brenner* (Brenner notebooks), 2: 9–19. Tel-Aviv: Tel-Aviv Univ.

Talmi, Efraim, and Menachem Talmi. 1981. *Leksikon Tziyoni* (Lexicon of Zionism). Tel-Aviv: Ma'ariv.

Tavori, Zvi. 1977. "Ayngezamlt tsu zayn Folk" (Gathered to his people). In *Yerusholaymer Almanakh,* 8: 219–20. Jerusalem: Yidishe Shrayber-grupe in Yerusholayim, Farlag Eygens.

Tchernichovsky, Shaul. 1990. *Kol Kitvey Shaul Tchernichovsky* (Collected works of Shaul Tchernichovsky). Vol. 1. Tel-Aviv: Am Oved.

Tidhar, David. 1966. *Entsiklopediyah le-Chalutzey ha-Yishuv u-Vonav* (Encyclopedia of the pioneers and builders of the Yishuv). Tel-Aviv: Sifriyat Rishonim.

Tilo Alt, Arthur. 1987. "A Survey of Literary Contributions to the Post–World War I Yiddish Journals of Berlin." *Yiddish* 7, no. 1: 42–52.

———. 1991. "Ambivalence toward Modernism: The Yiddish Avant-Garde and Its Manifestoes." *Yiddish* 8, no. 1: 42–62.

Tzemach, Shlomo. 1930. "ha-Kever ha-Rishon" (The first grave). In *Shiv'a-asar Sipurim* (Seventeen stories), 88–94. Tel-Aviv: Devir.

———. 1934. "Ya'arot Makbet" (Macbeth's forests). *Moznayim* 2, no. 6: 529–33.

———. 1968. "ba-Avotot he-Havai" (In the shackles of the present). 1918. Reprinted in *Masot u-Reshimot* (Essays and comments), 39–61. Ramat-Gan: Masada.

Vishny, Michele. 1974. *Mordecai Ardon*. New York: Harry N. Abrams.

Wallach, Jehuda. 1974. *Atlas Karta le-Toldot Eretz-yisra'el: me-Reshit ha-Hityashvut ve-ad Kom ha-Medinah* (Carta's atlas of the history of Palestine: From the beginning of settlement to statehood). Jerusalem: Carta.

Weinreich, Max. 1980. *History of the Yiddish Language*. Chicago: Univ. of Chicago.

Weinreich, Uriel. 1968. *Modern English-Yiddish Yiddish-English Dictionary*. New York: Schocken.

White, Hayden. 1985. *Tropics of Discourse*. Baltimore: Johns Hopkins Univ. Press.

Wolitz, Seth A. 1979. "Velt-Barg-Arop." *Yiddish* 4, no. 1: 98–106.

———. 1981. *"Di Khalyastre:* The Yiddish Modernist Movement in Poland." *Yiddish* 4, no. 3: 5–19.

———. 1988. "The Kiev-Grupe 1918–1920." *Yiddish* 3, no. 3: 97–106.

———. 1991. "Between Folk and Freedom: The Failure of the Yiddish Modernist Movement in Poland." *Yiddish* 8, no. 1: 26–51.

Ya'akobi, David, and Yoram Tsafrir, eds. 1988. *Yehudim, Shomronim ve-Notzrim be-Eretz-yisra'el ha-Bizantit* (Jews, Samaritans, and Christians in Byzantine Palestine). Jerusalem: Yad Ben-Zvi.

Ya'ari-Poleskin, Ya'akov. 1922. *Cholmim ve-Lochamim* (Dreamers and warriors). Petach-Tikvah, Israel: Gissin.

Yablonkin. 1910. "Din ve-Cheshbon shel Mo'etzet ha-Miflagah be-Sukkot 5671" (Report of the party convention, Sukkot 1910). *ha-Achdut* 2, nos. 2–3: col. 27.

Yatziv, Meri. 1947. "Pegishot u-Reshamim" (Meetings and impressions). 1945. Reprinted in *Sefer ha-Aliyah ha-Sheniyah* (The book of the Second Aliyah), edited by Brakhah Chabas, 564–72. Tel-Aviv: Am Oved.

Yehoshua, Abraham B. 1977. *ha-Me'ahev* (The lover). Jerusalem: Schocken. (Translated as *The Lover*. Translation by Philip Simpson. Garden City, N.Y.: Doubleday, 1978.)

Yehoyesh (Solomon Bloomgarden). 1917. *Fun Nyu-York biz Rechovot un Tsurik* (From New York to Rechovot and back). Vol. 3. New York: Farlag Oyfgang.

Zalmona, Yigal. 1981. "History and Identity." In *Artists of Israel: 1920–1980,* Susan Tumarkin Goodman, exhibition curator, 27–46. Detroit: Wayne State Univ. Press.

———. 1998. "Kadima? Kadima!" (To the East? To the East!). In *Kadima: ha-Mizrach be-Omanut Yisra'el* (To the East: Orientalism in the arts in Israel), Yigal Zalmona and Tamar Manor-Friedman, curators, 47–93. Jerusalem: Israel Museum.

Zerubavel, Ya'akov. 1910. "Pe'ulateinu ha-Tarbutit" (Our cultural activity). *ha-Achdut* 2, no. 2–3: cols. 11–14.

———. 1914. "Me-inyana de-Yoma" (Issues of the day). *ha-Achdut* 5, no. 35: cols. 5–11.

———. 1956. *Bleter fun a Lebn* (Pages from a life). Tel Aviv: Perets Bibliotek.

Zerubavel, Yael. 1995. *Recovered Roots: Collective Memory and the Making of Israeli National Tradition*. Chicago: Univ. of Chicago Press.

Zhitlovsky, Chaim. 1953. "Tsernovitser Shprakh-konferents un Parizer Kultur-kongres" (The Czernowitz language conference and Paris culture congress). 1937. Reprinted in *Mayne Ani-Mamins* (My credos), 396–410. New York: Yidishe Kultur-Farband.

Index

Italic page number denotes illustration.